PRENTICE-HALL

HISTORY OF MUSIC SERIES

H. WILEY HITCHCOCK, editor

MUSIC
IN THE UNITED STATES:
A Historical Introduction

second edition

MUSIC
IN THE UNITED STATES:
A Historical Introduction

H. WILEY HITCHCOCK

Professor of Music and Director,
Institute for Studies in American Music
Brooklyn College
City University of New York

PRENTICE-HALL, INC., ENGLEWOOD CLIFFS, NEW JERSEY

Library of Congress Cataloging in Publication Data

HITCHCOCK, HUGH WILEY, date
    Music in the United States.

    (Prentice-Hall history of music series)
    Includes bibliographies.
    1. Music—United States—History and criticism.
I. Title.
ML200.H58 1974   781.7'73   73-19751
ISBN 0-13-608398-6
ISBN 0-13-608380-3 (pbk.)

Printed in the United States of America

10 9 8 7 6 5

PRENTICE-HALL INTERNATIONAL, INC., *London*
PRENTICE-HALL OF AUSTRALIA, PTY. LTD., *Sydney*
PRENTICE-HALL OF CANADA, LTD., *Toronto*
PRENTICE-HALL OF INDIA PRIVATE LIMITED, *New Delhi*
PRENTICE-HALL OF JAPAN, INC., *Tokyo*

FOREWORD

Students and informed amateurs of the history of music have long needed a series of books that are comprehensive, authoritative, and engagingly written. They have needed books written by specialists—but specialists interested in communicating vividly. The Prentice-Hall History of Music Series aims at filling these needs.

Six books in the series present a panoramic view of the history of Western music, divided among the major historical periods—Medieval, Renaissance, Baroque, Classic, Romantic, and Contemporary. The musical culture of the United States, viewed historically as an independent development within the larger western tradition, is discussed in another book, and forthcoming will be similar books on the music of Latin America and Russia. In yet another pair, the rich yet neglected folk and traditional music of both hemispheres is treated. Taken together, the eleven volumes of the series will be a distinctive and, we hope, distinguished contribution to the history of the music of the world's peoples. Each volume, moreover, may be read singly as a substantial account of the music of its period or area.

The authors of the series are scholars of national and international repute—musicologists, critics, and teachers of acknowledged stature in their respective fields of specialization. In their contributions to the Prentice-Hall History of Music Series their goal has been to present works of solid scholarship that are eminently readable, with significant insights into music as a part of the general intellectual and cultural life of man.

H. WILEY HITCHCOCK, *Editor*

PREFACE

Surely no lengthy justification is needed for a historical survey of American music and musical life. For reasons suggested in Chapter 3 of this book, we know less about our own music than about that of western Europe, although in recent years there has been a considerable increase of interest in our musical past (if not, composers of today would claim, our musical present) and a decrease of the defensiveness about, the oblique view of, our country's music vis à vis that of Europe, that prevented us for so long from enjoying our musical selves. My attempt in this book is to view our music head-on, to measure it in its own terms, and to seek the "why" behind the "what" in American music. I have also attempted to view it in the round, believing that pop songs as well as art songs, player-pianos as well as piano players, rock as well as revival hymns, are important parts of the American musical experience.

In this second edition, I have added to my earlier discussions of music in the Colonial and Federal periods and of popular music in the twentieth century, and have revised particularly the sections on recent music in the light of trends since 1968, when the book was first written.

My approach to nineteenth-century American music has been in terms of what I call our "cultivated" and "vernacular" traditions. In dealing with the latter, as with secular music in the Colonial era, I discuss a considerable amount of music now considered "folk" music—but in its function as the "popular" music of earlier days; folk music per se is considered more broadly by Bruno Nettl in his companion-volume in The Prentice-Hall History of Music Series, *Folk and Traditional Music of the Western Continents*. In discussing American music since the First World War, I have emphasized the principal stylistic trends and the predominant musical attitudes. Many fine composers have thereby gone unmentioned; they have had to make way, with my apologies, for those who seem to me to have been the ones in whose work the major themes of twentieth-century American music have been expressed most clearly, boldly, and influentially. I make no apologies for devoting an entire chapter of a rather brief book to Charles Ives: both his thought and his music stand as continuing, fertile challenges to American musical evolution.

Bibliographical notes follow each chapter, and, although scholarly apparatus is not used extensively in this book, I have attempted to cite in footnotes primarily works that can serve as useful further references; one that I do not have occasion to cite but that should certainly be mentioned is Richard Jackson's *United States Music: Sources of Bibliography and Collective Biography* (Brooklyn: Institute for Studies in American Music, Brooklyn College, 1973), an invaluable reference-tool in the form of an annotated bibliography of about 100 books. Wherever possible in the text, I have quoted composers on their own music. Among the books and periodicals listed in the table of abbreviations below, a special word is in order about "*MinA*": the reader is urged to have close at hand a copy of this anthology of earlier American music, as I often refer to it. The same is true of "*EAM*," an ongoing series of facsimile reprints that makes available scores otherwise often difficult to locate.

I express with pleasure my gratitude to the two teachers who, many years ago, awakened my interest in the history of American music: Glenn McGeoch and Raymond Kendall. My greatest debt is to those who have shaped my attitudes about American music; I have been influenced most by the ideas of Charles Seeger and of Gilbert Chase, particularly his *America's Music*, and by the American music scholar (and friend) Irving Lowens. Others who have aided me include Henry Leland Clarke, Richard Crawford, Paul Echols, Leonard Feist, John Kirkpatrick, Josef Marx, Kenneth Roberts, Howard Shanet, Brooks Shepard, Frank Tirro, Margaret Bostwick Vaill, and Charles Wuorinen. Many libraries have served beyond the call of duty, especially the Music Re-

Preface continued

search Division of the New York Public Library, and its chief, Frank Campbell; the Music Division of the Library of Congress, and two of its scholar-librarians, William Lichtenwanger and Carroll Wade; and the library of the Union Theological Seminary. For her extrasensory perception in transferring my manuscript to typescript I thank Judy Kanazawa. As a teacher, I can hardly over-emphasize the role my students have played in shaping my thought—greater, perhaps, than mine in shaping theirs—and I am ever grateful.

In preparing the second edition of the book, I was given helpful criticisms of the first by several colleagues and fellow-scholars, and was assisted in various ways (sometimes unconsciously) by others; to all, but especially the following, my thanks: Allen P. Britton, Gilbert Chase, David Diamond, Ross Lee Finney, Ruth Hilton, Hugh J. Hitchcock (my son, of particular importance to my views of rock), Jean Ishizuka, Richard Jackson (head of the Americana Collection in the Music Division of the New York Public Library), Rita Mead, Wilfrid Mellers, Dorothy Morris, Vivian Perlis, Eric Salzman, Wayne D. Shirley, Lynn Siebert, Augusta Siegel, Francis Thorne, and Richard D. Wetzel.

The main themes of the book were sketched in an essay written for *American Civilization: An Introduction*, edited by A. N. J. den Hollander and Sigmund Skard (London: Longmans, Green & Co., 1968); others were developed from articles published in *The Musical Quarterly* and *Hi Fi/Stereo Review*. To these I am appreciative for permission to expand on ideas they were the first to publish. And for their patience and care in seeing the book into print I thank my editors at Prentice-Hall, Alan Lesure, Norwell F. Therien, Jr., Carole Richardson, and Raeia Maes.

To my wife, Janet, I am grateful for many things, among them the model of her own impeccable scholarship; her contribution to whatever accuracy and grace of expression may be found herein; and her cheerful sufferance, for several years, of my humming, singing, whistling, and playing through three and a half centuries of American music.

H. W. H.

CONTENTS

ABBREVIATIONS

ACS   *The American Composer Speaks,* ed. Gilbert Chase (Baton Rouge: Louisiana State University Press, 1966).

AM   Gilbert Chase, *America's Music* (rev. 2nd ed.; New York: McGraw-Hill Book Company, 1966).

EAM   *Earlier American Music,* ed. H. Wiley Hitchcock (New York: Da Capo Press, 1972–)

MinA   *Music In America: An Anthology from the Landing of the Pilgrims to the Close of the Civil War. 1620–1865.* Ed. W. Thomas Marrocco and Harold Gleason (New York: W. W. Norton & Co., Inc., 1964).

MM   *Modern Music* (1924–46)

MMEA   Irving Lowens, *Music and Musicians in Early America* (New York: W. W. Norton & Co., Inc., 1964).

MQ   *The Musical Quarterly* (1915–)

OAM   John Tasker Howard, *Our American Music* (4th ed.; Thomas Y. Crowell Company, 1965).

PNM   *Perspectives of New Music* (1962–)

ONE

SACRED MUSIC
IN NEW ENGLAND
AND OTHER COLONIES

In his poem *The Gift Outright,* Robert Frost remarked that "the land was ours before we were the land's./She was our land more than a hundred years/Before we were her people." Acknowledging that there was an "American music" of long standing among the Indians, that French Huguenots sang psalms on their arrival in Spanish Florida in 1564, that Englishmen under Sir Francis Drake sang psalms in Spanish California in 1579, and that there is evidence of the use of trumpets and drums, popular and religious song in Virginia long before the colonization of New England, we still must recognize that the heart of "our land . . . before we were her people" was New England. It is with the music of early New England, then, that our historical introduction must begin.

The musical world left behind by the earliest English-speaking American colonists was a rich one, perhaps the richest England has ever known. At Court and in the mansions of the British peerage was heard elegant and sophisticated music of many kinds—madrigals, balletts, ayres,

1

canzonets, and other part-songs by such Renaissance masters as William Byrd, Thomas Morley, Thomas Weelkes, and John Dowland; variations, dance pieces, preludes, and other fanciful works for harpsichord by Elizabethan virginalists like Orlando Gibbons, John Bull, and Giles Farnaby; fantasies and suites for ensembles of viols and other instruments. The music at the Chapel Royal and in the great cathedrals was no less elaborate and magnificent: both Catholic and Anglican services were permitted under Elizabeth I, and choirs of good size performed intricate and resonant motets and Mass-settings in the one, anthems and great Services in the other.

The American colonists, however, could hardly maintain such kinds of music in the New World. Most of them were not of the wealthy aristocracy that had created and supported such music in England. The leisure necessary to enjoy such purely artistic music was, needless to say, not their lot. Cargo space was at a premium on the tiny colonial ships, and large instruments like organs or harpsichords could not be accommodated.

So far as we know, the colonists could and did enjoy only music that was quite simple and fully functional: social music and worship music. Of the former we have few specific details; of the latter we know more. The history of "American music," in the first century of British colonization, must begin with New England worship music, specifically the psalmody, sung in religious meetings and at home, that had originated in mid-sixteenth-century Protestant sects of Western Europe.

PROTESTANT BACKGROUNDS

John Calvin, austere leader of the Swiss-French Protestant movement, believed that the only proper music for the church had to be based on the lyric poetry of the Bible, the Psalms. Like Martin Luther, Calvin encouraged a congregational music in the language of the people, not a choral music in the ecclesiastical Latin of the Roman Catholic Church. But, unlike Luther, Calvin thought that polyphonic music, instruments, hymns, and other non-biblical texts were too much associated with Catholicism; he replaced them with the unaccompanied congregational unison singing of psalms, translated into metrical French verse. By 1562 the Calvinists had published in their center at Geneva the complete psalter in translations by Clément Marot and Théodore de Bèze (Beza, in Latin), with melodies composed or adapted by Louis Bourgeois.[1] Similar psalters for congregational use were prepared by Dutch Prot-

---

[1] Two French psalms are printed in *MinA*, Nos. 1a, 5a.

estants, and, in the same year as the Geneva psalter, the London printer John Day published a complete English psalter, with translations of the psalms by Thomas Sternhold and John Hopkins and with melodies partly of English origin, partly of continental, the latter brought back, after Queen Elizabeth's ascendancy, by English Protestants who had sought asylum in Geneva during the reign (1550–58) of Mary, a Catholic (see *MinA*, Nos. 7–11).

The music of these Protestant psalters was adapted from a variety of sources. Some melodies were derived from popular songs of the day; some were older hymn tunes; some were altered versions of Catholic chants. They must have been sung with fervor and gusto: apparently because of their sprightliness, the French Huguenot psalms were dubbed "Geneva jigs" and "Beza ballads"; Shakespeare, in *The Winter's Tale* (Act IV, scene 3), has the clown say, "Three-man song men all [i.e., singers of part-songs], and very good ones . . . but one Puritan amongst them, and he sings psalms to hornpipes!"

In view of the character of this music and considering the popularity of part-songs in the sixteenth century, it should not surprise us that polyphonic arrangements of psalm tunes, for enjoyment at home, were soon forthcoming. In England, Damon's psalter of 1579 contained four-part settings, and in 1592 Michael East (Este) enlisted the aid of prominent composers of the day (John Dowland, Giles Farnaby, Michael Cavendish, and others) to provide polyphonic settings for his psalter. Two later and very popular collections of harmonized psalm tunes were Richard Alison's of 1599 and Thomas Ravenscroft's of 1621 (see *MinA*, No. 6).

EARLY NEW ENGLAND PSALMODY

That the fiercely devout New England colonists regarded the singing of psalms as an integral part of life is suggested by a comment of one of the little group of Pilgrims that sailed from Delftshaven, Holland, in 1620:

> They that stayed at Leyden feasted us that were to go at our pastor's house, [it] being large; where we refreshed ourselves, after tears, with singing of Psalms, making joyful melody in our hearts as well as with the voice, there being many of our congregation very expert in music; and indeed it was the sweetest melody that ever mine ears heard.[2]

[2] Edward Winslow, *Hypocrisie Unmasked* (1646), quoted in Waldo Selden Pratt, *The Music of the Pilgrims* (Boston: Oliver Ditson Company, 1921), p. 6.

The "joyful melody" sung by "many . . . very expert in music" was doubtless a group of the psalms collected, translated, and published in 1612 for his congregation by the pastor of the English Separatists at Amsterdam, Rev. Henry Ainsworth. Ainsworth's psalter included both prose and poetic translations, copiously annotated, of the entire Book of Psalms; it also included 39 melodies borrowed by Ainsworth from "our former Englished Psalms [and from] the French and Dutch Psalms" (see *MinA*, Nos. 1–5). In variety of length, meter, and rhythm Ainsworth's choices were remarkable: compare, for example, the lilting asymmetry of Psalm 21, which is of English origin and which Ainsworth probably got from Damon's psalter, with the powerful, stomping regularity of Psalm 44, a Huguenot tune first printed in Genevan psalters, then taken over in the Sternhold-Hopkins English psalter (Example 1-1).

EXAMPLE 1-1. Psalms 21 and 44 (first verses of text only) from Ainsworth's psalter (1612), after the Amsterdam edition of 1618: *The Psalmes in Metre* (no author, place, or publisher given). Their music duplicates that of the first edition: H[enry] A[insworth], *The Book of Psalmes: Englished both in Prose and Metre. With Annotations* . . . (Amsterdam: Giles Thorp, 1612).

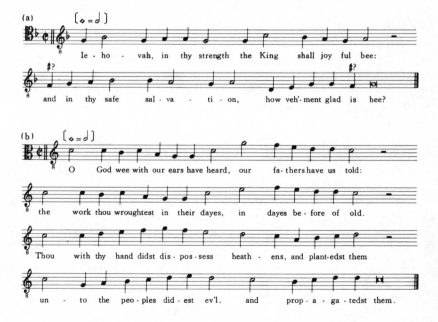

Used by the Pilgrims of the Plymouth colony and also by settlers at Ipswich and Salem, Ainsworth's psalter was finally replaced in 1692 by another, the so-called *Bay Psalm Book*. This psalter, famous as the first real book to be published in the British colonies, was a product of the

Massachusetts Bay Colony. The committee of thirty which compiled it sought not only to make "a plain and familiar translation" of the psalter more accurate than the Sternhold-Hopkins version they had brought with them from England, but also to differentiate their Puritan, Bay Colony psalter from that of the Pilgrims at Plymouth. First printed in 1640, the *Bay Psalm Book* (or "New England version") originally included no music, but directed that most of its verses could be sung either to Ravenscroft's tunes or those of "our english psalm books"—i.e., Sternhold-Hopkins. Enormously popular, the Bay psalter was published in nine editions in the seventeenth century alone. To the ninth edition of 1698 (or possibly to an earlier, missing one) were appended 13 melodies, with basses as well (see *MinA*, Nos. 12–17), which the unknown compiler had borrowed from various editions of John Playford's *Introduction to the Skill of Music* (London, 1667 and later).

That only 13 melodies could suffice for all 150 psalms suggests that the psalms of the Bay psalter were less diverse metrically than those of earlier psalters, and perhaps that the New England congregations of the late seventeenth century were less "expert in music" than their forebears. Indeed, "almost all this whole book of psalmes," declared the preface of the 1640 edition, was composed in three meters: Common Meter (8, 6, 8, and 6 syllables for the four-line verses); Long Meter (8, 8, 8, 8); and an irregular meter of 6, 6, 8, 6. The decline in the number of psalm tunes regularly sung was a reflection of a general decline in the quality of psalmody in the colonies. By the early eighteenth century, Puritan ministers were raising horrified outcries at the poor singing in their churches; one complained in 1721 that "the tunes are now miserably tortured, and twisted, and quavered . . . into an horrid Medly of confused and disorderly Noises." Precentors, who were appointed to "line out" the psalms for their congregations—that is, to set the pitch and remind their fellows of a psalm tune by chanting it, line by line, echoed by the congregation—were altering the melodies at will: "every Leading-Singer would take the Liberty of raising any Note of the Tune, or lowering of it, as best pleas'd his Ear, and add such Turns and Flourishes as were grateful to him," wrote Rev. Thomas Symmes of Bradford, Massachusetts in 1720.

Like clergymen before and after them, the Puritan ministers of New England set out to reform music in their churches. In so doing, they created the first music instruction books in America, established a unique kind of musical education, and paved the way for the first school of American composers.

First came sermons, pleading for a return to "regular" singing, by note instead of by rote; one such plea was Symmes's sermon on "The Reasonableness of Regular Singing" (1720). The earliest practical attempt to improve matters, and the first American music textbook, was a small volume by the Rev. John Tufts of Newbury, *An Introduction to the Singing of Psalm-Tunes,* first published in 1721. Tufts wrote a brief preface explaining the rudiments of music and a new method of musical notation (by letter rather than by note) that he had devised (see the reproduction of one page in *MinA,* plate [5]) and followed these with a collection of English psalm tunes. The fifth edition of 1726, the earliest extant, includes 37 such tunes, with two other harmonizing parts (see *MinA,* Nos. 21–23). Among them is one, *100 Psalm Tune New,* which has not been found in earlier publications and which may perhaps be claimed as the first American composition; whether Tufts wrote it himself we do not know. The little piece (Example 1-2) is worth a brief look: not un-

EXAMPLE 1-2. J. Tufts, *100 Psalm Tune New, An Introduction to the Singing of Psalm-Tunes . . . The Fifth Edition* (Boston: Printed for Samuel Gerrish, 1726), p. 10.

graceful, it has nevertheless an angularity of melody (the Cantus is the principal air) and a predilection for unisons, octaves, and bare fifths— not to mention the parallel fifths at the end of the second phrase—which distinguish it from British psalm tunes of the period. As we shall see, it was precisely such features of style that would characterize native American music of the later eighteenth century.

At almost the same time that Tufts first published his *Introduction,* another manual appeared, also including a number of psalm tunes with accompanying parts. This was *The Grounds and Rules of Music Explained* (Boston, 1721), by Rev. Thomas Walter of Roxbury, a nephew of the well-known Cotton Mather and, like Tufts, a graduate of Harvard

College (see *MinA*, Nos. 24–26). These two "tunebooks," as such works came to be known, were the first of many hundreds that were published in the eighteenth century. They marked the beginning of a significant movement in American music, the singing-school movement, to which I shall return shortly. Meanwhile, I should mention briefly the expansion of New England worship music by the addition of hymns to the traditional psalmodic repertory.

Calvin had limited the texts of church song to biblical psalms in metrical vernacular translations. The other great leader of the Protestant Reformation, Luther, had not been so restrictive; from the beginning he had permitted, and even composed himself, original hymns. Hymnody flourished under Lutheranism, and even before the eighteenth century it found its way into the English Puritan services. The first significant writer of English hymns was the Rev. Dr. Isaac Watts. From 1707 he published "hymns and spiritual songs" as well as paraphrases of psalms, and for a century or more his works were the most popular source of texts for English and American hymnody. A further impetus to hymnody was provided, from the 1730's on, by the evangelical movement of Wesleyanism and by the series of "awakenings" and "revivals" which, beginning with the "Great Awakening" of 1735, studded the evolution of American Protestantism.

THE SINGING-SCHOOL MOVEMENT

As we have seen, agitation among Puritan ministers for better singing in their churches resulted in the first American music instruction books. At their call too was instituted the first kind of American music school. Rev. Symmes asked in 1720:

> Would it not greatly tend to promote singing of psalms if singing schools were promoted? . . . Where would be the difficulty, or what the disadvantages, if people who want skill in singing, would procure a skillful person to instruct them, and meet two or three evenings in the week, from five or six o'clock to eight, and spend their time in learning to sing?

That is precisely what happened. As early as March, 1722, Boston had a Society for Promoting Regular Singing, with a core of about ninety who had learned to read music. From that time on, the singing school, convened to learn, practice, and demonstrate the skill of reading music at sight, became an important institution in the colonies, social as well as musical. Although originally begun in an attempt to improve church music, and although their music was for the most part religious, the sing-

ing schools were as much secular institutions as sacred, as much social
outlets as pious assemblies. One student at Yale, for example, wrote to a
friend with characteristic undergraduate querulousness:

> At present I have no inclination for anything, for I am almost sick of the
> World & were it not for the Hopes of going to the singing-meeting to-
> night & indulging myself a little in some of the carnal Delights of the
> Flesh, such as kissing, squeezing &c. &c. I should willingly leave it now.[3]

In a society that recognized no split between religion and everyday life,
the singing school was a popular meeting-ground for both. Not only in
New England but in the more southerly colonies, singing-school instruction became popular in the eighteenth century: we hear of it in South
Carolina by 1730, in New York by 1754, in Pennsylvania from the late
1750's, and in Maryland by 1765.

A broadside or a newspaper advertisement would alert a community that a singing school was to be organized. Arriving on the scene, the
singing master would enroll students for classes once or twice a week
for a month or more. Their texts were sometimes manuscript copybooks,
into which they laboriously wrote the music they were learning to sing,
or sometimes printed "tunebooks," partly composed by the singing master,
partly borrowed from other sources. (Copyright was nonexistent until
late in the eighteenth century, and piracy was as common among literary
landlubbers as on the high seas.)

Characteristically oblong (thus sometimes called an "end-opener")
and headed by some sociable title like *The Chorister's Companion, The
American Singing Book, The Rural Harmony,* or *The Easy Instructor,* the
typical tunebook was a how-to-do-it manual, containing an introduction
to the rudiments of music theory and notation, and also a what-to-do
anthology, with a collection of psalm tunes (and, later in the century, of
hymn tunes, anthems, and even secular songs) harmonized in three or
four parts for men's and women's voices. There was no instrumental accompaniment provided; the old Calvinist suspicion of instruments as
belonging not to the Lord but to the Devil (or the Catholics) died hard,
and the prejudice was only gradually given up during the eighteenth
century.

The classes of a singing school would typically culminate in a
"singing lecture"—essentially a choral concert embellished by a sermon
from the local minister—or a "singing assembly," without the sermon.
Having taught his pupils to sing accurately by note, having enlarged his
reputation and the use of his tunebooks, and perhaps having got in a few
licks for some other business interest (many of the singing masters were

[3] Quoted in *MMEA,* p. 282.

veritable prototypes of the Yankee peddler), the singing master would move on to another community to begin a new singing school.

In this way the first group of American composers developed. Perhaps "tunesmiths" is the better word, for most of the itinerant singing masters regarded themselves unpretentiously as artisans, not artists. They forged a distinctive style of music, rugged, powerful, and homogeneous (if also, as we shall see, awkward-seeming and archaic-sounding to later, more genteel ears).

YANKEE TUNESMITHS: THE FIRST NEW ENGLAND SCHOOL

Singing schools of the middle decades of the eighteenth century must have relied mainly on British psalters and hymnals, for after the pioneer efforts in the 1720's of Tufts and Walter no important colonial tunebook was published until 1761. This was *Urania,* "a choice Collection of Psalm-tunes, Anthems, and Hyms" compiled by the New Jersey-born James Lyon (1735–1794) and published at Philadelphia. Lyon apparently culled most of the 96 compositions in the work from various English tunebooks in circulation at the time (see *MinA,* No. 40). Among the 70 psalm settings are some of special interest to us: they are "fuging psalm tunes" with a form and texture that were to be taken up lustily by the Yankee tunesmiths. *The V Psalm Tune* (Example 1-3), borrowed perhaps

EXAMPLE 1-3. *The V Psalm Tune,* in J. Lyon, *Urania* (Philadelphia: William Bradford, 1761), pp. 42–43.

from Abraham Adams's *Psalmist's New Companion,* 6th edition (London, ca. 1760), is characteristic: beginning with a four-part setting of the tune (in the tenor voice), it reaches a cadence (here on the dominant) in measure 12; then it starts afresh with imitative entries for the individual voices—the so-called "fuge" (fugue) or "fuging section"—which soon lead to a final cadence. Aside from some peculiarities in harmony—for instance, the characteristically British use of cross-relations (F♯ vs. F♮) in measures 1 and 2 and the clash of soprano and alto in measure 16—there is a smoothness about the little piece that betrays its transatlantic origin; American fuging tunes would tend to be simpler in rhythm, more angular in melody, less chromatic in harmony, and in some ways stronger in general effect.

The Yankee tunesmiths—our "First New England School" of composers—made their appearance in the 1770's. The first such composer to make his mark was William Billings (1746–1800), a Boston tanner turned tunesmith and one of the most picturesque personalities in American music. Billings's first tunebook, *The New-England Psalm-Singer; or, American Chorister,* was engraved in 1770. The title-page was engraved by Paul Revere, which reminds us of Lexington and Concord, of the Colonies vs. Britain, of growing national consciousness and the spirit of independence during the Revolutionary decade of the 1770's. In his prefatory "Thoughts on Music" (portions reprinted in *ACS,* pp. 29–31), the twenty-four-year-old composer made no bones about *his* independence:

> I don't think myself confined to any rules for composition laid down by any that went before me. . . . Nature is the best Dictator, for all the hard dry studied rules that ever were prescribed will not enable any person to form an Air any more than the bare knowledge of the four and twenty letters [*sic*], and strict Grammatical rules will qualify a scholar for composing a piece of Poetry.

Warming to the analogy between music and poetry, Billings went on: "As I have often heard of a Poetical Licence, I don't see why with the same Propriety there may not be a Musical Licence." Here spoke the rebellious, self-confident young American of 1770. Here was a composer with a mind of his own. Nevertheless, after stating his conviction that "I think it best for every Composer to be his own Carver," Billings proceeded to instruct his readers in the rudiments of music, and even to make some qualifications in his eulogy of native genius:

> Perhaps some may think I mean and intend to throw Art intirely out of the Question. I answer by no Means, for the more Art is display'd, the more Nature is decorated. And in some sorts of Composition, there is dry Study requir'd, and Art very requisite. For instance, in a *Fuge,*

where the Parts come in after each other, with the same Notes; but even there, Art is subservient to Genius, for Fancy goes first, and strikes out the work roughly, and Art comes after, and polishes it over.

Many years later—in the preface to his last tunebook, *The Continental Harmony* of 1794—Billings was still the self-confident autodidact, putting his faith not in dry-as-dust rules declared by others, but in himself, and insisting on the pre-eminence of self-expression and of "fancy":

> Musical composition is a sort of something, which is much better felt than described (at least by me). . . . But in answer to your question, although I am not confined to rules prescribed by others, yet I come as near as I possibly can to a set of rules which I have carved out for myself; but when fancy gets upon the wing, she seems to despise all form, and scorns to be confined or limited by any formal prescriptions whatsoever.

The music of *The New-England Psalm-Singer* consists of 108 psalm and hymn settings and 15 anthems and canons for chorus, all of Billings's own composition. The four-part canon "When Jesus Wept"[4] is one of Billings's loveliest melodic inspirations; similar to it in style is another *Canon 4 in 1*, ".Thus saith the high, the lofty one" (Example 1-4). These canons suggest Billings's flair for graceful melody. But perhaps it

EXAMPLE 1-4. Billings, *Canon 4 in 1, The New-England Psalm-Singer* (Boston: Edes and Gill, 1770); original a whole-tone higher.

was his patriotic pieces which accounted for Billings's early popularity. Among the pieces in *The New-England Psalm-Singer* was one, *Chester*, which so caught the fancy of young America that it became a rally-

---

[4] Reprinted in *AM*, p. 132, and in *MinA*, No. 42.

ing song of the Revolution. When he published his second tunebook, *The Singing Master's Assistant* (Boston, 1778), at the height of the Revolutionary War, Billings reprinted in it the stirring, stomping, march-like tune and added to its patriotic text (his own) new verses that spoke for—shouted for—his whole generation:

> *Let tyrants shake their iron rod,*
> *And Slav'ry clank her galling chaines.*
> *We fear them not, we trust in God,*
> *New-england's God for ever reigns.*

Later verses went on with even more fire and sarcasm:

> *Howe and Burgoyne and Clinton too,*
> *With Prescot and Cornwallis join'd,*
> *Together plot our Overthrow,*
> *In one infernal league combin'd.*
>
> *The Foe comes on with haughty stride,*
> *Our troops advance with martial noise.*
> *Their Vet'rans flee before our Youth,*
> *And Gen'rals yield to beardless Boys.*[5]

The Singing Master's Assistant also includes an address "To the Goddess of Discord" with a short choral piece, *Jargon* (*MinA*, No. 44), accompanying it. Billings's reasons for writing these are not clear. Perhaps his first tunebook had been criticized as lacking dissonance, for he begins his manifesto to Lady Discord by saying: "I have been sagacious enough of late, to discover that some evil-minded persons have insinuated to your highness, that I am utterly unmindful of your Ladyship's importance." But, if he was retorting to critics, he affirmed his fealty to concord: "I shall be so condescending as to acquaint your uglyship, that I take great pleasure in subscribing myself your most inveterate, most implacable, most irreconcilable enemy." Then follows the notoriously dissonant *Jargon*, a musical joke full of harsh intervals and awkward harmonic progressions. The text is a brief quatrain:

> *Let horrid Jargon split the Air,*
> *And rive the Nerves asunder.*
> *Let hateful Discord greet the Ear*
> *As terrible as Thunder.*

Billings gives mock instructions for performance with a rough humor that prefigures some of Charles Ives's salty marginal comments (see p. 154):

[5] The music and complete text in *MinA*, No. 43.

In order to do this piece justice, the concert must be made of vocal and instrumental music. Le it be performed in the following manner, *viz.:* Let an Ass bray the base, let the filing of a saw carry the tenor, let a hog who is extremely weak squeal the counter [i.e., the alto part], and let a cart-wheel, which is heavy-loaded, and that has long been without grease, squeak the treble; and if the concert should appear to be too feeble, you may add the cracking of a crow, the howling of a dog, the squalling of a cat, and what would grace the concert yet more, would be the rubbing of a wet finger upon a window glass. This last mentioned instrument no sooner salutes the drum of the ear, but it instantly conveys the sensation to the teeth; and if all these in conjunction should not reach the cause [i.e., should not suffice], you may add this most inharmonious of all sounds, "Pay me what thou owest."

By 1781 Billings had published two more tunebooks. The first, *Music in Miniature* (1779; the title referred to its unusually tiny size), included mainly reprints of successful earlier pieces. The second, *The Psalm Singer's Amusement*, had plenty of new pieces, among them two that must have been great favorites in the singing schools. One, *Consonance*, is a setting of a poem by Rev. Mather Byles titled "On Musick." It begins, "Down steers the Bass with grave majestick air/And up the Treble mounts with shrill career." Billings is at his most melodious as he graphically "explains" each of the lines in a technique of musical word-painting that goes all the way back to the Elizabethan madrigal composers. The other, *Modern Music* (*MinA*, No. 45), explains several musical matters even more explicitly, commencing with the lines, "We are met for a Concert of modern invention./To tickle the Ear is our present intention." The singers chant liltingly that ". . . we all agree/To set the tune on E,/The Author's darling Key/He prefers to the rest," and they go on to sing, in various meters, modes, tempos, and textures, a naïve but engaging demonstration of "modern" American music.

Billings was to offer to the public two more tunebooks, *The Suffolk Harmony* in 1786 and *The Continental Harmony* in 1794. In the preface to the latter, he exclaimed ecstatically over "fuging music" (which he had been composing since *The Singing Master's Assistant* back in 1778):

There is more variety in one piece of fuging music than in twenty pieces of plain song. . . . The audience are most luxuriously entertained, and exceedingly delighted; in the mean time, their minds are surprizingly agitated, and extremely fluctuated. . . . Now the solemn bass demands their attention, now the manly tenor, now the lofty counter, now the volatile treble, now here, now there, now here again. —O inchanting! O ecstatic! Push on, push on ye sons of harmony.

Why was Billings so excited about "fuging music"? The answer lies in the fact that Billings, and after him many other Yankee composers, was rediscovering the pleasures of counterpoint. Their predecessors, the earlier tunebook compilers of the pre-Revolutionary period, had been content to offer their singers nothing but simply harmonized versions of traditional psalm tunes, but the idea of contrapuntal imitation between the voice-parts seemed to offer a much better world of musical pleasure to the singers than had the old "plain song." No wonder Billings called the idea of imitative counterpoint—not a new idea, by any means, but one with which the early Americans had lost contact—a "most ingenious and . . . most grateful" one. It may be true, but it is certainly irrelevant, that neither Billings nor, perhaps, any of the other Yankee tunesmiths had the background or the technical skill needed to write real fugues (which is why it is useful to preserve the archaic spelling and thus to distinguish the New Englanders' fuging style from the classical European fugue). What they were after, and what they achieved, was music grateful to perform—music that would give every voice a good tune to sing. It was enough for them that the regular, foursquare chordal texture of the music would occasionally give way to a "fuge," and, as put by Billings, each part would seem to be "mutually striving for mastery, and sweetly con-tending for victory."

Billings has captured the imagination of American music historians by virtue of his colorful personality, his apostleship of artistic freedom and individuality, his sense of humor, and his flair for tuneful melody. If he was not, as some have implied, the most original, the most typical, or the most popular of the First New England School, he does symbolize perfectly the cheerful, unselfconscious pride, the honest journeyman ex-cellence of our nation's first composers. Nevertheless, he died "poor and neglected." Other composers, from outside the Boston area, had even more successfully caught the popular fancy in the post-Revolutionary War period. Like Billings, they were singing masters and singing-school tunebook compilers. Most of them came from Connecticut or central Massachusetts, and for many of them music was but a part-time oc-cupation.

Daniel Read (1757–1836) was one of the most active, and gifted, composer-compilers. He also ran a general store in New Haven. His immense popularity as a composer can be suggested by the fact that his pieces were pirated time and again by other tunebook compilers; one of his Christmas hymns, for instance, *Sherburne*, was reprinted (with or without permission) no less than 71 times between 1785 (when it first appeared in Read's *American Singing Book*) and 1810 (see Figure 1-1). Timothy Swan (1758–1842), of Worcester, Massachusetts, was first apprenticed to a merchant, then to a hatter; in later life he was termed "poor, proud, and indolent" by his neighbors. Supply Belcher (1751–1836) was a tavernkeeper in Stoughton, Massachusetts before he moved to the northern frontier, published his *Harmony of Maine* (1794), and came to be known as the "Handel of Maine." Justin Morgan (1747–1798) is perhaps best known as breeder of the Morgan horse; he was also known in West Springfield, Massachusetts and later in Vermont as a schoolmaster, tavernkeeper—and singing master. Andrew Law (1749–1821) was a minister, with several college degrees, but eventually all his energies went to organizing singing schools and to engaging in endless angry correspondence with musical pirates who were, he claimed, "pillaging my books." Other flourishing composers and compilers of music for the singing schools (and a few of their representative tunebooks) were Jacob French (b. 1754; *New American Melody*, 1789); Jacob Kimball (1761–1826; *The Rural Harmony*, 1793); Samuel Holyoke (1762–1820; *Harmonia Americana*, 1791; *The Columbian Repository of Sacred Music*, copyright 1802); Jeremiah Ingalls (1764–1828; *The Christian Harmony*, 1805); Oliver Holden (1765–1844; *The Union Harmony*, 1793); Stephen Jenks (1772–1856; *The Musical Harmonist*, 1800); and many others.[6]

The kind of piece which the New Englanders liked best was the fuging tune; about one-quarter of their total production is made up of this characteristic type which, as we have seen, was modeled on English fuging psalm tunes of the sort Lyon had borrowed for *Urania*. The typical American fuging tune usually proceeds like this: beginning like a choral hymn, in three-part or four-part harmony with the principal air in the tenor voice, it gives way about halfway through to a series of staggered entrances by each of the voice-parts (the fuging section), which are then led to a full close; then the "fuge" is repeated. A good example, and one very popular during the Federal era (it was "borrowed" for reprinting some 101 times before 1810, after its initial publication in 1782), is *Greenfield*, by Lewis Edson (1748–1820) of Bridgewater, Massachusetts. Example 1-5 gives the piece one whole-tone lower than its original pitch, to facilitate comparison between the Yankee musical style in fuging tunes and the style of their British prototypes, represented in Example 1-3.

Some fuging tunes are strophic settings of metrical psalms or hymns; the same music serves for each of the poetic stanzas. Similarly strophic are "plain tunes," which are syllabic settings of one poetic stanza, with three-part or four-part harmony throughout, no fuging section, and the principal air in the tenor voice; see, for example, Billings's *Conquest* (*MinA*, No. 46), Read's *Windham* (*MinA*, No. 50), or Swan's *China* (see Example 1-6; another version in *MinA*, No. 53). The New Englanders essayed larger types of works also: the set piece, a through-composed setting of poetry longer than a single stanza, and the anthem, a through-composed

---

[6] Pieces by most of these composers are reprinted in *MinA*, Nos. 50ff. Lowens has pointed out numerous inaccuracies of fact in this section of *MinA*; see his review in *MQ*, L (1964), 393–98.

EXAMPLE 1-5. L. Edson, *Greenfield,* as originally printed in Simeon Jocelin's tunebook *The Chorister's Companion* (New Haven: T. and S. Green, 1782), p. 18.

setting of a prose text from Scripture. While the set piece is typically chordal throughout, like an extra-long plain tune, the anthem is characterized by varied textures—now a chordal passage, now a fuging section, now individual voice-parts in alternation. These longer pieces are not always successful: the Yankee tunesmiths had a very limited vocabulary of harmony and virtually no concept of modulation, and their attempts to build larger formal structures often become tedious for lack of harmonic variety.

The melodies of all this music are apt to be of a folkish quality, now simple and flowing, now angular and rhythmically powerful, if somewhat rigid. They derived partly from the Anglo-Celtic folk-song tradition, and indeed in many of the tunes can be heard echoes of such airs as *Greensleeves* and *Lord Randal*. One of the most striking is that of Swan's *China* (*MinA*, No. 53), a piece that so caught the fancy of New Englanders that it was sung at funerals "down East" for about a century after it first appeared in 1790. Example 1-6 gives the entire piece; the air is, of course, in the tenor voice.

EXAMPLE 1-6. T. Swan, *China* (1790), after the version printed in William Little and William Smith, *The Easy Instructor* (Albany: Websters & Skinner and Daniel Steele, [1809]), p. 99.

The harmony of the Yankee fuging tunes and other works is perhaps the most characteristic feature of their style. Abounding in open fifths, parallel fifths and octaves, modal inflections, surprising dissonances, it seems almost a throwback to an earlier style of European music, long before the development of the highly organized tonal syntax of the century of Handel and Haydn. Yet the Americans were consistent in their taste, and their music is perfectly homogeneous stylistically; in its own terms, it is as "stylish" as the more complex and sophisticated European music of its time.

In performing these choral pieces, some women usually doubled the leading tenor part in a higher octave; conversely, some men might double the trebles an octave lower. Thus the New England style often resulted in an organ-like sonority of six parts. Billings emphasized the desirability of a really solid bass: he complained in *The New-England Psalm-Singer* that "in most Singing Companies I ever heard, the greatest Failure was in the Bass," and he cautioned that "in order to have good Music, there must be Three Bass to one of the Upper Parts. So that for instance, suppose a Company of Forty People, Twenty of them should sing the Bass."

Most of the texts found in the Yankee tunebooks are, of course, religious. Isaac Watts was by far the most popular source for the hymns and fuging tunes. His doughty translations and paraphrases of the psalms fit the rough-hewn, forthright New England music perfectly, and on occasion he could rise to greatness; witness a stanza of his that was set as a hymn by Justin Morgan under the title *Amanda*:

> *Death, like an overflowing stream,*
> *Sweeps us away; our life's a dream;*
> *An empty tale; a morning flow'r,*
> *Cut down and withered in an hour.*

Nahum Tate and the Wesleys were also favorite poets, and so was John Newton, whose *Olney Hymns* (1779) were full of powerful (some said extravagant) imagery and emotionalism.

Patriotism and religion were often intermingled. One can imagine the political overtones that singing-schoolers must have read into Supply Belcher's lusty *Jubilant* (*MinA*, No. 59), set to a text by Charles Wesley and published not long after the United States was proclaimed a new constitutional republic:

> *Blow ye the trumpet, blow*
> *The gladly solemn sound;*
> *Let all the nations know,*
> *To earth's remotest bound:*
> *The year of jubilee is come,*
> *Return, ye ransom'd sinners, home!*

Stephen Jenks voiced the same sentiments even more directly in his fuging tune *Liberty*:

> *No more beneath the oppressive hand*
> *Of tyranny we groan.*
> *Behold the happy, smiling land*
> *That freedom calls her own.*

In 1775, Andrew Law found appropriate verses for *Bunker Hill* (*MinA*, No. 47) in Nathaniel Miles's poem, "The American Hero":

> *Why should vain Mortals tremble at the sight*
> *Of Death and Destruction in the Field of Battle,*
> *Where Blood and Carnage clothe the Ground in Crimson,*
> *Sounding with Death-Groans?*

. . .

> *Life, for my Country and the Cause of Freedom,*
> *Is but a Trifle for a Worm to part with;*
> *And if preserved in so great a Contest,*
> *Life is redoubled.*

We may find Billings's paraphrase of the 137th Psalm amusingly presumptuous, but certainly it was no smiling matter to him when, remembering the siege of Boston, he wrote:

> *By the rivers of Watertown we sat down and wept.*
> *We wept when we remembered thee, O Boston. . . .*

> *Forbid it, Lord God, that those who have sucked*
> *Bostonians' breasts should thirst for American blood.*

Such a piece as the last-mentioned, Billings's *Lamentation Over Boston* (1778), points to one of the most appealing aspects of the singing-school music of the Yankee tunesmiths: this was a music completely in tune with the society for which it was written. These journeyman composers had a secure and respected function in Colonial and Federal-era life in general; viewed historically from a point two hundred years later, theirs was a sort of golden age of musical participation in which teachers, composers, singers, and populace in general worked together fruitfully. If ever there was truly a popular music, the music of the New Englanders was popular: it arose from deep, old traditions of early America; it was accessible to all and enjoyed by all; it was a plain-spoken music for plain people; and, assessed on its own terms, it was a stylistically homogeneous music of great integrity—really the first indigenous music of the United States.

Diffusion of the Yankee idiom outside of New England was aided not only by the peripatetic singing masters—Andrew Law, for instance, conducted singing schools throughout his native New England and in New York, New Jersey, Pennsylvania, Maryland, and even the Carolinas —but also by the evangelistic revival movements, like the "Great Revival"

FIGURE 1-1. Daniel Read's fuging tune *Sherburne* (1785), as printed in shape-notes in an 1802 edition of *The Easy Instructor*. Courtesy of The New York Public Library; Astor, Lenox and Tilden Foundations. Music Division.

of 1800. It may also have been encouraged by the development of new systems of music notation, especially the "shape-note" notation of William Smith and William Little, in whose *Easy Instructor* (Albany, 1798) the musical notes were shaped differently according to their position in the scale (see Figure 1-1). At that time, instead of *do, re, mi, fa, sol, la, ti, do* the syllables *fa, sol, la, fa, sol, la, mi, fa* were used; hence, four shapes sufficed to distinguish the syllables: ◁ (*fa*), ○ (*sol*), □ (*la*), ◇ (*mi*). Little and Smith's invention, reminiscent of other less successful American attempts (e.g., Tufts's) both earlier and later to make easier the task of learning to read music, had the simplicity of genius. Their four-shape notation was widely adopted in other tunebooks: it would seem that Andrew Law, who claimed shape notes as his own idea, borrowed them from *The Easy Instructor* for his *Art Of Singing* (4th ed., 1803), and other tunebook compilers followed suit, especially those who favored the New England style of music.

But not every post-colonial American did favor it. With the new wave of immigration that followed the successful establishment and consolidation of the United States of America came a new wave of foreign influence in American music. In the cities along the eastern seaboard, wealth began to accumulate, and so did a taste for European standards of culture—and cultural models as well. The tendency of more-or-less aristocratic Americans to look to Europe for "lessons in living well" had been latent for some time; it was reinforced as Americans, at least those in the eastern cities, sought increasingly to act "urbane." Ironically, in the very place that had seen its beginning, and for the same reason—cultural improvement—the Yankee music began to be attacked. One articulate spokesman for reform was John Hubbard, a sometime musician himself but also professor of mathematics and natural philosophy at Dartmouth College in New Hampshire. Hubbard's *Essay on Music* (1808) was a harsh criticism of the New England style and its artisan composers. It attacked the "common fuge" as a music that "can never be of more consequence than an oration well pronounced in a foreign language," and as for the tunesmiths:

> Almost every pedant, after learning his eight notes, has commenced author. With a genius, sterile as the deserts of Arabia, he has attempted to rival the great masters of music. On the leaden wings of dullness, he has attempted to soar into these regions of science, never penetrated but by real genius. . . .[7]

Elias Mann, whose tunebook appeared in 1807 in Boston, made a point of saying in his preface that he had included "none of those wild fugues, and rapid and confused movements, which have so long been the disgrace of congregational psalmody." Andrew Law, after a lengthy career

[7] John Hubbard, *An Essay on Music* (Boston: Manning & Loring, 1808), pp. 17–18.

as partisan of his native style, turned his back on it completely. Increasingly, as his knowledge of the "sublime and beautiful compositions of the great Masters of Music" grew, he sought to substitute "serious, animated, and devout" music for "that lifeless and insipid, or that frivolous and frolicksome succession and combination of sounds" which the New Englanders had created. Even Daniel Read, perhaps the most gifted of the Yankee composers, felt the impact of the new wave. Read never became, as did Law, a self-styled reformer; nevertheless, in some oddly touching words written in his old age, he confessed to changed musical values:

> Since studying the writings of such men as D'Alembert [and others], since carefully examining the system of harmony practically exhibited in Handel's *Messiah,* Haydn's *Creation,* and other similar works . . . my ideas on the subject of music have been considerably altered; I will not say improved.[8]

In later chapters, we shall see how completely the music of the Yankee tunesmiths was submerged beneath the new wave of musical taste in eastern America—but not extinguished completely.

SOUTH OF NEW ENGLAND

If the British colonists of the New World must, because of their predominance among the early settlers, be considered the mainstream of early American culture, there were nevertheless important minority groups very early. In general, these groups—notably German Pietists in Pennsylvania and Moravian brethren in Pennsylvania and the Carolinas—were culturally insular; their communities tended to remain "foreign" enclaves even in a land of immigrants. Nevertheless, their musical cultures deserve brief mention.

A number of Protestant German sects settled in Pennsylvania for religious motives. Each differed in its worship-music practice, but all were alike in their emphasis on congregational song, especially chorales. To Germantown in 1694 came a group of Pietists under the leadership of Johannes Kelpius (1673–1708). Known as the Hermits of the Ridge (or Wissahickon Mystics, or True Rosicrucians), they sang hymns, psalms, and anthems and apparently used instrumental accompaniment. Kelpius compiled for his flock a hymn book with the Pietist title *The Lamenting Voice of the Hidden Love at the Time when She Lay in Misery and forsaken* (the manuscript is now at the Historical Society of Pennsylvania),

8 Quoted in *MMEA,* p. 175.

containing ten hymn tunes, some with basses, of a harmonic richness un-known to the New England Puritans.

Conrad Beissel (1690–1768), who emigrated to Pennsylvania in 1720, founded in 1732 a semi-monastic community at Ephrata, in what is now Lancaster County, 65 miles from Philadelphia. Urging on his band an active musical seventh-day observance, Beissel turned from Pietist hymns and traditional chorales to original compositions, some of great length and in as many as eight voices. In 1747 he published at Ephrata a massive collection of sacred choral pieces, *The Song of the Lonely and Forsaken Turtle Dove, namely the Christian Church*, the pages of which give some idea of the uniquely mannered notation of Beissel, even better viewed in the beautifully illuminated manuscripts that emanated from the cloister.[9] Beissel's music is purposely ultra-consonant, avoiding any dissonant harmony on accented text syllables, which produces a monolithic if somewhat tedious result only slightly relieved by occasional antiphonal treatment of the choristers, who are said to have numbered 25, 15 women and 10 men.

The richest and most sophisticated musical culture in colonial America was that of the Moravians in Pennsylvania and the Carolinas. They came from German-speaking Bohemia for the most part, members of the Unitas Fratrum, the first independent Protestant sect, founded in Bohemia and Moravia in the mid-fifteenth century. The first Moravians to reach America came to the West Indies in 1732; a sizable community settled in Bethlehem, Pennsylvania, in 1741. Other Moravian centers were created at Lititz and Nazareth and at Salem (now Winston-Salem) in North Carolina.

The musical life of the Moravian brethren was extraordinarily intense. Theirs was the first concerted sacred music in America: instruments joined soloists and choirs in anthems, sacred arias, motets, and chorales. At the major Moravian musical centers, Bethlehem and Salem, brass ensembles serenaded the communities of brethren and played for weddings, christenings, funerals, and other solemn occasions. Collegia Musica—groups meeting regularly to practice music, especially instrumental music—were organized, and substantial libraries of European music of the seventeenth and eighteenth centuries accumulated. Some of this country's earliest and best instrument makers helped to supply the Collegia; especially notable is the Lititz organ builder David Tannenberg (1728–1804), who designed and constructed almost 50 organs, for Lutheran and Roman Catholic as well as Moravian churches.

---

[9] A reproduction of one page of the published version of the *Turtle Dove* is printed in *MinA;* No. 31 is a transcription of it. The largest and most stunning of the manuscript versions, once possessed by Benjamin Franklin, is in the Library of Congress.

Like most of the Yankee tunesmiths to the north, many of the
Moravian composers were occupied in other tasks for a living. Indeed,
some might never have composed at all had not a demand for new music
existed. Jeremias Dencke (1735–1795) arrived from Germany in 1760
as pastor and business manager in Bethlehem. He was the first to compose sacred music with instruments, notably three sets of sacred songs
for soprano, strings, and organ, among them the lovely aria *Ich will
singen von einem Könige.* Johannes Herbst (1734–1812) came to Pennsylvania in 1786, was pastor at Lancaster and later Lititz, and pastor and
bishop at Salem in the last year of his life. The most prolific of the Moravian composers, Herbst wrote some 125 sacred songs and anthems. John
Antes (1741–1811), American-born, was a string-instrument maker who
was later ordained a pastor and sent to Egypt as a missionary. There, between 1779 and 1781, he composed three trios for two violins and cello,
the earliest chamber music written by an American.[10] Johann Friedrich
(John Frederick) Peter (1746–1813) was probably the most gifted of the
Moravian composers: almost 100 works, mostly anthems and arias but
also six string quintets (Salem, 1789), reveal him as a sensitive and highly
expressive minor master of the early Classic style.[11] David Moritz
Michael (1751–1825), a German who was in Pennsylvania from 1795
to 1815 in various administrative posts, put his first-hand knowledge
of woodwind instruments to good use in 16 suite-like works for wind
sextet;[12] he is also notable for having conducted a performance of
Haydn's *Creation* in America as early as 1811.

The Moravian culture was essentially insular: although it was
known and spoken of admiringly by other Americans in the eighteenth
century, it had little influence outside the Moravian communities themselves. On the other hand, the music of the American Moravians has a
special stamp, the result of the New World environment. One specialist
in their music has cogently described the source of this "American"
quality:

> The Moravians were devout people. Colonial life for them had a religious
> purpose and religious ideas dominated their activities. This gives their
> music a special character. In Europe, the average late 18th century com-
> poser wrote an occasional piece of church music between the symphonies,
> sonatas, operas, and other secular works which were his chief concern.

[10] Trio II, 1st movement, in *MinA*, No. 34. Antes's moving aria *Go, Congregation, Go!* and the choral anthem *Surely He has Borne our Griefs* (which some claim
to be a companion piece for the aria) in *MinA*, Nos. 32, 33.
[11] Quintet V, 2nd movement, in *MinA*, No. 35; the sacred song *Ich will mit
euch einigen ewigen Bund machen* in *MinA*, No. 36.
[12] The first movement of No. 1 of these, which were called *Parthien* by
Michael, in *MinA*, No. 37.

To the Moravian musicians in America, however, church music was the most important expression of their inner lives. Their music therefore is better suited to the purpose and more touching than most religious music written in Europe during the same period.[13]

The story of sacred music in the middle Atlantic and Southern British colonies is less well documented than in the German-speaking communities or in New England. The German immigrants maintained and even enriched their European musical life; thanks to the singing-school movement, the New Englanders created a whole repertory of published sacred-secular music. Little is known, however, of sacred music in the Quaker center of Philadelphia until the 1760's; Virginia, almost wholly an agricultural colony, has left us almost no colonial music; and South Carolina, especially its largest city Charleston (Charles Town at the time), had an active secular music life that has somewhat obscured its special activity in sacred music.

Two native-born composers (the first Americans securely identifiable as such) figured in the sacred music of Philadelphia in the early 1760's. These were James Lyon and Francis Hopkinson (1737–1791; see below, pp. 39–41). Lyon began the history of Philadelphia music publishing in 1761 with *Urania* (see p. 9). He indicated in the index that six of the 96 pieces in it were "completely new"; some of these may have been by Lyon himself, but the music for *The 23d Psalm* is by Hopkinson, better known as a cultivated dilettante specializing in secular music (Example 1-7). One of the hymns in *Urania, Whitefield's*, is a setting of a text from the 1757 *Hymn Collection* of the famous British Methodist revivalist George Whitefield; its music is the first American publication of the tune *God Save the King*, later (1831) to be used as the melody for Samuel Francis Smith's "My Country 'tis of Thee."[14]

Charleston, by 1775 the largest city south of Philadelphia, was a brilliant center of church music, as it was of secular. Free from the restrictions on instruments observed in Puritan New England, Charleston's Anglican churches of St. Philip's and St. Michael's allowed organs to be heard, and peals of bells. Organist at St. Philip's from 1737 to 1750 was Charles Theodore Pachelbel (1690–1750), son of the famous Nuremberg organist Johann Pachelbel. Of Charles Theodore's music we have a fine *Magnificat* for two choirs and organ, written, however, before the composer left Germany for America.

---

[13] Hans T. David (ed.), *Ten Sacred Songs*. Music of the Moravians in America . . . , No. 1 (New York: New York Public Library, 1947), p. v.

[14] The hymn is in *MinA*, No. 40. The tune has been put to various uses by Americans; one version from the Federal period begins with the words "God save great Washington," another with "God save America."

EXAMPLE 1-7. Hopkinson, *The 23d Psalm Tune,* in J. Lyon, *Urania* (Philadelphia: William Bradford, 1761), p. 50; measures 1-12. The cut-time signature reversed indicates a quick tempo, $\frac{2}{2}$.

BIBLIOGRAPHICAL NOTES

Robert Stevenson's *Protestant Church Music in America* (New York: W. W. Norton & Company, Inc., 1966) is a rich reference source for material in this chapter.

The music of Ainsworth's psalter has been transcribed, not without errors, in Waldo Selden Pratt's *The Music of the Pilgrims* (Boston: Oliver Ditson Company, 1921). The most extensive study of the *Bay Psalm Book,* emphasizing textual rather than musical matters, is Zoltán Haraszti's *The Enigma of the Bay Psalm Book* (Chicago: University of Chicago Press, 1956), published together with a facsimile of the first edition of 1640.

"The Singing School Movement in the United States" was the subject of a round-table discussion at the Eighth Congress of the International Musicological Society; the illuminating paper by Allen P. Britton on which the discussion was based is printed in Volume I of the *I.M.S. Congress Report (1961),* a summary of the discussion in Volume II

(1962). Britton and Irving Lowens have collaborated on a number of articles in the *Journal of Research in Music Education* and the *Journal of the American Musicological Society;* Lowen's independent work, especially an invaluable series of bibliographical studies, has been revised and reprinted in *MMEA.* Tufts's *Introduction* (1726 edition) has been published in facsimile (Philadelphia: Musical Americana, 1954) with an introduction by Lowens.

I have written on "William Billings and the Yankee Tunesmiths" in *HiFi Stereo Review,* XVI, 2 (February 1966), 55–65. Billings's *Continental Harmony* is available in a facsimile reprint, introduced by Hans Nathan (Cambridge: Harvard University Press, 1961); *The Psalm Singer's Amusement* is reprinted in the *EAM* series (as is Belcher's *Harmony of Maine*). Another of the tunebook compilers, Andrew Law, is the subject of a fine lengthy study by Richard Crawford: *Andrew Law, American Psalmodist* (Evanston: Northwestern University Press, 1968).

The American Moravians have been extensively studied by researchers affiliated with the Moravian Music Foundation (Winston-Salem, N.C.), especially its former director Donald McCorkle.

TWO

SECULAR MUSIC
IN THE NEW WORLD

We have very little hard evidence of secular music-making in the Colonial period, at least until the mid-eighteenth century and even later. As Oscar Sonneck commented in his monumental bibliography of American secular music to 1800, "Before 1790 practically nothing but psalm and hymn books were published, with here and there an issue of secular character as in the various 'Almanacks' and literary periodicals—also a very few songsters with music" (as opposed to the great majority, which were simply printings of song texts).[1] But it is impossible to believe that the colonists, for all the strictures of Puritan and Calvinist mores, did not enjoy secular songs and dances along with psalmody and hymnody (and much of that, as we have seen, was put to secular, social use in the singing schools, although it was ostensibly sacred). And, in fact, there is plenty of circumstantial evidence that they did.

[1] Oscar George Theodore Sonneck, *A Bibliography of Early Secular American Music (18th Century)*, revised and enlarged by William Treat Upton (Washington: The Library of Congress, Music Division, 1945), p. 575.

BRITISH-AMERICAN FOLK AND POPULAR SONG

To begin with, there is the large repertory of Anglo-Scottish-Irish "folk songs" that have come down to us. These were, of course, the "pop songs" of the day—a living music of everyday use by all. During the Colonial period, virtually none were written down: not only were they part of an ages-old tradition whereby popular music was transmitted orally from performer to performer and from one generation to the next, but also the press, in early America, was almost entirely in the control of the clergy, and the clergy had no interest in propagating or memorializing secular music. Nevertheless, that the "underground" popular culture of the American Colonies was a very lively one indeed is suggested, for instance, by the fact that about 100 of the 300-odd traditional British ballads—the "Child ballads," so called after Francis James Child (1825–1896), their great collector and commentator—have been traced (and are still sung) in this country—more than in living British tradition. The colonists were selective: older songs on themes irrelevant to the Colonial experience (e.g., courtly or chivalric) tended to be dropped; many that were preserved have to do with sexual rivalry as seen through feminine eyes (*Barbara Ellen, The Gypsy Laddie, Little Musgrove, Jimmy Randall*) or relate directly to the New World experience (*Captain Kidd, The Golden Vanity*). The colonists of course changed the details of many British songs in terms of the American context and developing character. One example is a song from southern England (known also in Ireland), "My Jolly Herring" or *The Red Herring Song*, which was transformed into a tale of Yankee resourcefulness and thrift (with a comic note) as "The Sow Took the Measles."[2] Another is *The Foggy Dew*, of which the original explicit sexuality ("I rolled my love all over the foggy dew") was tempered by Puritan sensibility ("The only thing I did that was wrong/ Was to keep her from the foggy dew").

Against the background of this British ballad tradition, Americans of course created their own popular ballads. The earliest that can be dated with certainty is *Springfield Mountain*, a re-creation in song of the death by snake-bite on August 7, 1761, of Timothy Myrick of Springfield Mountain (now Wilbraham), Massachusetts (Example 2-1).[3]

In addition to British ballads and other songs brought to the New

---

[2] For some of these points, and the specific example of this song, I am indebted to Alan Lomax, *The Folk Songs of North America in the English Language* (Garden City, New York: Doubleday & Co., Inc., 1960), pp. xv–xxii.

[3] *Ibid.*, p. 6; verses 2–7 of this version of the song, not given in Example 2–1, are found in Lomax, p. 13.

EXAMPLE 2-1. *Springfield Mountain,* as collected by Alan Lomax in Town-shend, Vermont (1939); stanza 1 of text only. From FOLK SONGS OF NORTH AMERICA by Alan Lomax. Copyright © 1960 Alan Lomax. Copyright © 1960 Cassell & Co., Ltd. Reprinted by permission of Doubleday & Company, Inc.

World and preserved through oral tradition, the colonists also had copies of various British publications containing popular and traditional songs and tunes. One was Thomas Ravenscroft's three-part collection of 1609–11: *Pammelia. Musick's Miscellanie; Deuteromelia: or the Second Part of Musick's Melodie* (which includes the first published version of "Three Blind Mice"); and *Melismata. Musicall Phansies.* Another was John Play-ford's *The English Dancing Master,* dated 1651 (*recte* 1650; many more editions through 1728). Across the Atlantic came also Thomas d'Urfey's six-volume collection, *Wit and Mirth; or Pills to Purge Melancholy* (London, 1719–20), as did John Watt's *The Musical Miscellany* (also in six volumes; London, 1729–31) and John Walsh's *The Compleat Country Dancing Master* (London, 1731).

Examples from one or two of these printed collections of British popular tunes can suggest the sturdy musical stock from which sprang early American secular songs and dances. *Newcastle,* from Playford's *English Dancing Master,* is a bold, stomping tune with a short-long, iam-bic syncope ("x" in the example) we shall meet again in several later kinds of American popular music (Example 2-2a). The traditional *Pack-ington's Pound* tune is the basis for anonymous verses about the "gallants of Newgate"—denizens of London's most infamous prison—which were printed in Watts's *Musical Miscellany;* the tune alternates between minor and modal flavor (now using E♮, now E♭) and at one point broadens out marvelously from $\frac{3}{4}$ to $\frac{3}{2}$ meter (bracketed in the example) (Example 2-2b).

With Example 2-2, which relates textually to the subject-mat-ter (London's underworld) of the first popular English "ballad opera," *The Beggar's Opera* (1728) of John Gay and Christopher Pepusch (and whose tune is actually the basis of Air XLIII, in Act III), we approach a more formal kind of secular music than the ballads of oral tradition: music that was heard in concert and on stage in the eastern seaboard American cities, from the 1730's on. These cities had developed remark-ably in size and wealth during the first three-quarters of the eighteenth century. If by 1690 substantial towns had been established at Boston,

EXAMPLE 2-2. a. *Newcastle;* my transcription from John Playford, *The English Dancing Master* (London, 1651 [recte 1650]), No. 77; the original is a minor third higher;

EXAMPLE 2-2 b. "Newgate's Garland," anonymous verse to be sung to the tune *Packington's Pound,* John Watts, *The Musical Miscellany* (London, 1729–31), V, 42.

New York, Philadelphia, Charleston, and elsewhere, by 1774—on the eve of the Revolution—they had mushroomed into real cities, which grew even more rapidly in the next quarter-century. The following table[4] shows the growth during this period.

[4] Adapted from Charles A. and Mary R. Beard, *A Basic History of the United States* (Philadelphia: The Blakiston Company, 1944), p. 44, and from Russell B. Nye, *The Cultural Life of the New Nation, 1776–1830* (New York: Harper & Brothers, 1960), p. 124.

	1690	*1774*	*1800*
New York (founded 1625)	3900	25–30,000	60,000
Boston (founded 1630)	7000	20,000	25,000
Charleston (founded 1672)	1100	10,000	18,000
Philadelphia (founded 1682)	4000	40,000	70,000

Other growing cities were Salem, Providence, New Haven, Perth Amboy, Baltimore, Richmond, and Savannah. Although the population of these cities was but a fraction of the total population of the colonies, their concentration of wealth and of social, political, and intellectual activity made them the cultural centers of the new land. As commercial cities, they tended to reflect the artistic life of similar European cities with which they had close contacts. Thus, among other kinds of art, art-music gained its first Anglo-American expression in the cities, where from the 1730's we have records of concerts, operas, and other secular music.

THE RISE OF CONCERTS AND OPERA

The New World was hardly behind the Old in the establishment of a secular music culture based on public concerts. This would be a matter for nationalistic pride were it not for the fact that public concerts in Europe were a reflection of the rise of the middle class as patron of music, in contrast to the traditional aristocratic and churchly patronage; lacking a true aristocratic class, America's was basically a middle-class culture from the beginning, and it was natural that some of its musical energy was directed very early into public concerts. Thus, from the 1730's we hear of concerts in Boston, Charleston, New York, and other cities. The first of these we know about was announced in the *Boston Weekly News Letter* of December 16, 1731 as a forthcoming "*Concert of Music* on sundry Instruments at Mr. Pelham's great Room. . . . Tickets to be delivered at the place of performance at *Five shillings* each. The concert to begin exactly at Six o'clock. . . ."[5]

Opera too was heard in America from the 1730's, not of course the lavish, costly, and aristocratic Baroque opera but English ballad operas, those plays-with-songs which had captivated London's public with the immensely successful run in 1728 of John Gay's *The Beggar's Opera*. To Gay's text, which satirized the social, political, and musical establishment, John Christopher Pepusch adapted well-known popular songs and ballad airs—also, with tongue in cheek, some music from Handel's Italian

[5] Quoted in O. G. T. Sonneck, *Early Concert-Life in America* (Leipzig: Breitkopf & Härtel, 1907), p. 251.

operas. (The satiric thrust of *The Beggar's Opera* and its many immediate imitators, and their use of pre-existent music, were gone from ballad
operas later in the eighteenth century; they were largely sentimental
dramas with newly-composed songs interpolated in them.) New York
audiences heard *The Beggar's Opera* in 1750 and 1751, as produced by
a company of "comedians from Philadelphia," but the record of ballad
opera in America had begun even before that with *Flora, or Hob in the
Well* (London, 1729), produced at Charleston in 1735 (both the libretto
and the music lost), and Coffey's *The Devil to Pay* (adapted in Germany
as one of the first *Singspiele* under the title *Der Teufel ist los*) in 1736,
also at Charleston. The operatic centers of America in the eighteenth
century were the cities from New York south: at Boston, the anti-theater
blue law of 1750 had put an effective check on the establishment of
ballad opera there. By the end of the eighteenth century two major opera
companies were renowned. One was William Hallam's London troupe,
which started its American career in 1752 at Williamsburg, moved to
New York, named itself the American Company (and later the Old American), went back to England during the Revolution, then returned after
the war to New York. The Old American Company's rival was the New
Company founded in 1792 at Philadelphia by Thomas Wignell, English
actor and singer, and Alexander Reinagle (see p. 36). The Wignell-
Reinagle company played in the celebrated New Theatre on Chestnut
Street, a handsome hall with a stage 36 feet wide and 71 deep and with
some 2000 seats, 900 of them in two tiers of boxes, above which was a
large gallery.

Early American concerts and ballad operas were understandably
dominated by emigrant professional musicians, unlike the singing schools
which, arising from a long native tradition, were led by American-born
journeyman composers. The cities could support these emigré "professors" of music, particularly in the post-Revolutionary period of economic
and commercial consolidation between 1783 and 1812, and indeed their
standards and taste were to have a shaping influence on American musical culture in general. They were aided by, in fact they led, the remarkable development in the late eighteenth century of music publishing in
America. In little more than a half-century before 1820, American publishers issued an estimated 15,000 separate works in sheet-music editions,
plus more than 500 different "songsters"—pocket-size collections of song
texts. Instrument manufacture was also on the rise: the simpler instruments had probably been made in America almost from the beginning,
but as early as the 1740's we learn of a harpsichord builder, Gustav Hes-
selius of the Old Swedes' Church in Philadelphia, and of piano builders
from 1775, when John Behrent of Philadelphia announced the manufacture of "an extraordinary instrument, by the name of the pianoforte, in

mahogany in the manner of a harpsichord."[6]

Concerts and opera performances in the cities were paralleled by a dramatic rise of secular music in the urban home. "Almost every young lady and gentleman, from the children of the judge, the banker, and the general, down to those of the constable, the huckster and the drummer, can make a noise upon some instrument or other, and charm their neighbors with something which courtesy calls music," wrote a correspondent in the Philadelphia *Mirror of Taste and Dramatic Censor* in 1810.[7] Even if professional musicians could not make a living solely by performing, they could eke out an existence by hanging out a shingle as teachers or as proprietors of music stores—"magazines" or "repositories," as they were more often called. In short, secular music was becoming a real business in America as the eighteenth century closed and the nineteenth opened.

We should not, however, expect to find in the secular music of eighteenth-century America anything to match the scope or seriousness of purpose of, say, the music of Vienna, Rome, or Paris. The American ballad opera was an unpretentious entertainment with simple songs, enjoyable to all. The American concert was a mixture of short instrumental pieces delivered by a few performers and songs or duets of no great dimensions. The American music publishers addressed themselves mainly to amateurs: like the singing-school tunebooks, the thousands of music sheets and songsters aimed to satisfy the modest abilities of music-makers at home, to offer them practical or topical sources of mild diversion. It would remain for a later generation to distinguish between such "popular" music and a more selfconsciously high-flown "classical" music with serious artistic pretentions.

Representative of the socially useful and surprisingly diversified output of our early publishers is a collection of the 1790's with the informative title page *Evening Amusement. Containing fifty airs, song's, duett's, dances, hornpipe's, reels', marches, minuett's, &c., &c., for 1 and 2 German flutes or violins. Price 75 cents. Printed & sold at B[enjamin] Carr's Musical repositories, Philadelphia and New York, & J[oseph] Carr's, Baltimore*. Published in 1796, this potpourri of pieces designed for "evening amusement" typifies the kinds of secular music enjoyed by American townspeople of the early Federal period.

Traditional popular songs (we would call them folk songs today) of the English, Scottish, and Irish past are well represented, among them *Soldier's Joy, The Irish Washerwoman*, and *O Dear, What Can the Matter Be?* Newer songs, many of them from ballad operas, are present,

---

[6] Arthur Loesser, *Men, Women and Pianos* (New York: Simon & Schuster, 1954), pp. 442–43.

[7] Quoted *ibid.*, pp. 456–57.

like *What a Beau your Granny Was, Thou Softly Flowing Avon,* and *How Happily My Life I Led* (the last taken from the ballad opera *No Song No Supper* of British composer Stephen Storace). Patriotic songs furnished tunes for several of the items: *God Save Great Washington, Yankee Doodle,* Reinagle's *America, Commerce, and Freedom,* and *The Marseilles Hymn.* A variety of dance tunes appears—several hornpipes, a highland reel, a "minuet de la cour," *Mrs. Fraser's Strathspey*—and so do marches, including *General Washington's March, The Duke of York's March,* and a march from *The Battle of Prague* by the Czech-English composer Franz Kotzwara. Haydn is represented by a minuet and "airs" from two symphonies.

Here, then, is what our early urban secular music consisted of: martial and patriotic music, opera airs and traditional songs, dance tunes, and a smattering of programmatic or absolute instrumental music.

MARCHES AND PATRIOTIC SONGS

As we might expect, both the Revolutionary and Federal periods produced their share of military music, including marches and patriotic songs. Sometimes both were combined, as in *Hail! Columbia.* The poem by Joseph Hopkinson (son of Francis) was written in 1798 to be sung to the tune of *The President's March;* the latter, a sturdy foursquare tune, was the work of Philip Phile, who may have composed it after George Washington's inauguration as President of the new United States in 1789, but did not publish it until 1793 or 1794. It was very popular: arrangements for two flutes and for piano duet appeared, as well as many other versions adapted from Phile's original piano setting. *Hail! Columbia* was first published in Philadelphia by Benjamin Carr "for the Voice, Piano Forte, Guittar and Clarinet" (*MinA*, No. 111).

Yankee Doodle has all the earmarks of a march, too, and in fact the earliest known separate edition of the song, published in England in the 1780's, carries the mocking title *Yankee Doodle, or (as now Christened by the Saints of New England) The Lexington March.* A subtitle instructs: "NB. The Words to be Sung thro' the Nose, & in the West Country drawl & dialect"—a jibe at the rural, plebeian backgrounds of most English emigrants to America. Popular here even before the Revolution,[8] *Yankee Doodle* appeared in 1797 or 1798 with bold new words

---

[8] It is mentioned in the libretto of *The Disappointment: or, the Force of Credulity* (New York, 1767), where its tune is to be sung to Air IV of that ballad opera (which seems to have been the first actually written in America).

from the press of James Hewitt, leading New York composer in the post-Revolutionary period (*MinA*, No. 110).

The song destined to become the national anthem was anything but patriotic to begin with. Addressed "to Anacreon in Heav'n," the tune later sung as *The Star-Spangled Banner* originated as a British drinking song, celebrating the twin delights of Venus and Bacchus. Taken up by Americans, it was given new patriotic words in 1798 by a (not *the*) Thomas Paine, who sang of "Ye sons of Columbia, who bravely have fought/For those rights, which unstained from your Sires had descended." The *Star-Spangled Banner* text, which was composed in 1814 by Francis Scott Key after the bombardment of Fort McHenry by the British, was applied to the old tune, and the resulting song was made the national anthem in 1931 (all three versions, among many variants, printed in *MinA*, Nos. 113–115).

OPERA AIRS AND OTHER SONGS

The song *America, Commerce, and Freedom* found in *Evening Amusement* has a patriotic text, but it originated as a theater air. The composer was Alexander Reinagle (1756–1809), who came to New York in 1786 from his native England but soon moved to Philadelphia, where he dominated the musical scene for over two decades. An indefatigable composer, pianist, arranger, conductor, and impresario, Reinagle typified the emigrant professional musicians of the Federal period. A competent if not extraordinary composer, he wrote many of the airs for the ballad operas produced at the New Theatre on Chestnut Street, where he was musical director. (Its opening concert of February 2, 1793, offered an elaborate program of overtures, concertos, symphonies, songs, a quartet, and glees.) *America, Commerce, and Freedom* was composed for the "ballet pantomime" *The Sailor's Landlady*; lusty and virile, it is one of Reinagle's best songs. Example 2-3 gives the beginning of the verse and the sturdy refrain.

More characteristic of the American ballad opera air than *America, Commerce, and Freedom* was a tender, lyrical effusion in the tradition of English or Irish love songs, and modeled on the pleasant if somewhat effete airs of the middle and later eighteenth-century English composers of ballad operas like Thomas (1710–1778) and Michael (1741–1786) Arne, Charles Dibdin (1745–1814), William Shield (1748–1829), and Stephen Storace (1763–1796). Reinagle surely contributed many of this kind to Philadelphia productions, although surprisingly few of his airs

EXAMPLE 2-3. A. Reinagle, *America, Commerce, and Freedom* (Philadelphia: B. Carr, [1794]), measures 9–16, 29–42.

are extant today.[9] The general nature of the "tender" airs, and of their usually vapid poetry, is well seen in *Why, Huntress, Why?*, composed by Benjamin Carr (1768–1831) for a ballad opera on the tale of William Tell

---

[9] One, *When I've got the ready rhino*, a humorous song to a hornpipe tune, printed in *AM,* 1st ed., pp. 115–16; omitted from 2nd ed.

(*The Archers; or, the Mountaineers of Switzerland*), produced by the
Old American Company in New York in 1796 (*MinA*, No. 76). Carr, who
came to New York from London in 1793, established with his brother
and his father a chain of music stores in Philadelphia, New York, and
Baltimore and was a prolific publisher as well. He also had a nice, if
modest, talent as a composer of songs, as suggested by his *Hymn to the
Virgin* ("Ave Maria"), No. 3 of *Six Ballads from the Poem of "The Lady
of the Lake"* (Philadelphia, 1810), which is perhaps the most impressive
American song before Foster's best, and, on a smaller scale, by his sensitive little setting of the "Willow Song" from Shakespeare's *Othello*. It is
so inconclusive, however, as to suggest that it was not intended as an
independent work but as an interpolation in the play (Example 2-4).

EXAMPLE 2-4. B. Carr, "Shakespeare's 'Willow,' " *Musical Journal*, Vol. I,
Vocal Section (Philadelphia: Carr and Schetky, [1800]), 22.

Lacking a lyric theater tradition, New England did not produce a large body of secular song in the eighteenth century, at least not of the sort I have been discussing. The Yankee singing-school tunebooks served, as noted above, for secular diversion even though their contents were mainly sacred; and into them, as the eighteenth century neared its close, secular texts crept more frequently. Supply Belcher's *The Harmony of Maine* (Boston, 1794) included no less than eight secular, nonpatriotic songs to texts in the English lyric tradition and was intended for use in both "singing schools and musical societies." Belcher meant by the latter term those urban rivals of the singing schools which were beginning to be organized in the cities—choral or instrumental groups established (usually under emigrant professional musicians) to perform the "new, scientific" music of Europe. The most famous of these was Boston's Handel and Haydn Society, organized in 1815 by Gottlieb Graupner (1767–1836), who had settled in Boston in 1797 to become an influential entrepreneur of concerts and musical organizations. The invitation to the organizational meeting of the Society was explicit about its aim: ". . . cultivating and improving a correct taste in the performance of sacred music, and also to introduce into more general practice the works of Handel, Haydn, and other eminent composers."

Organist of the Handel and Haydn Society was the corpulent Dr. George K. Jackson (1745–1823), deemed the most learned musician of Boston. Composer of an affecting *Dirge for General Washington* with a complementary *Dead March* for instruments, Jackson also wrote "songs, serenades, cantatas, canzonetts, canons, glees, &c. &c.," as we read in the subtitle of his undated collection *New Miscellaneous Musical Work*. One of its songs, *Cancherizante,* suggests he was indeed musically learned: planned as a demonstration of *cancrizans* or retrograde melodic technique, it is, as Dr. Jackson pedantically explains at the head of the music, "a song to be sung forwards & then backwards beginning at the last note & ending with the first." Pedantic or not, the little song comes off rather well, its music matching nicely the gentle pastoral text (Example 2-5).

Gilbert Chase has neatly pinpointed (in *AM,* Chapters 5 and 6) the two kinds of musicians who fostered eighteenth-century urban secular music: emigrant professionals and "gentleman amateurs." Among the latter, best-known are Thomas Jefferson, who if not a practicing musician or composer was still an aristocratic patron of art music; Benjamin Franklin, who was a practicing musician on the guitar, harp, and musical glasses and who may have composed (although not the string quartet sometimes claimed to be his); and Francis Hopkinson. According to John Adams, Hopkinson was a "pretty, little, curious, ingenious" man, "genteel

EXAMPLE 2-5. G. K. Jackson, *Cancherizante, New Miscellaneous Musical Work* (n.p., n.d. [after 1800]), p. 9.

and well-bred." He was something of a poet (his *Battle of the Kegs* is well known) and a political figure (his signature is on the Declaration of Independence, and he was our first Secretary of the Navy). Hopkinson's interest in music extended beyond performance and composition to mechanical improvements for the harpsichord (somewhat belatedly, since the instrument was already being superseded by the pianoforte).[10] In 1788 Hopkinson dedicated a set of *Seven Songs for the Harpsichord or Forte Piano* to George Washington (an eighth was added after the title page was set in type), remarking in the dedication (reprinted in *ACS*, pp. 39–40) that "I cannot, I believe, be refused the credit of being the

[10] In March, 1771, Jefferson wrote to his agent in Philadelphia, sending a list of purchases to be made in Europe. Nine weeks later he wrote again to the agent, who was by then in England, correcting the list to include a piano: "I have since seen a Fortepiano and am charmed with it. Send me this instrument instead. . . ." Quoted in O. G. Sonneck, *Suum cuique* (New York: G. Schirmer, 1916), p. 51.

first native of the United States who has produced a musical composition." Hopkinson probably knew the music of the New England Yankee tunesmiths, some of whom doubtless antedated him as native-born composers, but he must have adjudged his genteel songs for the "republican court circle" of Philadelphia as *real* music, compared to the folkish singing-school tunes of his northern contemporaries. Nevertheless, the first composition we can unequivocally attribute to a native American is a manuscript song by Hopkinson dated 1759, *My Days Have Been So Wondrous Free*. The music does not quite live up to the charm of its first verse line; it is a bit stiff, if innocuously pleasant (*MinA*, No. 38). The *Seven Songs*, written (or at least published) almost thirty years later, show hardly any advance in style or technique, although one of them, *My Gen'rous Heart Disdains*, is a lilting rondo of considerable verve and wit; Example 2-6 is its refrain.

EXAMPLE 2-6. F. Hopkinson, *My Gen'rous Heart Disdains, Seven Songs . . .* (Philadelphia: Thomas Dobson, 1788), No. 7, measures 21–48.

Song and instrumental music were combined in a special way in a few turn-of-the-century theater works which mingled the English ballad-opera tradition with the descriptive incidental music of French and German "melodrama," a term at that time denoting a play with background music. Such a mélange was the historically interesting "operatic melodrame" *The Indian Princess* by the American playwright James Nelson Barker and the British-born actor-composer John Bray (1782–1822), produced at the Chestnut Street Theatre in Philadelphia in 1808. The first surviving play on the story of Captain John Smith and Pocahontas, *The Indian Princess; or, La Belle Sauvage* contains an overture, solo airs, choruses, and vocal ensemble numbers in the manner of ballad opera; it also has snippets of instrumental music sounding in the background of the spoken dialogue to underscore the drama and heighten its emotional impact. Open-ended, to be repeated as many times as needed during a given scene, these mood-music miniatures are the precursors of later American background music for drama and films, and they point to the dawning Romantic era's impulse to exaggerated emotionalism (to "melodrama" in the later sense) and to a programmatic, narrative musical aesthetic.

DANCE MUSIC

One of the least-studied areas of early American music is that of the dance. Yet the colonists, even the earliest ones, were great dancers. Hawthorne's tale of *The Maypole of Merry Mount* is partly legendary, but its essence is confirmed by William Bradford's contemporary account (1647) of the revels at the Merry Mount settlement, where ". . . they also set up a May-pole, drinking and dancing about it many days together." Throughout the colonial and Federal periods, journals and letters are full of mention of dancing. The eminent justice Samuel Sewall of Boston refers in his diary in 1685 to "a Dancing Master who seeks to set up here and hath mixt dances"; by 1716 the *Boston News-Letter* was advertising instruments, instrumental instruction books, and ruled [music] paper "to be sold at the Dancing School of Mr. Enstone." Eighteenth-century concerts often concluded with a march, which served then to introduce a post-concert ball.

The main reason, of course, that the actual music of early American dances is not better known is that little of it was published or even written down: like most of the world's dance music, it was not transcribed but improvised by musicians according to the needs of the moment, elaborating upon, extending or shortening, repeating or varying the current repertory of dance tunes. Popular dancing, moreover, is traditionally done to the accompaniment of whatever instruments and/or voices are at hand. Thus when dance music *is* written down, it usually appears as a bare-boned skeleton, to be given flesh and blood in actual performance; the written music is often merely a cue-sheet for the musicians. Ultimately, a composer may base a fully-realized work on a well-known tune, a dance rhythm, or a typical dance form; but his music presents a somewhat flossy and stylized, if artistically valid, image of a particular dance.

By the late eighteenth century, American dance music found its way into manuscript and even printed music-sheets. Some of the pieces are stylized versions for pianoforte of well-known dance types, e.g., the "Tempo di Menuetto" movement of a *Sonata for the Pianoforte with an Accompaniment for the Violin* (1797? in *MinA,* No. 75) by Raynor Taylor (1747–1825), a teacher of Alexander Reinagle and active in Philadelphia's musical life from 1793. Many, however, are practical dances written out usually in abstract format on treble and bass staves (although often just the treble tune is given), to be fleshed out by actual instrumentation and improvisation on the spot.

The dances in the *Evening Amusement* collection of 1796 mentioned earlier suggest the types favored by the late eighteenth century: hornpipes, reels, minuets, strathspeys, and marches. To these might be added the gavotte, the allemande, the country dance, the cotillion, the quadrille and (the great novelty of the period) the waltz. The music of a "line dance" like the country dance (or "contra dance") was often the same as for a "square dance" like the cotillion or the quadrille: hornpipes, reels, cotillions, strathspeys served equally well for these dances of British origin. On the other hand, the minuet, gavotte, and allemande, introduced from France, each had its own tempo, steps, and rhythmic character.

Cotillions and country dances were the most popular in the late eighteenth-century American cities. The music comes as a surprise to the twentieth-century listener, since it is obviously the forerunner of square-dance music that he considers rural, not urban. It is not hard to hear *Harriet's Birthday* or *Jefferson's Hornpipe* (Example 2-7), both published

EXAMPLE 2-7. Two country dances, from James Hewitt (compiler), *A Collection of the Most Favorite Country Dances* (Philadelphia: J. Hewitt, [1802?]), pp. 5, 17.

(a) *Harriet's Birthday.*

(b) *Jefferson's Hornpipe.*

by James Hewitt about 1802 in *A Collection of the Most Favorite Country Dances,* as lusty, ongoing fiddle tunes, pattering along in running eighth-notes until, at the phrase endings, they land stompingly on repeated cadence chords. *Fitz James* (Example 2-8) is a lively dance tune

EXAMPLE 2-8. *Fitz James* ("First Set, No. 1"), from *A Collection of the most favorite Cotillions* . . . (Philadelphia: G. E. Blake, [1804?]), p. 2.

from a collection of "the most favorite cotillions" published at Philadelphia about 1804. The collection is interesting not only for the verve and unpretentious excellence of the tunes in it but for its arrangement in "sets" showing the actual order that the dances followed, and for the "figures" (directions for the dances) which follow each tune. *Fitz James* turns out to be a miniature group of variations on its first strain, which then returns at the end to round out the form neatly. The "figure" for this dance is:

> GRAND ROUND—NB. The Change must be danced at the beginning of every Cottillion—

> The leading couples chassez to the right—back again—chassez across each couple with your partners and back again—right and left.

Simple as such dance music is, it has a vitality, an infectious appeal, and a kind of rawboned integrity that transcend much other music of the period.

OTHER INSTRUMENTAL MUSIC

Aside from marches, dances, and some overtures for ballad operas, colonial America produced little instrumental music. The Federal period saw more extensive publication of independent instrumental music, mostly by European composers: by 1825, American presses had issued some 170 works by Mozart, almost 80 by Haydn, over 50 by Handel, and about 30 each by Beethoven and Weber. More highly favored than sonatas or even the flowery sets of variations coming into favor in the late eighteenth century were programmatic pieces of all kinds, especially "battle" pieces. The prototype among these, at least in terms of the number of American editions published, was *The Battle of Prague* by Franz Kotzwara (d. 1791), described as late as 1879 by Mark Twain as "that venerable shivaree" in a hilarious account of its performance by one young lady (*A Tramp Abroad*, Volume II, Chapter 3). Originally a piano work, *The Battle of Prague* (1789) was rearranged constantly by American musicians to fit their instrumental resources; one Boston program in 1810 proudly announced that its version would include "double-basses, cymbals, French horns, kettle drums, trumpets, cannon, etc." Other battle pieces were popular: Bernard Vignerie's *Battle of Maringo* [*sic*] came out in an American edition (1802) as "a military and historical piece for the piano forte," with cannon shots (expressed by the symbol ⊗) to be produced "by stretching the two hands flat on the three lower octaves in order to sound indistinctly every note." Like other battle pieces, *The Battle of Maringo* is an episodic work, its various sections titled "March," "Word of command," "Trumpet call," "Cries of the wounded," and such. The whole work ends with a gigantic ⊗.

One American composer of battle pieces was James Hewitt (1770–1827), who came to New York in 1792 as "leader of the band" for the Old American Company. The first concert he organized in New York included an overture by Haydn, a quartet by Pleyel, and a flute quartet by Stamitz, plus Hewitt's own *Overture in 9 movements, expressive of a battle* and an *Overture in 12 movements, expressive of a voyage from England to America* by Jean Gehot (b. ca. 1756), who had come to America with Hewitt. Hewitt also composed a *Battle of Trenton* (1797), duly dedicated to General Washington and enlivened with quotations from *Washington's March* and *Yankee Doodle*. This was not the first American publication of *Yankee Doodle* in instrumental guise, for three years earlier Benjamin Carr had included it along with the *Marseillaise, Ça ira, O Dear What Can the Matter Be*, and other popular tunes in a patriotic potpourri called *The Federal Overture*. Carr, whom we have met as an able songwriter, could when he wished write a graceful Haydnesque miniature for keyboard, if the six sonatas in *A New Assistant for the Piano-Forte or Harpsichord* (Baltimore and Philadelphia, 1796) attributed to him are indeed his (Example 2-9).

EXAMPLE 2-9. B. Carr (?), *Sonata 1, A New Assistant for the Piano-Forte or Harpsichord* (Baltimore, Philadelphia: B. Carr, 1796), second movement.

Carr's tiny sonata movements were aimed to instruct (the finger-ings of Example 2-7 are those of the original edition). Much more lengthy and probably written for his own performance are four sonatas left in manuscript by Alexander Reinagle. One of these may have been played by Reinagle at a concert in June, 1787, heard and noted in his diary for June 12 by George Washington, then in Philadelphia as a delegate to the Constitutional Convention. Example 2-10 shows the beginnings of the movements of Sonata III, a charming if somewhat over-extended essay in the style of C. P. E. Bach. (The second and third movements of Sonata II are printed in *MinA*, No. 74.)

EXAMPLE 2-10. A. Reinagle, Sonata III, beginnings of the three movements (after Library of Congress manuscript).

(3) Allegro

BIBLIOGRAPHICAL NOTES

Charles Haywood's *Bibliography of North American Folklore and Folk-song* (2nd ed.; New York: Dover Publications, 1961) and Ray M. Law-less's *Folksingers and Folkways in America* (rev. ed.; New York: Duell, Sloan and Pearce, 1965) are basic guides to music once popular, now folk. Alan Lomax's book on North American English-language folk songs (see footnote 3) includes the music of 317 songs.

Besides Francis Child's own basic work of 1883—*English and Scottish Popular Ballads* (reprinted New York: Folk Lore Press, 1957)—two other studies of British ballads are important: B. H. Bronson, *The Traditional Tunes of the Child Ballads,* in four volumes (Princeton: Princeton University Press, 1959–72), and Claude M. Simpson, *The British Broadside Ballad and Its Music* (New Brunswick: Rutgers University Press, 1966).

Several of the seventeenth- and eighteenth-century British publications of popular music are available in modern editions. Ravenscroft's *Pammelia, Deuteromelia,* and *Melismata* have been reprinted in facsimile (Philadelphia: American Folklore Society, 1961). Playford's *Dancing Master* is similarly reprinted, with an introduction and notes by Margaret Dean-Smith (London: Schott, 1957); a transcription of the music has been made by Leslie Bridgewater and Hugh Mellor (London: H. Mellor, 1933). D'Urfey's *Wit and Mirth* was published in a new edition in 1876; a facsimile of that edition, with an introduction by Cyrus L. Day, is published in three volumes (New York: Folklore Library, 1959).

The two basic sources on the early development of American concert music and opera are by O. G. T. Sonneck: *Early Concert-Life in America* (Leipzig: Breitkopf & Härtel, 1907; reprinted New York, 1949) and *Early Opera in America* (New York: G. Schirmer, Inc., 1915; reprinted New York, 1963). Sonneck's *Bibliography of Early Secular American Music* (Washington: Library of Congress, 1905) was revised and enlarged by W. T. Upton (Washington, 1945; reprinted New York: Da Capo Press, 1964). Taking up where Sonneck-Upton leaves off is Richard J. Wolfe's monumental three-volume bibliography, *Secular Music in America 1801–1825* (New York: New York Public Library, 1964).

H. Earle Johnson's *Musical Interludes in Boston, 1795–1830* (New York: Columbia University Press, 1943) is a model of what can (and should) be done by way of regional studies.

Several volumes of *EAM* are relevant to this chapter: Belcher's *Harmony of Maine* (*EAM*, No. 6); *The American Musical Miscellany*, a 1798 collection of more than 100 songs (No. 9); *The Indian Princess* (both Barker's play and Bray's music) (No. 11); and *Riley's Flute Melodies* (1814–20), containing more than 700 tunes. John Edmunds has edited *A Williamsburg Songbook* (Colonial Williamsburg, distributed by Holt, Rinehart and Winston, 1964) "from eighteenth-century collections [of British songs] known to have been in the libraries of colonial Virginians."

part two

1820-1920

THREE

CULTIVATED AND VERNACULAR TRADITIONS AND THE IMPACT OF ROMANTICISM

Americans distinguish colloquially between two broad categories of music: they speak of "classical" music and "popular" music. The terms may be poor ones, especially the former (because of its several meanings), but they bespeak a common realization of the existence of two major traditions in American music. These I shall call the "cultivated" and "vernacular" traditions. I mean by the term "cultivated tradition" a body of music that America had to cultivate consciously, music faintly exotic, to be approached with some effort, and to be appreciated for its edification, its moral, spiritual, or aesthetic values. By the "vernacular tradition" I mean a body of music more plebeian, native, not approached selfconsciously but simply grown into as one grows into one's vernacular tongue; music understood and appreciated simply for its utilitarian or entertainment value.[1]

---

[1] There is, of course, yet another great category of American music: folk music. This body of music, whether in its form of a legacy of older musical tradition still to be found in cultural backwaters (or taken up somewhat selfconsciously by the

As America entered the nineteenth century, a distinction between cultivated and vernacular traditions was hardly visible. The music of the ballad operas at New York and Philadelphia was also the music of broadsides and songsters, as it was of the popular products of sheet-music publishers. The fuging tunes of the New England Yankees aimed to improve church singing and thus to be spiritually edifying, but they served also as a popular social music for secular entertainment. The Alexander Reinagles of the late eighteenth century brought a cultivated professionalism to the New World, but they wrote and played and sang to the populace at large as well as to the gentlemen and gentlewomen.

However, as the nineteenth century unfolds we can distinguish with increasing clarity two bodies of American music, two attitudes toward music: cultivated and vernacular traditions become visible; an eventually profound schism in American musical culture begins to open up. On the one hand there continues a vernacular tradition of utilitarian and entertainment music, essentially unconcerned with artistic or philosophical idealism; a music based on established or newly diffused American raw materials; a "popular" music in the largest sense, broadly based, widespread, naive, and unselfconscious. On the other hand there grows a cultivated tradition of fine-art music significantly concerned with moral, artistic, or cultural idealism; a music almost exclusively based on continental European raw materials and models, looked to rather selfconsciously; an essentially transatlantic music of the pretenders to gentility; hopefully sophisticated and by no means widespread throughout all segments of the populace.

Many factors worked to create this dualistic musical culture in nineteenth-century America, among them the rapid geographical expan-

---

more sophisticated) or in its form of traditional communal music among various immigrant or ethnic minorities, is not treated *per se* at any length in this book; it is dealt with as such by Bruno Nettl in a companion volume in the Prentice-Hall History of Music Series: *Folk and Traditional Music of the Western Continents* (2nd edition; Englewood Cliffs: Prentice-Hall, Inc., 1973). On the other hand, as we have observed (see p. 29), whether one speaks of a certain music as "folk" or "vernacular" (in the broad sense of "popular") often depends on the point in time being considered. The British ballads of the Colonial era and the popular songs and dances of the Federal era, which functioned as (some of) the vernacular music of early America, eventually lost their broad popularity; and yet many of them still survive—but now as a folk music. Conversely, some folk music occasionally becomes vernacular: think of today's commercial "folksingers" and the music they have popularized to the point where it is now vernacular (actually, *two* shifts of function have occurred—from vernacular to folk and back to vernacular). For that matter, some cultivated-tradition music may also become a kind of vernacular music: in Germany and Austria, this has happened to some of Schubert's song melodies; in the United States, to some of Stephen Foster's. The rapidity with which such shifts in social function and "status" of various musics have occurred in the United States is one of the most striking things about our dynamic musical culture (reflecting, of course, our culture at large)—in fact, so far as I know, unique.

sion of the nation and distinctive new immigration patterns. Perhaps most significant were the impact of Romanticism's attitudes and ideals and the continued development of public concerts as a primary source of musical experience.

The extraordinary territorial growth of the United States in the nineteenth century accelerated a split between cultivated and vernacular traditions in American music because it diversified the cultural possibilities of American society. Dominating the entire social and cultural situation was the moving frontier, constantly being pushed westward and leaving behind it an ever-widening area of newly settled towns, with the old urban centers of the eastern seaboard behind *them*. Necessarily, musical life was vastly different in a pioneer settlement like Horse Creek, Nebraska, on the Mormon and Oregon Trails; in a relatively new but substantial and growing town like Pittsburgh, just beyond the Allegheny Mountains, which increased in population between 1810 and 1840 from less than 5,000 to more than 20,000; and in an old established urban center like New York or Boston. Music of cultivated taste was taken up first in the older eastern cities, which were closest in spirit and space to Europe's centers of an art-music tradition. The music formerly enjoyed in such cities by all levels of society then tended to become both a slightly déclassé "popular" music and part of a vernacular tradition accompanying the westerly push of Americans across the land. By 1853, for instance, a Boston writer remarked of the Yankee singing-school tunebooks, once enjoyed by Bostonians great and small, that "if used at all, [they] have been crowded to the far West, out of sight and hearing."[2]

The frontier settlements had virtually no contact with the developing cultivated tradition of the eastern urban centers. However, the newly established towns in between, rapidly growing in numbers, in population, in stability and ease of life, did have some contact and sought still more. But, lacking the urbanity, wealth, leisure, and comforting traditions of the eastern seaboard cities they were at once envious, fearful, and resentful of the culture "down East." The men, only one step removed from pioneering, viewed any time spent on non-productive, inutile art as wasteful or effete. Land and money needed cultivation, not their sensibilities. Music, the most intangible and "useless" among the arts, had their special disdain and hostility. Leave music to the women, or to the immigrant "professors." Thus crystallized an American view of fine-art music as essentially the province of females, foreigners, or effeminates, a view still common in the twentieth century although it weakened rapidly after World War I.

[2] Nathaniel Gould, *History of Church Music in America* (Boston: A. N. Johnson, 1853), p. 55.

New immigration patterns during the nineteenth century were also of great importance in shaping America's music, particularly that of the cultivated tradition. The flow of immigrants was immense: some 16,000,000 between 1840 and 1900, spurred on by the land-rich, broadening nation and by its manpower-hungry industrialization. Until the 1880's the main influx of immigrants continued to be from Great Britain, but from the 1830's came also, in roughly chronological order, Germans, Scandinavians, Italians, and eastern Europeans. The arrival of these continental Europeans was critical in the moulding of cultivated American taste because it diluted the traditional mainstream of Anglo-American culture and especially because it occurred at the peak of the Romantic movement in Europe. Early nineteenth-century America was ripe for Romanticism: indeed, someone has said that the American Revolution itself was perhaps the first and greatest example of Romanticism and, as Lewis Mumford has written, "pioneering may in part be described as the Romantic movement in action."[3] The ordinary American may not have been aware of the philosophic concepts of Romanticism—idealism, imagination, boundlessness, personal freedom, individualism—but his whole way of life and thought reflected them. And his musical attitudes were no less ready to be shaped along Romantic lines.

Romanticism had its earliest and strongest flourishing in Germany and, although springing initially from poets and novelists, it found its highest expression and made its greatest impact through German music and musicians. Outside the field of opera, in which Italy maintained a national identity, hardly any kind of nineteenth-century music escaped being touched by German influence; hardly any musician could avoid the impact of Beethoven, Schubert, Schumann, Mendelssohn, Liszt, Wagner. Essentially, the centers of nineteenth-century musical thought were Berlin, Leipzig, Munich, and Vienna; essentially, the ultimate in fine-art music was considered to be German music.

Even before massive crop failures and the 1848 revolutions brought a huge wave of Germans to the United States, some Americans were shifting their musical allegiance from England to Germany. The influential hymnodist Thomas Hastings spoke for his generation, poised on the brink of submission to German rather than English models, when he wrote in 1822 in his *Dissertation on Musical Taste:*

> We are the decided admirers of *German* musick. We delight to study and to listen to it. The science, genius, the taste, that every where pervade it, are truly captivating to those who have learned to appreciate it: but such, we presume, are not yet the *majority* of American or English auditors or executants.[4]

[3] *The Golden Day* (2nd ed.; Boston: Beacon Press, 1957), p. 20.
[4] *Dissertation on Musical Taste* (Albany: Websters and Skinner, 1822), p. 194.

Hastings was writing as one of the first spokesmen for the cultivated tradition of American music. Terms like "science," "genius," and "taste" bespoke special standards, not for all music but for the *art* of music; not for music as a utilitarian part of everyday life or a pleasant diversion on the surface of life but as an art whose holy mission it was to edify and uplift. "Appreciation" of such music required cultivation. As expressed by the highly respected and pontifical editor and critic of the later nineteenth century, John Sullivan Dwight, the aim of such music and of the other arts was to remedy the defects of a materialistic society by "familiarizing men with the beautiful and the infinite." This was the credo of the cultivated tradition. As the exponents of this attitude saw it, German music more than any other achieved the desired goals. One significant result of this view was a rejection of the American musical past, dominated as it had been not only by popular, "unscientific" taste but by British backgrounds. Both the friendly, folkish music of the Yankee tunesmiths and the great melodic reservoir of Anglo-American song were spurned as bases for the new "scientific" music of the cultivated tradition.

In their selfconscious, un-selfconfident striving toward a transatlantic taste for cultivated music, Americans also tended to reject the the American *present* as a source of musical subject-matter. The very aspects of American civilization that were unique had of course no models in Europe; they found scant celebration in American art-music. Europeans of the early nineteenth century were, after all, infinitely disparaging of American culture: "Who, in the four quarters of the globe, reads an American book, or goes to an American play, or looks at an American painting or statue?" asked the British author-minister Sydney Smith in 1820.[5] The European might grudgingly admit to American achievements in industry, technology, and science but considered them, if anything, inimical to art and edification. When the Philadelphia journalist-composer William Fry asked the director of the Paris opera if he might present at his own expense an open rehearsal of his opera *Leonora*, he was refused with the remark: "In Europe we look upon America as an industrial country—excellent for electric telegraphs, but not for art."[6] The American pianist Louis Moreau Gottschalk had a similar experience: "Zimmerman, director of the piano classes at the Paris Conservatoire, . . . without hearing me refused to receive me because 'l'Amérique n'était qu'un pays de machines à vapeur'."[7] Cowed by such attitudes, American musicians of the cultivated tradition were not about to celebrate their electric tele-

[5] Quoted from the *Edinburgh Review* by J. B. McMaster, *History of the People of the United States* (New York: D. Appleton and Company), I (1883), 82.
[6] Quoted in *OAM*, p. 245.
[7] Louis Moreau Gottschalk, *Notes of a Pianist*, ed. Jeanne Behrend (New York: Alfred A. Knopf, 1964), p. 52.

graphs or their steam engines, their reapers or railroads. (Vernacular-tradition composers, of popular songs for instance, did indeed celebrate them, as they did American steamboats and streetcars, balloons, baseball, and the Brooklyn Bridge.)

With the European music of Romanticism their main model, and with German music held up as the ideal, Americans welcomed German musicians. They came in large numbers. Gottschalk heard a volunteer military band in Williamsport in 1863: "Is it necessary," he wrote in his journal, "to say that it is composed of Germans (all the musicians in the United States are Germans)?" A year earlier he had only half facetiously noted that "It is remarkable that almost all the Russians in America are counts, just as almost all the musicians who abound in the United States are nephews of Spohr and Mendelssohn." The figure of the German music teacher came to be a familiar one in American towns; Gottschalk, Paris-trained and something of a Germanophobe (but with a perceptive eye and a sharp pen), wickedly described one:

> I was introduced [in St. Louis in 1862] to an old German musician with uncombed hair, bushy beard, in constitution like a bear, in disposition the amenity of a boar at bay to a pack of hounds. I know this type; it is found everywhere.[8]

It was inevitable that as the cultivated tradition of American music developed momentum in the nineteenth century, under the sway of European music and musicians here at home, young American musicians affluent enough to do so would go to the source, to Europe, for training. Not surprisingly, when they went, it was to Germany.

Some aspects of Romanticism, working in combination with a new domination of the economics of music by the middle class, confirmed the dichotomy between cultivated and vernacular traditions in American music.

Romantic art-music put a premium on the individuality of the composer and on an apparent subjectivity of artistic expression. One result was a broadening of the vocabulary of art-music, for to the degree that a composer used a vocabulary different from others' he could be viewed as unique, as one who was expressing his innermost thoughts as only he felt and knew them, a sort of extraordinary culture hero. Romanticism encouraged the virtuoso composer. But if individuality and novelty were most highly prized assets of the composer, they also collided with the fundamentally conservative tastes of the mass public which had become the principal patron of music. The agents of the new patronage

[8] This, and the previous two quotations, from *Notes of a Pianist;* in order, pp. 127, 102, 63.

were the public concert and the public opera, which had replaced the aristocratic soirée musicale and the cathedral service as the principal forums for musical performance. Public concerts depended for their existence on the approbation of a large, heterogeneous audience. Such an audience, with collective ears less finely tuned, less carefully cultivated than those of the earlier aristocratic patrons of music, tended to resist complexity and innovation in the musical language—just what the Romantic-era composer was striving for. The composer was trapped between the conflicting demands of Romantic individualism and the mass audience. Precisely to the degree that he spoke in a uniquely personal language, his communication with the public—which liked what it knew and knew what it liked—was attenuated. Inevitably, a fissure appeared between the taste of the composer of art-music and that of his ostensible patron, the public. Inevitably, the fissure widened as the nineteenth century wore on. Ultimately, the fissure now a chasm, the public concert would virtually exclude the contemporary composer; the public concert hall and the public opera house would virtually become musical museums. The composer would be forced to find other sources of patronage, or at least other sources of income than musical composition. The vernacular-tradition composer might be paid to exercise his craft, but not the cultivated-tradition composer his art.

If the virtuoso composer's lot was a problematic one, the virtuoso performer's was not. Not only was he a critical success for his unique gifts, which made him appear the inspired Romantic individualist par excellence; he was a popular success as well. Technical brilliance is confused with musical profundity in direct ratio to the naiveté of the listener, and the mass-public concert audience of the Romantic era tended to be naive. American concert audiences welcomed the virtuosos, equated virtuosity with artistry, mistook virtuosity for talent. European virtuosos appeared regularly in America. Robert Schumann commented:

> The [European] public has lately begun to weary of virtuosos, and . . . we have too. The virtuosos themselves seem to feel this, if we may judge from a recently awakened fancy among them for emigrating to America; and many of their enemies secretly hope they will remain over there; for, taken all in all, modern virtuosity has benefited art very little.[9]

To America came the Norwegian violinist Ole Bull (five American visits beginning in 1843); the "Swedish Nightingale," soprano Jenny Lind, brought over in 1850 by the notorious impresario P. T. Barnum; mezzo-

[9] *Gesammelte Schriften über Musik und Musiker* (5th ed.; Leipzig, 1914), II, 134, as trans. by Paul Rosenfeld, *Robert Schumann on Music and Musicians* (New York: Pantheon Books Inc., 1946), p. 81.

soprano Maria Malibran, 1825 to 1827; Henriette Sontag, celebrated German soprano, in the United States from 1852 to 1854; the pianists Henri Herz (1845 to 1851) and Sigismond Thalberg (1856 through 1857).

One result of the adulation of virtuosos was an emphasis on the performer of music rather than on the composer or even the music itself; that is to say, on the means rather than the end. Did it matter *what* Paganini or Liszt or Jenny Lind performed, so long as they performed? Symbolic of this view of the musical experience (and still common today) was the listing in announcements of a forthcoming concert not of the music to be heard but only its performer. In earlier eras, when the virtuoso was primarily an improviser, virtually composing the music as he performed, such an attitude was hardly peculiar and posed no threat to progressive trends in the musical vocabulary. But in the Romantic era, when the art of improvisation was dying under the effect of the composer-as-culture-hero idea and when at the same time the conservatism of the mass audience meant resistance to innovation, this attitude tended to freeze the concert repertory and to block any change in the musical vocabulary. In this sense the nineteenth-century virtuoso became the real musical hero while only lip-service was paid to the living composer, whose heroism often had to await posthumous recognition after the slowly changing taste of the concert public, finally catching up with the composer's vocabulary, allowed a change in the performance repertory.

The virtuoso conductor, a new kind of virtuoso, was born during the Romantic era. He was no longer merely *primus inter pares,* a musical chronometer keeping time for a group of co-equal instrumentalists, but a kind of super-performer playing a super-instrument, the Romantically expansive symphony orchestra. America welcomed increasingly this kind of virtuoso, as was reflected in a number of visiting orchestras and the development of American orchestras themselves, with a parade of European conductors to lead them, further emphasizing the faint exoticism, the "foreignness" from an American standpoint, of the cultivated tradition.

The premium put on virtuosity tended to create higher performance standards in general, thus to increase professionalism in music of the cultivated tradition. This was mirrored in the establishment of America's first musical conservatories. Perhaps more significant in terms of musical attitudes were the increasingly common attempts through private music lessons to train amateurs up to professional levels of accomplishment, often with futile and musically disenchanting results, and always with an affirmation of the distinction between cultivated and vernacular music traditions. A similar educative aim, but one hoping to train people up to "professional" levels of musical understanding, lay behind the phenomenon of "music appreciation" lectures; the music in question, whose appreciation had to be cultivated, was of course exclusively cultivated-tradition music.

If the rise of the middle class altered the system of musical patron-age and accelerated a musical professionalism, it also tended to create a vast new army of amateur performers of art-music, persons with the leisure time to spend on music-making and the aspiration to do so, but with only modest talent or artistic judgment. Reflective of this aspect of middle-class musical culture was the rapid growth of the sheet-music publishing industry, which in America had reached impressive propor-tions even by the last decade of the eighteenth century and continued to expand throughout the nineteenth. The main output of the publishers was naturally music simple enough to be sold in quantity to amateur musi-cians across the land, music which in one sense of the word would be "popular." At first this published popular music was indistinguishable from the music to be heard on concert programs. This is true, for ex-ample, of late eighteenth-century American sheet music, which more often than not made an advertising pitch for its desirability by actually citing its use in concert or opera: Alexander Reinagle's opera air *Rosa* (1800), ". . . sung with great applause by Mrs. Merry in the comedy of *The Secret*," or Benjamin Carr's *Federal Overture* (1794) ". . . as per-formed at the theatres in Philadelphia and New York." But here too a fissure appeared—between the taste and capability of the amateur per-former and the music of the professional concert and opera performers. As the latter became ever more professionalized and as virtuosity tended to increase, concert music outstripped amateur ability, and the "popular" music of the music sheets came to be a different thing from the "classical" music of the concerts.

Some of this sheet music was music of the vernacular tradition. But much of it (songs and piano pieces for the most part) had an aura of pretentious gentility about it; it derived from and lay within the cul-tivated tradition rather than the vernacular, although its accessibility to both performer and listener kept it near the latter. As composed by in-numerable musical poetasters, it actually represented a subdivision of the cultivated tradition that might best be termed "household" music, a term we find in the title of a collection of the 1850's: *Household Melodies, a Selection of Popular Songs, Duets, Trios & Quartettes, Arranged to Household Words*, issued first by W. C. Peters & Sons of Cincinnati and then by other publishers and distributors in St. Louis, Nashville, Cleve-land, Pittsburgh, and Louisville. The term "household music" seems ap-propriate, for it suggests an analogy with the other household artifacts of the period like silverware, ceramics, glass, furniture, rugs and draperies which although utilitarian were never acquired solely for their utility but with an eye to their attractiveness and their reflection of fashionable cul-tivated taste. The early twentieth century would call such music "semi-classical" or "light classical," thus perfectly describing its ambiguous status.

By that time, the two main traditions of American music, cultivated and vernacular, came to be less independent, and in fact the cultivated tradition began to draw on the vernacular. By the mid-twentieth century, "popular" music was even beginning to draw on "classical," and once again the lines were not so clearly drawn in American musical taste.

In the following three chapters, I shall discuss that period in American music when the two traditions diverge and remain more or less separate: from about 1820 until the end of World War I. It will be most convenient to speak first of the cultivated tradition (including the genteel household music) up to the Civil War; next of vernacular-tradition music during the whole period; and finally, in Chapter 6, of cultivated-tradition music from the Civil War through World War I.

FOUR

THE CULTIVATED TRADITION,

1820-1865

American music of the cultivated tradition between about 1820 and the end of the Civil War can perhaps best be approached through a discussion of its main genres: church music, song, piano music, orchestral music, and opera.

CHURCH MUSIC

As we have seen (pp. 21–22), the New England school of composers of psalm tunes, hymns, anthems, and patriotic pieces, of fuging tunes and other sacred-secular works in a characteristic, indigenous style, came under criticism towards the turn of the nineteenth century. As early as 1791, when Samuel Holyoke published at Boston a collection titled *Harmonia Americana,* he specifically called attention to his omission of "fuging pieces," claiming in his preface that "the principal reason why few were inserted was the trifling effect produced by that sort of music; for the parts, falling in, one after another, each conveying a different idea, confound the sense, and render the performance a mere jargon of words." But this argument, an old one against vocal counterpoint, was only part of the reason for the new disfavor in which the Yankee composers found themselves. More significant was the developing taste for "the sublime and beautiful compositions of the great Masters of Music," to recall Andrew Law's phrase—that is, the masters of continental Europe.

Symptomatic of the shift in taste are the collections of church music published by Thomas Hastings (1784–1872), whom we have met as a "decided admirer of German musick" and who was a major figure in nineteenth-century cultivated church music. In 1815 Hastings brought out his first compilation, *Musica Sacra: A Collection of Psalm Tunes, Hymns, and Set Pieces.* Along with original tunes and works by other Americans, he included adaptations from the following Europeans: Giardini (to whose melody the hymn "Come Thou, almighty King" is sung even today in Protestant American churches), Purcell, William Croft, Handel (*Messiah*), Burney, and Madan. The English bias is clear; Hastings had not yet submitted to "the science, genius, the taste" of "German musick." He turned to it increasingly, however, for tunes to include in later hymn collections. By 1849 he could even title one hymn book *The Mendelssohn Collection.* To its main body he added as a sort of appendix a group of older hymns and psalm settings, a concession, apparently, to those who still wanted to sing the old New England favorites. Among them we find Timothy Swan's *China* (see p. 17), but in a completely bowdlerized version. Hastings's condescending footnote reads: "Extensively sung in former times, at funerals. The original harmony was, of course, inadmissible."

Hastings's own output as a hymnodist was considerable: he is said to have written some 600 hymn texts and composed 1000 hymn tunes. Among the best known are "Gently, Lord, O gently lead us," "How calm and beautiful the morn," "Return, O wand'rer to thy home," and, most popular of all, "Rock of ages" (*MinA*, No. 86), which appeared as a setting for A. M. Toplady's text in *Spiritual Songs for Social Worship* (1832), a collection compiled jointly by Hastings and the other dominant figure in the cultivated tradition's church music, Lowell Mason.

Mason (1792–1872) has been conceded by even so unsympathetic a critic as Gilbert Chase (see *AM*, Chapter 8) to have had "the strongest, the widest, and the most lasting impress on the musical culture" of any nineteenth-century American musician. His first musical success came with sponsorship by the weighty Handel and Haydn Society of Boston, which aimed not only ". . . to introduce into more general practice the works of Handel, Haydn and other eminent composers" but to support the publication of approved church music. Upon the recommendation of its esteemed organist, Dr. Jackson, the society accepted a hymn collection assembled by Mason, then a young bank clerk working in Savannah, and in 1822 there appeared the first of many editions of *The Boston Handel and Haydn Society Collection of Church Music.*

Mason's father and grandfather were both musical, and by the time he went to Savannah from his native Massachusetts he was proficient on several instruments. In Savannah he was taught by a German musician, one F. L. Abel, who probably contributed to Mason's esteem for "scientific" music as opposed to the less suave and polished American style. Already in his collection of 1822 Mason was basing his own style on continental European models and even included some six hymn tunes based on music by Beethoven. Other sources he was to tap included German chorales, Gregorian chants, and works of Gluck, Handel, Haydn, Mozart, Nägeli, and Pleyel.[1]

The Boston Handel and Haydn Society Collection was an immediate and continuing success: 22 editions were published between 1822 and 1858. Mason returned to Massachusetts in 1827, to become president of the Handel and Haydn Society and to found in 1832, together with George J. Webb (1803–1887) and other Boston musicians, the Boston Academy of Music; its purpose was to instruct children in music on principles based on the inductive methods of the Swiss educator, Johann Pestalozzi. Mason continued to compose, compile, and adapt hymns: later successful collections were *The Choir; or Union Collection of Church Music* (1832); *The Boston Academy's Collection of Church Music* (1835); *The Modern Psalmist* (1839); and *Carmina Sacra: or Boston Collection of Church Music* (1841), among others. With the income from these four major publications and from his original 1822 collection, Mason's fortune was assured; along with it went extraordinary fame and influence.

The musical style of Mason's hymns, based on European Classic-era music, is one of genteel correctness, neat and tidy in harmony and form, mild in rhythmic vitality and melodic thrust. The airs are now in the tenor voice in the old manner, now in the treble; not infrequently, they are oddly awkward, perhaps because Mason's musical thought as a whole was dominated by considerations of harmony and as a result even the air is sometimes made to accommodate the harmony rather than fulfilling its own directional impulse. Two of Mason's best-known hymns, *A Missionary Hymn* ("From Greenland's icy mountains"; *MinA*, No. 83) and *Olivet* ("My faith looks up to thee"; *MinA*, No. 84) share this trait.

[1] See Henry L. Mason, *Hymn-Tunes of Lowell Mason: A Bibliography* (Cambridge: The University Press, 1944).

It hardly seems coincidental that Mason chose, among British sources, the century-old *St. Thomas* by Aaron Williams to arrange, alter, and expand (in *New Carmina Sacra*, 1852; *MinA*, No. 85), for its air too is of this type.

Mason was not only a composer of some 1200 original hymn tunes and adapter of almost 500 melodies from other composers. He was also a dedicated teacher: to him must go credit for getting music admitted into the public-school curriculum of Boston, and indirectly into public-school programs over the entire country. The beginning was the Boston Academy, which provided free extracurricular music classes for schoolchildren. In 1838, after years of propagandizing by Mason, the public schools of Boston began to include musical instruction as a part of the regular curriculum, with Mason appointed as superintendent of music for the city system. It was a historic moment in the history of American music and musical attitudes; for better or worse, Mason's ideals and tastes, and those of a huge circle of musicians and educators associated with him, could now be directed where they would have the greatest impact: among the children.

It may be appropriate here to pause and consider the unique place in American culture that has been held by music education, which since Mason's day has been considered an essential part of the school curriculum. In fact, from the time of Tufts and Walter early in the eighteenth to the present, musical indoctrination has been considered a matter of importance by Americans. This attitude is uniquely American: as Allen Britton has put it in a thoughtful essay, music education has been "an American specialty."[2] Significantly, Americans have viewed musical education as important not just for itself but as a means to a higher goal. In the singing-school era, the end was a greater perfection in religious observance; from Mason's time on, it has been a kind of aesthetic and moral improvement. Throughout our history, these goals have been sought through education in "better music"—better, that is, than the vernacular music of the period in question. In Tufts's and Walter's day, the "better music" was that on the written page, and their main aim was simply to teach students how to read music. At the turn of the nineteenth century, the "better music" for the reformers among the singing-school masters was almost any music other than "those wild fugues" of the Yankee tunesmiths. For Mason and his circle, and indeed for many music educators up to the present, the "better music" was the music of Europe's Classic era. At the same time, because of that lag between the musical thought of the composer and the musical understanding which

[2] "Music Education: An American Specialty," *One Hundred Years of Music in America*, ed. Paul Henry Lang (New York: G. Schirmer, Inc., 1961), pp. 211–29.

we explored in Chapter 3 above, education in the elaborately artistic music of Europe was considered unrealistic. Thus, just as folk and vernacular music was rejected by school music teachers, so was the very best of "classical" music. Instead, a bland and bloodless, if correct and irreproachable, music of second- and lower-rate composers was taught. A lasting result was, as Britton remarks, that music education has always operated "at a certain distance from the well-springs of American musical life, both popular and artistic. . . . The term 'polite' is perhaps as good as any other to characterize much of the music utilized in schools from the time of Lowell Mason to the present day." Thus we see a paradox in American educational philosophy: on the one hand, a unique acceptance of music's importance in the education of every American and, on the other, a narrowly restricted *kind* of music that Americans are to be "educated" in—a music that has little to do with either the American past or present, nor with either the rough-hewn virility of folk music or the craftsmanly elegance of art music. The effect on many Americans has been one of disenchantment with music, both as listeners and participators, in the years after schooling: not only has formal music education, limited only to the blander and "politer" kind of music, tended to dull the impulse to lusty, unselfconscious participation in music-making for the fun of it; it has also provided very little understanding, let alone high standards for performance, of any highly artistic music. A great many Americans, since the mid-nineteenth century, have come to adulthood without much enthusiasm for *any* kind of music—at least, until fairly recently, when the folk-song revival and the supplanting of the piano by the guitar as the principal "household-music" instrument have reawakened American youth (at least) to the pleasures of informal music-making.

SONG

The Anglo-American tradition of the genteel air was maintained during the entire nineteenth century. Songs were the staples of the mid-nineteenth-century concert repertory; hardly any concert of exclusively instrumental music was to be heard, and the majority of public concerts were essentially song recitals. Up to the Civil War, at least, the songs of the public concerts were also heard in the parlor, the very center of middle-class polite society; there, beside horsehair-stuffed chairs and sofas and polite, instructive family magazines, could be found—ever more commonly as the century wore on—a square or an upright piano or a reed organ. Here, in the home, their cultural life dominated by the new breed of middle-class woman, nineteenth-century Americans gathered to hear a favorite daughter or bride sing the latest concert-household songs.

If eighteenth-century American songs only occasionally borrowed the sentimental tone and the high-flown language of Thomson's *Seasons* and Goldsmith's *Deserted Village,* nineteenth-century songs went the whole way, reflecting the tastes of an age which reveled in Scott's poems and Gothic romances, after a turn-of-the-century preparation by way of Richardson's *Pamela* and Susanna Rowson's *Charlotte Temple: A Tale of Truth.* Almost entirely vanished were the sturdy unforced optimism of Reinagle's *America, Commerce, and Freedom* or the lightly mocking bow to conventional love of Hopkinson's *My Gen'rous Heart Disdains the Slave of Love to Be.* In their place were set texts of the most extreme sentimentality, descending to bathos and ascending to manic ecstasy.

Models for American songs of the period were provided by the English singers who barnstormed through the eastern half of the country in the 1830's and '40's. One such was Henry Russell (1812–1900; in America from 1833 to 1841), who left the organ bench of Rochester's First Presbyterian Church to make a name for himself as a baritone soloist and songwriter. Mining the vein of sentiment for the aged that ran so deep in mid-nineteenth-century America, Russell concentrated on "old" songs (*The Old Bell, The Brave Old Oak, The Old Sexton,* and many others), for a total he claimed to be over 800 songs. Among the most renowned were *Woodman, Spare That Tree* (". . . Touch not a single bough,/In youth it shelter'd me,/And I'll protect it now") and *The Old Arm Chair* (*MinA,* No. 123). *The Old Arm Chair,* published in 1840 at the peak of Russell's popularity, illustrates in every detail the genre of the household song. The text is embarrassingly maudlin: the poet gazes on the armchair "with quivering breath and throbbing brow"; religion and filial love are identified ("I almost worshipp'd her when she smiled,/And turn'd from her bible to bless her child"); the chair itself is an object of sentimental veneration ("I love it, I love it, and cannot tear/My soul from a mother's Old Arm Chair"). The cover page, with its lithograph showing Mother and the chair (reproduced in *MinA*), is characteristic: nineteenth-century song sheets aimed to be visually seductive as well as vocally attractive. The music is quite simple, the melodic style essentially declamatory, in easy $\frac{4}{4}$ rhythms, with an occasional touch of affective chromaticism and a climactic, shuddering diminished-seventh chord. The form is strophic. The most frequent harmonic progression is the gentle I-IV-I, often made even softer by a tonic pedalpoint. One of Russell's songwriting successors was John Hill Hewitt (1801–1890), composer of some 300 songs, among them the Civil War ballad *All Quiet Along the Potomac Tonight* (1861; *MinA,* No. 118). He claimed that because of Russell's limited vocal range *The Old Arm Chair* has "but five notes in its melodic construction." This is untrue, but it *is* restricted to one octave and virtually sings itself, with a predictable curve of line and falling sequences. Most characteristic of the melodic method are the many sighing, drooping appoggiaturas, which strive to confirm the text's tone of deep emotion. One paradox of the song, typical of the genre, is that despite its lachrymose subject it is in the major rather than the minor mode; the latter must have been viewed as *too* potent a musical purveyor of sadness.

I have dwelt at this length on *The Old Arm Chair* not because it is either the best or the worst song of the period, but because it epitomizes so perfectly the concert-household song repertory. Far more extreme examples could be cited, and by composers highly thought of: perhaps the nadir was reached in *The Lament of the Blind Orphan Girl* (1847) by W. B. Bradbury (1816–1868), who compiled hymn books in collaboration with Hastings and was thought of as a rival by Mason. In this song, the doubly afflicted heroine is made to voice her lament in incongruously skipping rhythms and a modest coloratura (derived in part, certainly, from the Donizetti and Rossini arias that Bradbury would have heard in New York in the 1840's). It is a remarkable lesson in how to turn sentiment into sentimentality (Example 4-1).

EXAMPLE 4-1. W. Bradbury, *The Lament of the Blind Orphan Girl* (New York: Atwill, 1847), measures 25–30, 73–84.

The Lament of the Blind Orphan Girl was published "as sung with distinguished Applause, by Abby Hutchinson." Abby was the female member of the most celebrated American "singing family" of the period from 1840 to 1860: the Hutchinsons. They were one of a number of American troupes formed in imitation of European family groups, like the Rainer family from the Tyrolean Alps, which toured the States during the 1840's and after. The Hutchinsons specialized not only in laments—Oh! I'm in Sadness, Last Year's Flowers, Give That Wreath to Me, The Guardian of the Grave—but also in "Alpine" songs. Precisely at the moment (1846) when the Donner party battled to get to settlements in California across the mountain walls of the Rockies, Americans in the East were hearing about

> The mountain top! the mountain top!
> Oh! that's the place for me;
> I love to mount each craggy steep
> With shout of joyful glee!

And on an Albany program in 1842 the Hutchinsons sang The Snowstorm, its concluding verses a classic of American melodrama:

> And colder still the wind did blow,
> And darker hours of night came on,
> And deeper grew the drifts of snow.
> Her limbs were chilled, her strength was gone.
> "Oh God!" she cried in accents wild,
> "If I must perish, save my child!"

It is against this background, of the nostalgic sentimentality of *The Old Arm Chair*, the crocodile tears of *The Blind Orphan Girl*, the hysterical unreality of *The Mountain Top*, that one must view the household songs of Stephen Collins Foster, a few of which so sublime or mitigate the conventions of the genre, and so transcend the songs of his contemporaries, that Foster must be adjudged America's first great songwriter.

Born in 1826 on the Fourth of July, fifty years to the day after the Declaration of Independence, near the still small but booming commercial and industrial town of Pittsburgh, Foster had a typical middle-class upbringing in a family to which household music was no stranger (his older sister played the piano, and his father fiddled a bit). Drawn to music from early childhood (his father commented when Foster was sixteen that "his leisure hours are all devoted to musick, for which he possesses a strange talent"), he nevertheless got scant encouragement. His brother later claimed that Foster "studied deeply, and burned much midnight oil over the works of the masters, especially Mozart, Beethoven, and Weber. They were his delight, and he struggled for years and sounded the profoundest depths of musical science."[3] But Foster's music itself leaves no room for illusions about the extent of his training: there is ineptitude and amateurishness on virtually every page. On the other hand, there is an obvious and undeniable natural gift for melody.

Foster's debut as a songwriter was with *Open Thy Lattice, Love* (1844). Text and music are both remarkably restrained for the period, and we seem to be back in the very early nineteenth century, with a typically cool if amorous air set to music that reflects Foster's Anglo-Irish descent (Example 4-2). Within the next twenty years, until his

EXAMPLE 4-2. Foster, *Open Thy Lattice, Love* (Philadelphia: Willig, 1844), measures 5–8.

death in New York in 1864, Foster was to publish about 150 such household songs. Most are love songs, but the sweetheart is usually unattainable, either dead or distant, and the poet (usually Foster himself) can dwell with her only in a dream of love. Nostalgic yearning for the ir-

---

[3] Morrison Foster, *My Brother Stephen* (1896, privately printed; reprinted Indianapolis: Foster Hall, 1932), p. 32.

retrievably lost is the keynote, but the poet finds the mournful dream delicious. "I dream of Jeanie with the light brown hair," sang Foster in 1854—but Jeanie is gone:

> Many were the wild notes her merry voice would pour,
> Many were the blithe birds that warbled them o'er.

and we see her only through a gentle haze of nostalgia, "floating like a vapor on the soft summer air." Gentle tenderness, or temperate gentility, characterizes the music as well as the texts of Foster's best household songs. *Gentle Annie* (1856) and *Gentle Lena Clare* (1862) are stereotypes, but both heroines are depicted in memorable melodies (Example 4-3).

EXAMPLE 4-3. (a) S. Foster, *Gentle Annie* (New York: Firth, Pond & Co., 1856), measures 5–12 (piano part omitted); (b) S. Foster, *Gentle Lena Clare* (New York: S. C. Gordon, 1862), measures 9–16 (piano part omitted).

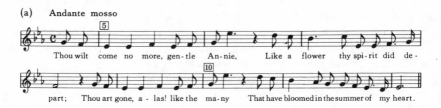

In one of the most thoroughly "composed" loved songs, *Come Where My Love Lies Dreaming* (1855), it is the sweetheart who is dreaming, hence asleep, hence for the moment unattainable. *Come Where My Love Lies Dreaming* is set, atypically for a household song, for vocal quartet, with the soprano part set in relief against three lower voices and given an arching line that just barely hints at the Italian opera to be heard in New York, where Foster had lived for most of 1854 (Example 4-4). The last love song written by Foster is one of the best, musically: *Beautiful Dreamer,* copyrighted shortly after his death (1864).

As in the love songs, nostalgia suffuses an extraordinary proportion of the other household songs of Foster. Perhaps from Henry Russell,

EXAMPLE 4-4. Foster, *Come Where My Love Lies Dreaming. Quartette* (New York: Firth, Pond & Co., 1855), measures 13–16 (piano part omitted).

whom he had heard in concert in Pittsburgh, comes the favorite adjective "old." But Russell's "old" usually means simply "aged"; Foster's usually means "of the past": *Old Memories* (1853), *When Old Friends Were Here* (1864), *Farewell, Old Cottage* (1851), *My Old Kentucky Home, Good Night* (1853). Beloved ones lost through death are mourned in *Bring My Brother Back to Me* (1863), *Our Willie Dear is Dying* (1861), and *Little Belle Blair* (1861). In *Ah! May the Red Rose Live Always* (1850), one of Foster's richest works harmonically, the poet asks "Why should the beautiful die?" (Example 4-5).

EXAMPLE 4-5. S. Foster, *Ah! May the Red Rose Live Alway* (Baltimore: F. D. Benteen, 1850), measures 9–16.

There are, of course, some happy ones among Foster's household songs. *Fairy Belle* (1859); *If You've Only Got a Moustache* (1864), an

Irish reel with coy advice to bachelors; and *There's a Good Time Coming* (1846) are a few. But for the most part a sense of loss and nostalgia for the lost are pervasive. An apostrophe to the family hound, *Old Dog Tray* (1853), leads Foster to mourn a "once happy day":

> *The morn of life is past*
> *And evening comes at last;*
> *It brings me a dream of a once happy day,*
> *Of merry forms I've seen*
> *Upon the village green. . . .*

Some historians have seen more than simple sentimentality in the insistent nostalgia of the American mid-nineteenth century, so typified by Foster. The "once happy day," they say, was an unspoiled early America, fresh for clearing and settling, since, as Lewis Mumford has put it, "ruin and change lay in the wake of the pioneer, as he went westering." A sense of uneasiness, of dislocation, of transition and change must have permeated post-pioneer life. Mumford reminds us of the fascination the legend of Rip Van Winkle held for the period:

> The old landmarks have gone; the old faces have disappeared; all the outward aspects of life have changed. At the bottom, however, Rip himself has not changed; for he has been drunk and lost in a dream, and . . . he remains, mentally, a boy.[4]

Foster, too, perhaps remained mentally a boy; he did musically, for there is no essential stylistic difference between his early works and his late ones among the household songs. (There is, however, between his household songs and his minstrel-show songs, as we shall see). But with his natural talent as melodist, despite his artlessness, Foster spoke for pre-Civil War America; not for the frontier or for the seaboard cities, perhaps, but for that broadening span in between, settled but unsettled, no longer a frontier to be pierced and conquered but an America to be made into something else, and perhaps frighteningly so.

Foster's last years coincided with the Civil War, which evoked (as all wars have) a spate of songs from American composers. Foster himself contributed a few (as a Northerner, though a Democrat)—*We are Coming, Father Abraham, 300,000 More,* a poem set by several composers; *We've a Million in the Field;* and others—but they are of no particular distinction. Two other composers seem to have caught in a few of their songs the militant spirit of the Civil War far better than did Foster: George Frederick Root (1820–1895) and Henry Clay Work (1832–1884).

---

[4] Both quotations from *The Golden Day,* pp. 32–33.

Work, an otherwise undistinguished composer incapable of sustained effort, produced in *Marching Through Georgia* (1865) a jaunty valedictory to the war, following on Sherman's unopposed march through Georgia to the sea (*MinA*, No. 121). Root, after an early association in Boston with Lowell Mason, enlisted Mason's cooperation in opening his own Musical Institute in New York in 1853 but then moved west to Chicago where, in the 1860's, he was music editor for the important music publishing firm of his brother, Root and Cady. Of his 200-odd songs, almost 30 are Civil War songs, among them *The Battle Cry of Freedom* (1863), *Just Before the Battle, Mother* (1863), and *Tramp! Tramp! Tramp!* (1864). An amusing and revealing footnote to Root's career: having decided to try for some of the popular household-song market occupied by Foster but taking a patronizing attitude toward it, Root sought a pseudonym; in view of the adulation of German musicians at the time, a German translation of his own name was the choice: Friedrich G. Wurzel.

Another kind of song, the glee, was also popular during the period and, like the solo song, was sung both in concerts and at home. A part-song for three or four unaccompanied male voices, the glee (from the Anglo-Saxon *glíw* or *gléo*: "entertainment, music") had been enormously popular in eighteenth-century England. Unpretentious, set to friendly doggerel, glees were written by most of the composers we have mentioned above (though not by Foster) for household use and for male singing societies (glee clubs) usually of amateur musicians.[5] The influence of this tradition is sometimes seen in the solo songs themselves, which not infrequently end with a three- or four-part "chorus." Male chorus singing in America, which preserved the tradition of the glee long after it had waned in England, was stimulated by the influence of the German *Männerchor*; a German singing society of this name was organized at Philadelphia in 1835, and similar groups were formed elsewhere, particularly in the Midwest where many German immigrants settled.

PIANOS AND PIANO MUSIC

If any single instrument can be called the Romantic-era instrument par excellence, it is the pianoforte. Indeed, its invention in early eighteenth-century Florence by Bartolomeo Cristofori, its gradual supersession of the harpsichord during that century, its triumphant hegemony among keyboard instruments during the nineteenth, and the decline in its importance during the twentieth reflect a whole cycle in Western

[5] Two glees by Isaac B. Woodbury (1819–1858) are printed in *MinA*, Nos. 89, 90.

musical history.[6] Unlike the harpsichord and organ, and more resound-ingly than the clavichord, the piano responds directly to the player's touch: not only can it play *piano* and *forte* but all the dynamic levels above, below, and between. Not only is it appropriate for intimate music-making at home but, as enlarged and extended in range during the nine-teenth century, it can rival an orchestra in power. Not only can it simulate the sustained, affective melodic curve of a single voice but it can produce dense polyphonic textures. In a period like the Romantic era, which viewed tonal flux as a musical mirror of life itself, whose centers of music were the parlor and the concert hall, and whose musical fabric was a blend of cantabile melody and rich harmony, the piano was the ideal instrument. If the organ was still viewed as the imperious king of instruments, the piano was a responsive and versatile queen.

Manufacture and sale of pianos in America boomed in the nine-teenth century. It has been estimated that whereas in 1829 some 2500 instruments were built, or one for every 4800 persons in the nation, in 1851 more than 9000 were produced and sold. By 1860 the figures had risen again, to 21,000 pianos manufactured, one for every 1500 Amer-icans, with sales across the country of 30 pianos every working day.[7] If we take into account the longevity of a sturdy pianoforte and its low depreciation and degeneration rates, even the last figures must be low as a reflection of the number of people who had access to a playable piano on the eve of the Civil War.

American piano builders (many of them immigrants, of course) were among the best in the world, making significant improvements in the instrument during the period. From the 1820's through the '40's, Jonas Chickering (1798–1853) of Boston was pre-eminent. Like other manufacturers, he concentrated on the heavy, four-footed "square" (actu-ally rectangular) piano that was most popular in America during the nineteenth century, but he and his sons made wing-shaped "grands" as well, and very grand they were: the virtuoso pianist Gottschalk com-mented in his journal in June, 1863 on "two mastodons, which [Thomas] Chickering made expressly for me. . . . The tails of these monster pianos measure three feet in width. Their length is ten feet; they have seven and a half octaves." Piano builders were among the German immigrants of the 1830's and later. Among them were William Knabe, who settled

---

[6] And in social history as well, has been shown with brilliance and wit by Arthur Loesser in *Men, Women and Pianos: A Social History.*

[7] See Loesser, *op. cit.*, pp. 469, 492, 511. The social necessity of a piano in a proper parlor is graphically shown in the design for an ideal *American Woman's Home* (New York, 1869) suggested by Catherine Beecher and Harriet Beecher Stowe. On their first-floor ground plan, they indicated only two pieces of furniture, both in the Drawing Room: one is a sofa, the other a piano. The design is reproduced in John A. Kouwenhoven, *Made in America* (New York: Doubleday, 1949), p. 77.

in Baltimore in 1837, and, most celebrated of all, Henry Steinway (*recte* Heinrich Steinweg, 1797–1871), who fled the revolutions of 1848, settled in New York in 1850, and with his sons established his own firm in 1853. America's own nineteenth-century dynasty of musicians, the Masons, figured in piano manufacturing through Lowell Mason's son Henry, a cofounder of the Mason & Hamlin Company in 1854. Initially the company built melodeons, the American term for small reed organs (harmoniums), which, because of their small size and price and their popularity mainly in rural America, Loesser has brightly called "the American piano's little country cousin."

The Romantic fondness for the piano, its versatility and its value both as cultural symbol and source of entertainment, resulted in an extraordinary output of piano music from American publishers. Most of it was frankly utilitarian, intended for household use as pleasant diversion and without pretensions to high artistic value, though with overt claims to cultivated gentility. Hundreds of dilettante composers appeared in print as writers of airy trifles; almost anyone, it seems, could gain publication in that era of a seller's market for parlor piano music. The nonentities are legion and need not detain us. One among them might be cited, however, partly because his music so completely typifies the kinds of piano music of the period and partly because of his fantastic prolixity: Charles Grobe.

We know next to nothing about Grobe; having served his purpose as composer of parlor pieces, he was promptly forgotten, all the more quickly since he seems not to have been a performer of any calibre. He is said to have been born in 1817 in Weimar and to have come to the United States in 1839. He was appointed music teacher in Wesleyan Female College (Wilmington) in 1841 and, according to John W. Moore (1807–1889), America's first musical lexicographer, "in 1842 his pianoforte publications became known, which are very numerous."[8] Moore was putting it mildly: Grobe's production of music, apparently all of it for piano, surpasses any other known composer's. By 1847, with *The Battle of Buena Vista* ("a descriptive Fantasie for the Piano"), he was up to Op. 101; six years later, he had trebled his output: the *Gothamite Quick Step* of 1853 is Op. 352. Another half-dozen years, and Grobe's extensive and thorough *New Method for the Piano-Forte* (Philadelphia, 1859) came out as Op. 1100. Practically in the same breath was issued an *Italian Medley*, Op. 1102, on opera airs by Rossini, Donizetti, Verdi, and others. The mid-century fad for the jog-trot rhythm of the polka was reflected in Grobe's *Tommy Polka* of 1860, Op. 1211, and the Civil War

---

[8] *Appendix to Encyclopaedia of Music* (Boston: Oliver Ditson Company, 1875), article "Grobe." Moore's *Complete Encyclopaedia of Music* (Boston, 1854) was the first comprehensive American music encyclopedia.

naturally elicited from him an "American Medley," *Music of the Union,*
Op. 1348 (Boston, 1861). Over 600 more opus numbers were yet to come.

Programmatic and patriotic pieces, marches and dances, medleys
of popular tunes and opera airs, and above all variation sets were the
order of the day, pianistically speaking. When Grobe published in 1854
his *Buds and Blossoms: 60 Sacred Melodies with Brilliant Variations for
the Piano* (among the melodies were Mason's *Missionary Hymn, Adeste
Fideles,* Haydn's "The Heavens are Telling," an air from Rossini's *Stabat
Mater,* another from "Mozart's 12th Mass"), the publisher obligingly
printed on the back cover a catalogue of representative compositions by
Grobe (Figure 4-1). One could write the history of early nineteenth-
century America from the 215 titles listed. For our purposes, it is interesting to note that the 68 sets of variations outnumber any other type of
piece; next come 52 waltzes, 28 duets (mostly dances: waltzes, polkas,
and schottisches), 25 marches and quicksteps, 18 "gallops," 11 polkas,
and a few each of "piano songs" and "rondos, etc."

The popularity of piano variations reveals several things about the
era. One was its love of the imaginative and inventive: to the ordinary
consumer-musician, what could be more delightfully titillating than to
hear, through a shower of fanciful passagework, the hidden outlines of a
familiar tune? what more suggestive of a composer's invention—tested, as
it is in variation sets, against the given material of a theme? Another,
closely related, was its love of the improvisatory in performance. The
concert pianist at that time was still expected as a matter of course to
improvise, sometimes on familiar tunes, often on themes called out to
him by the audience. Almost by definition, such improvisations took the
form of variations; and if not of variations, then of a "fantasy," less formally strict than variations but no less a matter of creating new shapes
out of old. In a survey of New York piano concerts between 1849 and
1865, one researcher found that one out of every three works presented
was a fantasy on popular themes.[9] Variations and fantasies were also the
simplest and most foolproof substructure for virtuoso scaffolding, since
neither form nor thematic content was problematic and all attention
could be paid by both performer and listener to the treatment of the
musical material. It is against this background that some comments made
by Gottschalk toward the end of his career about the improved taste of
American audiences must be read. He noted in his journal for December
8, 1864 that "at the time of my first return from Europe [1853] I was
constantly deploring the want of public interest for pieces purely sentimental; the public listened with indifference; in order to arouse it, it became necessary to astound it; grand movements, tours de force, and noise

---

[9] Andrew C. Minor, "Piano Concerts in New York City 1849–1865" (unpublished Master's thesis, University of Michigan, 1947), p. 475.

CATALOGUE
OF THE
COMPOSITIONS OF CHARLES GROBE,
Published by LEE & WALKER, (Successors to George Willig,) 188 Chestnut St., Philadelphia.

WALTZES.

A Home that I Love	12½
Alpine Rose	12½
L'Amarante	12½
Amusement de Salon	18¾
Barcarole	12½
Charity	12½
Chateau en Espagne	12½
Cologne Water	12½
La Confiance	12½
Court Ball	12½
L'Etoile du Matin	12½
Fillmore	25
Home of my Heart	12½
Snow Flake	12½
The Lone Star	12½
The Meteor	12½
Guadalquiver	12½
Hand in Hand	12½
Kate	12½
Ladies' Smile	12½
Mazeppa, (Grand)	25
Mnemosyne, (Valse Brillante)	12½
Monterey	12½
Night and Morning	12½
O Summer Night	12½
Queen of my Soul	12½
Ole Bull's Dream	12½
Orsini, (from Lucretia Borgia)	12½
Pet, (Call me pet names)	12½
Potpourri, (from the Bohemian Girl)	12½
Ray of Hope	12½
Rose Blanche	12½
Sans Souci	12½
Souvenir de Belleville	12½
Souvenir de Cape May	12½
Spring Flower	12½
'Tis Midnight Hour	12½
Ruby	12½
Don Pasquale	12½
Come to the Old Oak Tree	12½
By the Margin, etc	12½
Snails	12½
The Sky Lark	12½
The Magician	12½
Annie Laurie	12½
Couleur de Rose	12½
Thou art gone from my gaze	12½
True Love	12½
El Cabalera	12½
Metamores	12½
United States Grand Waltz	25
Sophie Waltz, (by Strauss)	12½

GALLOPS.

Banisher of Sadness	12½
Fausta	12½
Flying Cloud	12½
Homage aux Belles du Philadelphia	25
Hortensia	12½
Ice Cream	12½
Les plus beau de mes jours, etc	12½
Lucy Neal	12½
Maritana	12½
Pine Apple	12½
Ray of Joy	12½
Sentinel	12½
Strawberry	12½
Unassuming	12½
Ever be Happy	12½
Comet's Flight	12½
Short and Sweet	12½
Orlando	12½

DANCES, etc.

Mirror Dance	38
Les Nymphes	25

MARCHES AND QUICKSTEPS.

Adieu et Retour	12½
Brewer of Preston Grand March	12½
Capuletti i Montecchi	25
Captain Walker's Quickstep	12½
Clay Club Quickstep	12½
General Taylor's Grand March	12½
Les Amazones	12½
Lucrezia Borgia	12½
Old Rough and Ready Quickstep	12½
Philadelphia Gals' Quickstep	12½
Alpine Horn	25
Cuba	12½
March from Lucia	12½
Pestal Quickstep	12½
Spider and the Fly	12½
Virginia Rosebud Quickstep	12½
Mr. and Mrs. Jones's Quickstep	12½
March from "Il Crociato"	12½
Cuckoo Quickstep	12½
Swiss March	12½
Sixty Miles an Hour Quickstep	12½
Avant Courier Quickstep	12½
Going Ahead Quickstep	12½
Alpine March	12½
Gothamite Quickstep	25

DUETS FOR TWO PERFORMERS.

Flow gently, sweet Afton	12½
Venetian Gallop	12½
Louisville Gallop	12½
Elfin Waltz	12½
La Belle du Sud	12½
Baden-Baden Polka	12½
Affection Waltz	12½
Grand March from the Bohemian Girl	12½
Flower of America	12½
Hohnstock Polka	25
Mollie's Dream Waltz	25
Morning Star Waltz	25
Evening Star Waltz	25
National Schottisch	25
Redowa Waltz	25
Sounds from Home	25
Henriette Polka	25
Souvenir of Germany, (Schottisch)	25
Emerald Waltz	25
Gipsy March	25
Pet Waltz	25
Jenny Lind Polka	12½
Gertrude's Dream Waltz	12½
'Tis Midnight Hour, (Waltz)	12½
Les Vents, (No. 1, 2, 3, 4,) each	12½
London Polka Quadrilles	50
March Triumphale	25
Le Retour des Heroes	25

POLKAS.

Fidelia	12½
Lucilla	12½
La Mode	12½
My Heart and Lute	12½
Saratoga	12½
Rose Atherton	12½
Bona Fide	12½
Ne Plus Ultra	25
The White Violet	25
Fitzgerald's Gift Polka	25
Leap Year Polka	25

PIANO SONGS.

The heart, the heart, oh, let it be	12½
Kindred Hearts	25
Look how the Stars like jewels glisten	25
The Sabbath Bells	25

VARIATIONS.

L'Amitie, (La Fille du Regiment)	38
Amusement des Amateurs	50
Bachelor Polka	50
Les Bords du Hudson	50
Charity	38
Evening Song to the Virgin	38
Les Charmes de l'Amitie	38
Chasse d'Amour	50
Clochette Polka	62½
Dearest Mae	25
I dream of my Fatherland	38
The False Friend	38
Flow gently, sweet Afton	38
O Susanna	25
Oh! would I were a Boy again	50
Ravel Polka	50
Old Uncle Ned	25
Mary Blane	25
Rosà Lee	25
Virginia Rose Bud	25
Gipsy's Wild Chant	50
Hope and the Rose	50
Leonore	25
Les Ideals	50
Song of the Regiment	38
Salut a Philadelphie	25
Les Amoureux	25
Serenade March	38
Les Troubadours	62½
La Solitude	38
What's a' the Steer Kimmer	25
Come, ye Disconsolate	38
From Greenland's Icy Mountains	38
Jerusalem, my Happy Home	38
Henriette Polka	50
A Life on the Ocean Wave	50
Salut a Baltimore	25
La Liberte	50
Child of the Regiment	38
Song of the Drum	38
Rataplan	38
By the Sad Sea Waves	38
Love Not	25
Les Fleurs du Plaisir	50
Columbia the Gem of the Ocean	62½
Jenny Lind Polka	50
Vesper Hymn	38
I would not live alway	38
Strike the Cymbal	38
Peace, troubled Soul	38
Far, far, o'er Hill and Dell	38
Fading, still Fading	38
Messenger Bird	38
Widow of Nain	38
Adeste Fideles	38
There is nothing true but Heaven	38
Sicilian Hymn	38
Pleyel's German Hymn	38
Pilgrim Fathers	38
Prayer from Moses	38
Prayer from Zampa	38
Prayer from Tancredi	38
Watchman, tell us of the Night	38
Faith ... 38 Hope	38
Washington's March	38
Maretzek's Rondo Finale	50
Yes, I Remember, (answer to Ben Bolt)	38
Wings of a Dove	38

RONDOS, etc.

Bellone, (Polonaise à la Militaire)	38
Diane, (Rondeau de Chasse)	25
El Sinsonte de Camagne	25
La Tendresse, (Rondoletto)	12½
The Talisman, (Rondo Militaire)	50
Love's Influence, (Rondo)	25
Potpourri en forme de Rondeau	25

Just Published, 1st and 2d Nos. of GROBE'S WORLD OF MUSIC, an unsurpassable Collection of Music, consisting of 100 of the most charming Melodies ever offered to the Musical World.

LEE & WALKER'S Publications may be had of the principal Music Dealers in N. York, Boston, Baltimore, N. Orleans, Cincinnati, St. Louis, Louisville, Charleston, Savannah, Pittsburg, Detroit, Chicago, and other Cities of the U. States and Canada.

FIGURE 4-1. A list of piano works (incomplete) by Charles Grobe, from the back cover of his *Wings of a Dove* (1854).

had alone the privilege in piano music." Now, however, audiences were willing to listen to "pieces purely sentimental"—pieces which, in Gottschalk's terms, had real musical content and "feeling," not just spectacular fantasies and pyrotechnical variations.

If Grobe can represent for us the legion of minor composers of piano music for the household market, a few others of the period before the Civil War emerge as composers with higher aspirations and more distinct musical personalities. Most notable are Anthony Philip Heinrich, Richard Hoffman, William Mason, and Gottschalk.

Heinrich was born in Bohemia in 1781, emigrated to America about 1810, and died in New York in 1861. He was this country's first— and without a doubt its most wildly enthusiastic—Romantic in music. Intoxicated with the natural grandeur of the New World, fascinated with the history of his adopted country, enchanted with the American Indian as "noble savage," and above all eager to be called an "American Musician," he poured out hundreds of pieces of the most extravagantly bizarre Romantic programmatism. Most of these were on American subjects, although his musical speech remained essentially that of central Europe.

Heinrich came first to Philadelphia, where he was a merchant and served as volunteer director of music at the Southwark Theatre. Beset by financial reverses, in the fall of 1817 he decided to try his lot elsewhere and traveled via Pittsburgh to Lexington, Kentucky—still virtually a wilderness village. He began composing music at about that time; to a pathetic plea for funds written late in his life (1856) he added this postscript:

> P.S. The Composer did not commence writing music until verging upon the fortieth year of his age, when dwelling by chance in the then solitary wilds and primeval forests of Kentucky. It was from a mere accident that music ever became his profession. . . .[10]

Once embarked on composition, however, Heinrich poured out songs; piano works; marches and dances; choral music; and orchestral overtures, fantasies, concertos, and symphonies. His "opera prima," published at Philadelphia in 1820, was titled *The Dawning of Music in Kentucky, or The Pleasures of Harmony in the Solitudes of Nature,* a huge collection described by the composer as including "*Songs* and *Airs* for the *Voice* and *Pianoforte, Waltzes, Cotillions, Minuets, Polonaises, Marches, Variations* with some pieces of a national character adapted for the Piano Forte and also calculated for the lovers of the Violin" (preface reprinted in *ACS,* pp. 42–43; also in *EAM,* No. 10, a facsimile reprint of *The Dawning of Music in Kentucky* and of Heinrich's Op. 2, *The Western Minstrel*). Heinrich might also have noted that he included a minuet version of *Hail! Columbia* and a waltz version of *Yankee Doodle;* that the "military waltz," *Avance et Retraite,* is to be played from beginning to end, then backwards to the beginning again (note the title); that *A Chromatic Ramble, of the Peregrine Harmonist* is a tour de force of enharmonic complexity, a piece that literally must be seen to be believed; and that the collection is crowned with a fantastic quintet for piano and strings, *The Yankee Doodleiad,* based on trumpet calls, *Hail! Columbia,* and *Yankee Doodle* again (with fourteen variations, interrupted in the middle

---

[10] Heinrich, manuscript scrapbook, Library of Congress (Music Division), p. 836.

by an interlude on *The President's March* labeled "Huzza for Washington!").

Heinrich's was an expansive and mercurial muse: he himself characterized his music as being "full of strange ideal somersets and capriccios." (The pontifical J. S. Dwight of Boston said it was "bewildering . . . wild and complicated.")[11]

Richard Hoffman (1831–1909) came to America from his native England as a boy of sixteen, having already studied with a constellation of German pianists, among them Liszt and Leopold de Meyer. (The latter, renowned as the "Lion of Pianists," had been, in 1845–47, the first great European pianist to tour in America.) Hoffman settled in New York, where beside teaching and composing he played concerts. Competent and agreeable ("a perfect musician, a distinguished and modest man . . . an artist and a *gentleman*," said Gottschalk with unusual generosity), Hoffman wrote a piano music of flowery grace through almost one hundred opus numbers. *La Gazelle* (1858?) was a favorite, with its Lisztian arabesques (Example 4-6) and its fashionable French title evoking the image of Chopin.

EXAMPLE 4-6. R. Hoffman, *La Gazelle* (Mainz, New York: B. Schott's Söhnen, [ca. 1858]), measures 8–15.

William Mason (1829–1908), the third son of Lowell Mason, was also a pupil of Liszt, during the last of his five years' study in Germany (1849–1854). His main role, like that of his father, was more that of tastemaker and teacher than composer; he was also a most competent performer. He concertized in the northern states from the east coast to Chicago, offering solo piano recitals without the usual interpolations of song from an "assisting vocalist"; he played music of high calibre, if almost exclusively Germanic, although his recital-closing improvisations might, because of audience demand, have to be based on *Yankee Doodle* counterpointed with *Old Hundred*; he formed an influential chamber music group and for 13 years (1855–68) offered New York City its finest chamber music; he was also a renowned piano teacher. His own music seems proper but bloodless, without even Hoffman's airy Lisztian flair, although Liszt politely called Mason's *Amitié pour Amitié* (Example 4-7) "a charming little piece," his *Etude de concert*, Op. 9, and *Valse caprice*, Op. 17, "distinguished in style and of good effect."[12] Chopin's *Berceuse*, Op. 57, is certainly the model for Mason's *Lullaby* of 1857 (*MinA*, No. 126); the reference to *Three Blind Mice* is surely unconscious and unintended.

EXAMPLE 4-7. W. Mason, *Amitié pour Amitié* (2nd ed.; Boston: N. Richardson, 1854), measures 1–8.

Without question the most colorful personality, the most articulate intelligence, the most talented performer, and the most provocative composer among the mid-nineteenth-century pianists was Louis Moreau

[12] William Mason, *Memories of a Musical Life* (New York: The Century Co., 1902), pp. 88, 294.

Gottschalk (1829–1869). Born in the racial and ethnic melting-pot of New Orleans, Gottschalk's lineage was itself cosmopolitan: his father was a cultivated Englishman educated in Germany; his mother was of upper-class French descent. For thirteen years, Gottschalk lived in the Vieux Carré quarter, hearing among other kinds of music that of the many Negroes and Latin Americans in the southern trade center. In 1842 he was sent to Paris to study, not returning to America until 1853 as a renowned virtuoso and keyboard composer. From then on his life was virtually one long concert tour, all over the United States, up into Canada, down to the West Indies, Panama, Mexico, and South America, where he died at Rio de Janeiro, forty years of age.

Even as a youth in Paris, Gottschalk was praised by Chopin and Berlioz, his playing spoken of in the same breath with that of Liszt and Thalberg. He became the darling of the Paris salons not only for his virtuosity but for his early compositions, which were heard as exotic mélanges of Afro-Caribbean rhythms and Creole melodies, with a Chopinesque overlay of virtuoso passagework. According to a review by Berlioz of a concert in 1851, "everybody in Europe now knows [Gottschalk's] *Bamboula, Le Bananier, Le Mancenillier, La Savane,* and twenty other ingenious fantasies in which the nonchalant grace of tropical melody assuage so agreeably our restless and insatiable passion for novelty."[13] Back in the Americas and embarked on a career as traveling virtuoso, Gottschalk became a sort of living player-piano: "I have become stupid with it. I have the appearance of an automaton under the influence of a voltaic pile. My fingers move on the keyboard with feverish heat. . . . The sight of a piano sets my hair on end." He had just finished his last tour of 1862: "I have given eighty-five concerts in four months and a half. I have traveled fifteen thousand miles by train. At St. Louis I gave seven concerts in six days; at Chicago, five in four days. A few more weeks in this way and I would have become an idiot."[14] In an age of virtuosity, Gottschalk was the virtuoso incarnate. He has also rightfully been called "our first matinee idol": the young American music student Amy Fay lamented in Berlin upon hearing of his death, "The infatuation that I and 999,999 other American girls once felt for him, still lingers in my breast."[15]

Like Chopin and other pianist-composers of the era, Gottschalk published little of his music except solo piano compositions, of which

[13] Quoted in Behrend (ed.), *Notes of a Pianist,* p. xxii.

[14] Both quotations from *Notes of a Pianist,* p. 102. Gottschalk's journal, written between 1857 and 1868, is a fascinating, kaleidoscopic account of his travels in the West Indies, the United States, and Latin America.

[15] *Music-Study in Germany* (New York: The Macmillan Company, 1897), p. 42. It was Irving Lowens who first equated the idolatry of Gottschalk with that of later stage and screen stars; see *MMEA,* pp. 223–33.

there are just over 100. He composed in addition some songs, a few orchestral works, and purportedly three operas. The pieces mentioned by Berlioz are among the earliest and most interesting of the piano compositions, "New Orleans" pieces published in France and advertised there as the work of "Gottschalk de la Louisiane." Based mostly on Negro and Creole tunes, they tend to begin with marvelously fresh, strong ideas (see Example 4-8) which before long are overwhelmed by showers of scales, arpeggios, passagework of all kinds. Youthful, exuber-

EXAMPLE 4-8. L. M. Gottschalk, early "New Orleans" pieces. (a) *Bamboula,* Op. 2, measures 1–7. (b) *Le Bananier,* Op. 5, measures 1–8.

ant, and immensely promising, they are nevertheless overlong and lacking in tonal or formal interest, as the genuinely gifted fledgling composer gives way to the virtuoso prodigy. The slightly later *Le Banjo,* Op. 15 (1854 or 1855; a so-called *Banjo second* was actually composed first), probably has in common with Stephen Foster's *Camptown Races* (see Example 5-8) a source in American Negro song, if it was not based on Foster's. Full of ingenious strumming, *Le Banjo* (*MinA,* No. 125) is one of Gottschalk's best works, although even an enthusiast like pianist John Kirkpatrick admits to its "characteristic redundance and tonal monotony."[16]

[16] "Observations on 4 volumes and supplement of the works of Louis Moreau Gottschalk" (typescript; New York Public Library's Music Division).

Gottschalk mined other folk and popular song veins as he toured through Spain (*La jota aragonesa*, Op. 14), the West Indies (*Souvenir de Porto Rico*, Op. 31; *Souvenir de la Havane*, Op. 39), and South America (*Grande Fantasie triomphale sur l'hymne national brésilien*, Op. 69). Only occasionally, as in *Souvenir de Porto Rico* ("*Marche des Gibaros*"), does formal control restrain technical exuberance; however, in that piece of 1857 based on a native Christmas song (Example 4-9), Gottschalk achieves a minor masterpiece with the arching dynamic curve, waxing and waning, of a "patrol" piece and the strong syncopations of Afro-Caribbean dance music (Example 4-10). Perhaps Gottschalk's greatest *pastiche* on folk and popular source materials, and certainly the noisiest, was *L'Union*, Op. 48 (1862), a grand "paraphrase de concert sur les airs nationaux" (*Yankee Doodle, The Star-Spangled Banner, Hail! Columbia*, and some trumpet calls) written at the height of the Civil War and received in Philadelphia, according to the composer's journal, with "unheard-of enthusiasm . . . recalls, encores, hurrahs, etc.!"

EXAMPLE 4-9. Puerto Rican *aguinaldo*, beginning, and L. M. Gottschalk, *Souvenir de Porto Rico* (Mainz: B. Schott's Söhnen, 1859), measures 17–20.

EXAMPLE 4-10. L. M. Gottschalk, *Souvenir de Porto Rico*, climax (measures 189–193).

Another side of Gottschalk's art was that of the "purely sentimental" piece, as he called it, the genre piece of meditative and "poetic" reflection. Among the most carefully worked of these are *Ricordati*, "méditation," Op. 26, a Chopinesque nocturne; *The Last Hope,* "méditation religieuse," Op. 16 (1854), Gottschalk's monument to pious sentimentality, his most notoriously successful tear-jerker, but withal a shrewdly contrived series of daringly chromatic introductions to an indestructible arc of songful melody; *Berceuse,* Op. 47 (before 1863), based on a French folk song, *Fais dodo, mon bébé;* and *Suis-moi,* Op. 45 (ca. 1861). *The Dying Poet* (1863–64), one of "some contraband pieces that are to be published under the aegis of a borrowed paternity" (as Gottschalk archly described his pseudonym, "Seven Octaves"), and *Morte!!* (1868?), which had, said Gottschalk, "un succès de larmes," were famous pieces in the vein of *The Last Hope.*

Gottschalk noted in his journal one night in 1865 that his had been a life of "playing the piano, of having composed two or three hundred pieces, of having given seven or eight thousand concerts, of having given to the poor one hundred or one hundred and fifty thousand dollars, [and] of having been knighted twice." The remark may have been one of Romantic hyperbole, but so were Gottschalk's personality and his music.

ORCHESTRAS

The Romantics loved the orchestra. Convinced that instrumental music in general was the purest, most sublime music, they conceived of the orchestra as a kind of super-instrument. And seeking an ever-broader coloristic and expressive spectrum, they enlarged it from a smallish ensemble of one or two dozen players into a giant symphonic machine of more than a hundred. If, during the era, the organ was king of instruments, the piano the queen, the orchestra was emperor.

One of the most characteristic trends in American music since the mid-nineteenth century has been the proliferation of independent symphony orchestras. Whereas in Europe such orchestras have hardly existed apart from opera houses (although a few, typically state-subsidized, are now virtually independent), here the symphony orchestra has tended to develop as an independent entity, reflecting our penchant for concerts rather than opera. The American notion of a "permanent" orchestra, and one supported by public subscriptions and box-office receipts, has been a by-product of the rise of public concerts and a mass audience that I have discussed in an earlier chapter. Two decades before the Civil War, the first "permanent" orchestra still in existence today, the New York Philharmonic, was founded. By the late 1960's, the American Symphony Orchestra League counted some 1400 orchestras in the U.S.A. and Canada. The vast majority of these were community, college, school, or "youth" orchestras (all non-professional groups), but in the United States alone there were no less than 27 major, permanent, professional orchestras with annual budgets exceeding $500,000 and 62 other metropolitan orchestras with budgets between $100,000 and $500,000.[17]

The beginnings of this astonishing development go back to the early nineteenth century, when Gottlieb Graupner, who had been one of the musicians in Salomon's London orchestra during the famous visit of Haydn in 1791, organized a group of Boston instrumentalists into a "Philo-Harmonic Society" to meet informally and play through symphonies of Haydn and others. Notices of rehearsals appeared regularly in the semi-weekly Boston newspapers from October 4, 1809, and the society soon began playing for the public. John Rowe Parker, editor of the first American music periodical, *The Euterpeiad, or Musical Intelligencer* (1820–1822), signalized the historic importance of Graupner's instrumental organization (and the other society Graupner helped to found) when he wrote, "Until the formation of the Philo-Harmonic for instrumental, and the institution of the Haydn and Handel Societies, for vocal performances, regular concerts have never succeeded in this metropolis" (*Euterpeiad,* April 8, 1820). They did not succeed well enough, apparently, for the Philo-Harmonic Society of Boston gave its last concert late in 1824.

Meanwhile, in Philadelphia a Musical Fund Society was organized in 1820 by Benjamin Carr and others; it was active as a choral-orchestral organization up to 1857, and more sporadically to the present. In the nearby Moravian center of Bethlehem a Philharmonic Society was founded, also in 1820, which flourished until about 1839. And in 1842 a group of musicians led by Ureli Corelli Hill (1802–1875), Henry Christian Timm (1811–1892), and William Scharfenberg (1819–1895) founded the New York Philharmonic Society. Numbering about 55 players, give or take the few who found it impossible to give up other jobs to play in the three concerts of the first season (four in each season thereafter through 1858), the orchestra initially had no single conductor; six of the musicians shared the duties. From the 500-seat hall of the Apollo Rooms on Broadway below Canal Street, the orchestra graduated to Niblo's Theatre (Broadway and Prince Street), then in 1856 further uptown to the elegant Academy of Music at 14th Street and Irving Place.

That our first permanent orchestra should have been established in New York City reflected an important social development: New York's skyrocket rise, stimulated especially by the opening of the Erie Canal in 1825, to supremacy as the nation's first port, largest city, and principal commercial center. As such it became also the nation's center of those performing arts which rested on a foundation of mass-audience support. New York's pre-eminence as a musical performance center already by the mid-nineteenth century is confirmed by the fact that not until 1881 would the second permanent American symphony orchestra, the Boston Symphony, be established.

[17] *BMI Orchestral Program Survey,* in cooperation with the American Symphony Orchestra League (New York: Broadcast Music, Inc., 1970), p. 46.

Three other orchestras heard in pre-Civil War America should be cited briefly here for their catalytic influence on American music. One was the Germania Musical Society, a group of 25 young musicians who left Berlin in May of 1848, heading for the United States "in order to further in the hearts of this politically free people the love of the fine art of music through performance of the greatest German composers."[18] The Germanians' first concerts in New York led to others elsewhere, and the well-trained, well-balanced ensemble was heard, before its dissolution in 1854 (all its members by then American citizens), in many American and Canadian cities from Richmond to Minneapolis and from Boston to St. Louis (where one young woman, hearing Beethoven's Second Symphony for the first time, remarked, "Well, ain't that funny music!"). American attitudes as to the "standard repertory" of orchestral music were strongly shaped by this group's concentration on Germanic works from Haydn to Mendelssohn.

Another, briefer symphonic visitor was the orchestra brought from London to New York for one year by the French conductor Louis Antoine Jullien (1812–1860). "A splendid, bold, and dazzlingly successful humbug," wrote the New York *Courier and Enquirer*. To his 40-piece orchestra Jullien added 60 local musicians (among them two young violinists named George Bristow and Theodore Thomas, of whom more shortly); on August 29, 1853, after a strenuous advertising campaign, he initiated a series of "Monster Concerts for the Masses" at Castle Garden. The *Courier and Enquirer* had to admit that "the discipline of his orchestra is marvelous." *The New York Clipper* was not so charitable; that lively precursor of *Variety* and *Billboard*, which proclaimed itself "A Weekly Sporting Paper, devoted to the Ring, the Turf, Yachting, Pedestrianism, Cricket, Rowing Matches, Theatricals, Music, and the various sports of the Old World and the New," took up the cudgel against "these 'highfalutin' gimcracks" in its issue of September 3:

> There were not quite 3,000 persons in the building, and perhaps not quite 2,500 who paid for their tickets [at 50¢ each]. . . . It is now more difficult to humbug us than it was a few years since. . . . With encouragement, America can produce musical wonders as well as reaping machines; an American Forrest [Edwin Forrest (1806–1872), American actor] as well as American Clippers. . . . Several European celebrities have lately returned to their homes, not at all pleased with our reception of them. Stand fast, Americans! encourage those who are with us. . . . Monster concerts for the masses, indeed!

[18] H. F. Albrecht, *Skizzen aus dem Leben der Musik-Gesellschaft Germania* (Philadelphia. 1869), trans. H. Earle Johnson, "The Germania Musical Society," *MQ*, XXXIX (1953), p. 75.

The chauvinist tone is of interest: here spoke the vernacular tradition of American culture, weary of the European monopoly over American cultivated taste. In its next issue (September 10) the *Clipper* chuckled over the "but middling success" of Jullien's nightly concerts, and on September 17, headlining "A Failure in New York" for Jullien, it urged its readers to "encourage our own musicians, and endeavor to do away with the puffing system adopted by foreign professionals." Jullien's concerts had not in fact failed, but he got the message: he began to include some works by American-born composers on his programs, among them Bristow and William Fry. It was the first recognition that American composers of symphonic music had had.

A notable graduate of Jullien's orchestra and of nine years' playing experience with the New York Philharmonic (1854–63) was Theodore Thomas (1835–1905). His potential as a director was recognized when he was a violinist in the group organized by William Mason in 1855 for chamber music evenings: Mason conceded in his *Memories* that Thomas's "was the dominating influence, felt and acknowledged by us all." After some tentative beginnings in 1862 and 1863, Thomas initiated a long and brilliant career as conductor of his own orchestra late in 1864. An astute impresario and a canny program-builder, Thomas knew how to create and hold an audience with programs that might be called crescent-shaped, with the heaviest fare in the center; thus he might flank orchestral movements by Beethoven, Schubert, Mendelssohn, even the radical Wagner, with simpler music: the waltzes of Strauss, the Bach-Gounod *Ave Maria,* and other crowd-pleasers. It was an original format, which gave up the old reliance on maintaining interest by a potpourri of instrumental and vocal works, and one destined to become a stereotype. Characteristic is the following program[19] from one of Thomas's Summer Night Concerts in New York's Central Park Garden (August 7, 1868):

Coronation March	Johann Strauss
Overture to *Die Heimkehre aus der Fremde*	Mendelssohn
Waltz from *Masaniello*	Auber

Intermission

Overture to *Tannhäuser*	Wagner
2nd movement, Symphony No. 8	Beethoven
3rd movement (Scherzo), Symphony No. 7 (C major)	Schubert

[19] Adapted from Rose Fay Thomas, *Memoirs of Theodore Thomas* (New York: Moffett, Yard and Company, 1911), p. 49. Later programs of Thomas's Orchestra had fewer "light" works and included complete symphonies; some were one-man exhibitions of works by a single composer.

Intermission

Grand March for the Schiller Centenary	Meyerbeer
Overture to *Mignon*	Thomas
Ave Maria	Bach-Gounod
Waltz, "Die Sphärenklänge"	Johann Strauss
Turkish March [arranged from Piano Sonato, K. 311?]	Mozart

Between 1869 and 1878 the Thomas Orchestra made regular, lengthy tours through the East and the Middle West as far as Chicago, with a roster of about 50 players.[20] Both in New York and throughout the country, its influence on standards of performance and on ideas of a standard orchestral repertory was immense. The modern symphonic ideal, according to which dozens of players submit through careful rehearsal to the rigorous, not to say autocratic, direction of a conductor in the interests of polished perfection, was Thomas's ideal. His ideas on repertory were inevitably governed by an Austro-Germanic bias; nevertheless, he occasionally played music by American composers. They were very few, however; Thomas had high standards and, as he put it, "I do not believe in playing inferior works merely because they are American" (*Memoirs*, p. 67).

Thomas became conductor of the New York Philharmonic in 1877, resigned for an abortive year as first head of the Cincinnati College of Music, resumed the Philharmonic directorship in 1880, then moved permanently to Chicago in 1891 to become conductor of the newly established Chicago Symphony Orchestra. For the last half of the nineteenth century he was the acknowledged master of the symphony orchestra, the first American virtuoso conductor.

ORCHESTRAL MUSIC

What about American orchestral music, as opposed to American orchestras, in the period up to the Civil War?

With only a few orchestras in the land and with orchestral music, as distinct from music for solo instruments or small chamber groups, identified mainly with European composers and conductors, it is not surprising that American composers produced comparatively little symphonic music. Nevertheless, a few composers stand out as our first symphonists.

[20] When it played the opening concert of Harvard's Sanders Theatre, November 21, 1876, the make-up of the orchestra was eight first violins, eight second violins, four violas, four cellos, and four basses, plus woodwinds and brasses in pairs, according to *Dwight's Journal of Music*, XXXVI (March 3, 1877), p. 398. Presumably there was a percussionist as well.

"The Beethoven of America" is what Parker's *Euterpeiad* called Anthony Philip Heinrich in its issue of April 13, 1822. We have met Heinrich above (see pp. 78–79) as a composer of bizarre and extravagant virtuoso piano music, songs, and chamber works. He also had orchestral aspirations (and was to fulfill them), and in fact his first historically noteworthy act, upon arrival in Kentucky in the autumn of 1817, was to organize a benefit concert—the beneficiary was Heinrich himself—in which he not only played the violin and the piano but directed the "full band" in a "Simfonia con Minuetto" by Beethoven—perhaps the First Symphony, not one of the bigger, later ones, but certainly an extraordinary kind of work to present in the pioneer town of Lexington, Kentucky in November, 1817.

The major part of Heinrich's orchestral music consists of descriptive symphonies in several elaborately titled movements, or one-movement programmatic fantasies divided into contrasting sections. Their subjects are those of a hyper-enthusiastic, Romantic newcomer to America: Indian lore (*Pushmataha, a Venerable Chief of a Western Tribe of Indians,* 1831; *Manitou Mysteries; or, The Voice of the Great Spirit. Gran sinfonia misteriosa indiana,* before 1845); American history (*The Treaty of William Penn with the Indians. Concerto grosso. An American national dramatic divertissement, for a full orchestra, comprising successively 6 different characteristic movements, united in one* . . . , 1834, revised 1847; *Der Felsen von Plymouth; oder, Die Landung der Pilger Väter in Neu-England*); the American landscape (*The War of the Elements and the Thundering of Niagara. Capriccio grande for a full orchestra,* before 1845); hero-worship (*Schiller. Grande sinfonia dramatica,* in five movements composed at various times between 1820 and 1857; *The Tomb of Genius: To the Memory of Mendelssohn-Bartholdy. Sinfonia sacra, for grande orchestra,* after 1847 and before 1857; *To the Spirit of Beethoven,* in fourteen "tableaux," before 1845); and finally, patriotic encomiums (*The Jubilee. A Grand national song of triumph,* for orchestra and chorus, 1840).

The style of these extraordinary orchestral outbursts is indeed one of "strange somersets and capriccios" (to borrow Heinrich's own characterization of his music), mingling simple dance tunes (especially folkish Ländler types) and elaborately chromatic melodies; crystal-clear Classic-era harmonies and wildly modulating passages; basically homophonic, diatonic textures and a profusion of decorative chromatic counterpoints (most often solo woodwind voices over a background of strings); predictable, periodic phrase forms and surprising extensions (or, instead of the latter, the opposite: unexpected grand pauses of dead silence). For a latecomer to composition, Heinrich had a remarkable ear for orchestral color and an expansive imagination that led him to write for unusual instruments as well as the conventional orchestral core. The third ("The Adagio") of the four movements of the symphonically-scaled *Manitou*

Mysteries includes extensive and effective use of pizzicato. Among the instruments in the very large orchestra required for *The Indian War Council* is a "harmonicon" or "glassichord," a mechanized set of musical glasses invented by Benjamin Franklin (see *AM*, pp. 89–92). *Pushmataha* is a 14-minute fantasy for 33 different orchestral voices including piccolo, basset horn, serpent, contrabassoon, three kinds of drums, triangle, cymbals, and tambourine as well as the normal full orchestra. For reasons unclear (but possibly relating to the first public Independence Day celebration at which S. F. Smith's *America* was sung to the tune: July 4, 1831), this paean to a mighty Indian chief culminates with a majestic and characteristically chromaticized quotation of *God Save the King* (Example 4-11).[21]

EXAMPLE 4-11. A. Heinrich, *Pushmataha* (1831), measures 460–65 (reduced from the Library of Congress copy of the orchestral score).

[21] I am grateful to Professor Howard Shanet of Columbia University for making available to me tapes of performances he has conducted of several orchestral works by Heinrich.

It might be expected that the intense musical life of the German-speaking communities in Pennsylvania would have inspired some orchestral music, but the Moravians seem for the most part to have been content with European scores, and thus far we know of no orchestral productions of the other sects. Surprisingly, one of the earliest known American orchestral works, a Symphony in D in two movements, dated 1831, by a William C. Peters (d. 1866), was discovered in 1960 at the Harmony Society of Ambridge, beyond Pittsburgh in western Pennsylvania and hardly more than a frontier settlement in 1831. For Philadelphia's Musical Fund Society and Bethlehem's Philharmonic Society a few orchestral works seem to have been written by Americans. Charles Hommann (ca. 1800–ca. 1850) contributed an orchestral overture (ca. 1840) to the former society and dedicated to the Bethlehem organization a Symphony in E-flat (ca. 1840); both are well-crafted, Schubertian works. Another overture by Hommann has been discovered at Nazareth.

George F. Bristow (1825–1898) and William H. Fry (1813–1864) were the best-known mid-century composers of orchestral music in New York. Bristow was the better trained, a professional violinist and conductor who composed six symphonies in a polished Mendelssohnian style, among them a fine Symphony in F-sharp minor, Op. 26 (performed by the New York Philharmonic under Carl Bergmann in 1859) and a more lengthy Symphonie for Grand Orchestra, "The Pioneer" (Arcadian), Op. 49 (1874), which includes perhaps the first use of an American Indian melody in a work of art-music. The opera *Rip Van Winkle* (1855) and cantatas *The Great Republic* (1879) and *Niagara* (1898) have strong overtures. Fry, famous as a noisy champion of American composers amidst the deluge of Europeans just before the Civil War, composed four symphonies, *Santa Claus, The Breaking Heart, Childe Harold,* and *A Day in the Country,* all performed by Jullien's orchestra in 1853–54 and all provided with interminable programs which explain, but do not make coherent, the naive tone-painting and narrative forms of the works. An *Overture to "Macbeth"* (1862) reminiscent of Auber is well-scored and never dull.

The Romantic tendency to gigantism, exemplified by Jullien's "monster concerts," is suggested also by two in which Gottschalk was involved in Cuba and Rio de Janeiro. For a concert at Havana early in 1860 Gottschalk composed several works; the music of one of them, *Marcha Triunfal y Final de Opera,* long thought lost, is now in the New York Public Library. His orchestra, he reported in his journal, numbered 650, plus 87 choristers, 15 solo singers, 50 drums, and 80 trumpets—"that is to say, nearly nine hundred persons bellowing and blowing to see who could scream the loudest." And at Rio in 1869, for a concert which included the Andante of his symphony *La Nuit des tropiques* (1858–59),

Gottschalk dreamed of "eight hundred performers and eighty drums to lead."[22] He got about 650, made up from bands of the Brazilian National Guard, the Imperial Navy, the Army, the War Arsenal, and from three orchestras assembled for the occasion (November 11, 1869). *La Nuit des tropiques,* which may or may not be complete with the Andante and Finale movement that are extant, is a colorful work in the French tradition of Berlioz; John Kirkpatrick's "Observations . . ." cite its "poetic atmosphere" and "surprising expansion" of line. The brilliant, brassy Finale, which calls for separate sections of cornets, trumpets, trombones, and euphoniums, with each section divided, is overwhelming. Another symphony, in one movement, has recently been rediscovered: the "Montevideo" Symphony (1868?), subtitled "Romantique."

OPERA

Of all the kinds of art-music of the American cultivated tradition between 1820 and the Civil War, the least significant, and the least widely heard, was opera. The ballad opera of the eighteenth century, or at least plays with music, continued in unbroken tradition through the period. Their function, however, changed with the introduction of other kinds of music and musical theater, which tended to keep the musical play a vernacular entertainment without any growing pretensions to becoming "fine art." By the 1860's the ballad opera as such was virtually non-existent, except in transformations like *The Black Crook* (1866) (an extravagant mixture of Frenchy ballet and Germanic melodrama, to an American variation on the plot of Weber's *Der Freischütz*) or parodies like those of the minstrel shows at Buckley's Ethiopian Opera House in New York. European operas gained a foothold in America during the period, however, and the first "grand operas" by American composers were produced.

By far the most lively operatic center was New Orleans, where a cultivated French contingent of the cosmopolitan population had maintained support for French opera from 1796, when the theater on St. Peter Street produced Grétry's *Sylvain.* In the 1805–6 season alone, the St. Peter Theatre produced sixteen different operas by nine composers, among them Monsigny, Grétry, Dalayrac, Boieldieu, Méhul, and Paisiello —and all these for a town of only twelve thousand people. With the establishment of a permanent opera company at the Orleans Theater

---

[22] Octavia Hensel, *Life and Letters of Louis Moreau Gottschalk* (Boston: Oliver Ditson Company, 1870), p. 174.

in 1810, New Orleans was unrivalled as operatic center of America. Northern cities—Boston, Philadelphia, Baltimore—heard their first grand opera when the New Orleans company toured during the seven summers from 1827 to 1833; and New York admitted that the southern troupe was "fully equal to that we imported from foreigners," referring to Manuel García's Spanish company, which had given New York its first foreign-language opera in 1825.[23]

García's, the first of a number of traveling companies to play in New York, was to stay a year. Its repertory favored Rossini: *Il Barbiere di Siviglia* was the first production, followed by *Cenerentola, Semiramide, Tancredi, Il Turco in Italia,* and Mozart's *Don Giovanni.* Later troupes introduced other fare to those New Yorkers who went to the operas: Bellini, Donizetti, Auber, Halévy. The increasing numbers of German immigrants, especially after 1848, provided support for German opera; during the 1862–63 season, for instance, some 65 performances were heard, with the favorites being Weber's *Der Freischütz,* Beethoven's *Fidelio,* Mozart's *Magic Flute* and *The Abduction from the Seraglio.*

As with symphonies in New York, the names to reckon with in opera of the period are those of Fry and Bristow. Fry's early life was spent in Philadelphia, and it was at the Chestnut Street Theatre on June 4, 1845 that his *Leonora,* a full-scale three-act work on a libretto derived by Fry's brother from Bulwer-Lytton's *The Lady of Lyons* (1838), was first heard. Presented in what must have been an unusually lavish production for the time, at the hands of the English company of Arthur Seguin with an orchestra of 60 and a chorus of 80, *Leonora* had a successful run of sixteen performances. Its fashionably Romantic plot and Belliniesque music must have made it seem very up-to-date (two arias in *MinA,* Nos. 128 and 129; Fry's prefatory remarks in *ACS,* pp. 46–52). Fry composed three other operas, only one of which, *Notre Dame de Paris,* was produced.

Fry was perhaps less gifted as a composer than as a journalist. As such he was a belligerent and articulate champion of the rights of American composers to be heard in America. Ironically, however, it was not Fry but his friend Bristow who turned to American subjects: his *Rip Van Winkle* (1855) was successful; his *Columbus* was never finished. The former (two arias and chorus in *MinA,* Nos. 130, 131) is less derivative from Italian opera than is Fry's *Leonora* and reveals Bristow's solid grounding in German instrumental music of his time, although the gap between his fluid, chromatic harmony and his square-cut phrase structure is seldom successfully bridged.

---

[23] The quotation, from the New York *American* as cited in the New Orleans *L'Argus* of August 24, 1827, is given in Henry Kmen, *Music in New Orleans* (Baton Rouge: Louisiana State University Press, 1966), p. 125.

BIBLIOGRAPHICAL NOTES

Stevenson's *Protestant Church Music in America* is a well documented basic source for the material in this chapter, as well as for Chapter 1. The best biography of Lowell Mason presently in print is that by Arthur Rich: *Lowell Mason* (Chapel Hill: University of North Carolina Press, 1946). It is, however, superseded by the as-yet unpublished study by Carol Ann Pemberton, *Lowell Mason: His Life and Work* (Ph.D. dissertation, University of Minnesota, 1971). Mason's own *Musical Letters from Abroad* (1854) have been reprinted (New York: Da Capo Press, 1967); one reviewer of the reprint (in *American Quarterly*, XX, 1 [Spring 1968]) commented, "No serious student of nineteenth-century American priggery can afford to ignore them." The first edition of Mason's *Boston Handel and Haydn Society Collection of Church Music* is reprinted in *EAM*.

No really adequate study of American household and concert songs of the period 1820–65 has been made. W. T. Upton's *Art-Song in America* (Boston: Oliver Ditson Company, 1930; supplement, 1938) may be consulted. Carol Brink's *Harps in the Wind* (New York: The Macmillan Company, 1947) and P. D. Jordan's *Singin' Yankees* (Minneapolis: University of Minnesota Press, 1946) are both on the Hutchinson family. J. T. Howard's *Stephen Foster, America's Troubadour* (New York: Thomas Y. Crowell Company, 1934; rev. eds. 1953, 1962) is the standard biography, E. F. Morneweck's two-volume *Chronicles of Stephen Foster's Family* (Pittsburgh: University of Pittsburgh Press, 1944) the basic documentary source book. Twenty-two of Foster's household songs are reprinted from early editions in *EAM*, No. 12.

George Frederick Root's *Story of My Musical Life: An Autobiography* (1891) has been reprinted by Da Capo Press (New York, 1970). The publishing firm of Root & Cady has been authoritatively chronicled by Dena Epstein in *Music Publishing in Chicago Before 1871: The Firm of Root & Cady, 1858–1871* (Detroit: Information Coordinators, Inc., 1969). A volume of songs by Henry Clay Work has been reprinted in *EAM*.

The chapters on the U.S.A. in Loesser's *Men, Women and Pianos* make fascinating reading. Both Richard Hoffman and William Mason wrote their memoirs, characteristically devoting the most space to their European years; see Hoffman, *Some Musical Recollections of Fifty Years* (New York: Charles Scribner's Sons, 1910) and Mason, *Memories of a Musical Life* (New York: The Century Co., 1902). Jeanne Behrend's edition of Gottschalk's *Notes of a Pianist* (New York: Alfred A. Knopf,

Inc., 1964) is excellent, while Vernon Loggins's Gottschalk biography, *Where the Word Ends* (Baton Rouge: Louisiana State University Press, 1958), fictionalized and largely undocumented, must be read with caution. Robert Offergeld has made an important bibliographical contribution in his *Centennial Catalogue of the Published and Unpublished Compositions of Louis Moreau Gottschalk* (New York: Ziff-Davis Publishing Co., 1970). All of Gottschalk's works for piano, reprinted in facsimile from early editions, appear in a five-volume set, *The Piano Works of Louis Moreau Gottschalk* (New York: Arno Press & The New York Times, 1969); its substantial critical-biographical introductory essay is by Offergeld.

Jullien's flamboyant life is chronicled by Adam Carse in *The Life of Jullien* (Cambridge: W. Heffer & Sons, 1951). *Theodore Thomas: A Musical Autobiography,* edited by George P. Upton (Chicago: A. C. McClurg & Co., 1905), has been reprinted by Da Capo Press (New York, 1964), with an introduction by Leon Stein and some valuable appendices. A definitive history of the New York Philharmonic orchestra, by Howard Shanet, is scheduled for publication by Doubleday in 1974.

The basic (so far the only) biography of Heinrich is that of W. T. Upton (New York: Columbia University Press, 1939); two solid dissertations on different aspects of his music have been written at the University of Illinois, one by Neely Bruce, the other by David Barron. Upton is also the author of the biography, *William Henry Fry, American Journalist and Composer-Critic* (New York: Thomas Y. Crowell Company, 1954).

For opera in New Orleans to 1841, see H. A. Kmen's *Music in New Orleans* (Baton Rouge: Louisiana State University Press, 1966); in New York, Julius Mattfeld's *A Hundred Years of Grand Opera in New York* (New York: New York Public Library, 1927).

FIVE

THE VERNACULAR TRADITION,

1820-1920

Having considered the development of the cultivated tradition through the Civil War, let us go back to the early nineteenth century to consider vernacular-tradition music, carrying forward the discussion to the end of World War I and treating religious music, especially that of the revivals and camp meetings; the music of the popular lyric theater, the minstrel show; dance music; marches and other band music; and ragtime, at first a music of limited use among American Southern Negroes but by the turn of the twentieth century a music of national popularity.

SPIRITUAL FOLK SONGS, REVIVAL AND GOSPEL HYMNODY

We have noted in the foregoing chapter the rejection of the music of the First New England School in the very area that had spawned it.

Under the influence of the composers of "scientific" church music led by Lowell Mason and Thomas Hastings, the fuging tunes, anthems, and set-pieces of the Yankee tunesmiths were gradually eliminated from the churches as well as the singing schools, not only of New England but of the Middle Atlantic States as well. The imaginative shape-note notation of Smith and Little's *Easy Instructor* and its imitators was equally rejected in the North as being no more than "dunce notes" (Hastings's epithet). By 1853, as we have seen, a Boston historian of American church music believed that shape-note tunebooks and their music, "if used at all, have been crowded to the far West, mostly out of sight and hearing."[1]

He was wrong. Shape notes and the music of the New Englanders were still within "sight and hearing" of many Americans. They had indeed been crowded out of the Northern and Eastern cities, but they were flourishing in the Upland South and the Deep South, as well as in the "far West" (by which Gould probably meant any land west of the Appalachians). Spurned by the urban arbiters of cultivated taste in music, the tunesmiths' pieces had become essentially a rural music in the sparsely settled South and toward the frontier. There they would join with several other kinds of religious song to form the basis of a vernacular music tradition that is still alive today. These other kinds of song are our immediate concern: the spiritual folk songs and the revival hymns of the camp meetings, and the gospel hymns of the "City Revival" of the 1870's and later.

The beginnings of the migration to the South of the shape-note tunebooks are reflected in several Pennsylvania publications of the first two decades of the nineteenth century. For the English-speaking population appeared such imitations of *The Easy Instructor* as the 1807 edition of *Philadelphia Harmony; Ecclesia Harmonia* (1807); and *The Musical Instructor* (1808). German-speaking Pennsylvanians first learned shape-note singing from *Der leichte Unterricht* of 1810 (its title a literal translation of *The Easy Instructor's*) and *Die Franklin Harmonie* (1821). The latter two were published by a Harrisburg printer, John Wyeth (1770–1858), who also issued English-language tunebooks, among them *Repository of Sacred Music* (1810) and *Repository of Sacred Music, Part Second* (1813). The *Repository . . . Part Second* proved to be "the first really influential anthology of what the late George Pullen Jackson dubbed spiritual folksong."[2]

Spiritual folk songs are just what the term implies: religious songs set to folk melodies, whether secular song melodies, patriotic airs, or popular dance tunes. Three types of spiritual folk songs may be distin-

---

[1] Gould, *History of Church Music in America*, p. 55.
[2] Lowens, *MMEA*, p. 134. Lowens is referring to the pioneer studies of Jackson in a series of books from 1933 on, and specifically to his *Spiritual Folk-Songs of Early America*.

guished: religious ballads, folk hymns, and revival spiritual songs. Wyeth's collection of religious songs in two, three, and four voice-parts included both ballads and hymns, besides many tunes from earlier New England collections (Billings, Jenks, Law, Chapin) and 13 by Elkanah Dare (1782–1826), who may have been Wyeth's musical adviser. (*Fairton,* Dare's setting of Watts's "God of mercy! hear my call," is in *MinA,* No. 91.) *Heavenly Union,* for example, is a ballad in some ten strophes which begins with the balladeer's typical invitation to listen to a story:

> *Come, saints and sinners, hear me tell*
> *The wonders of Emmanuel,*
> *Who saved me from a burning hell,*
> *And brought my soul with him to dwell,*
> *And gave me heav'nly union.*

The tale goes on in a characteristically folkish, colloquial way:

> *When Christ the Saviour from on high*
> *Beheld my soul in ruins lie,*
> *He look'd on me with pitying eye,*
> *And said to me as he pass'd by,*
> *"With God you have no union."*

The folk hymns are briefer, non-narrative pieces; many are new settings to anonymous tunes of old favorite texts by Watts or Wesley. *Hallelujah* is one of three settings of the popular text of Robert Robinson, eighteenth-century English hymnodist, "Come thou fount of ev'ry blessing"; the tune, which was to be resecularized to the text "Tell Aunt Rhody," appears in print for the first time in Wyeth's *Repository* as an anonymous and presumably well-known folk tune (Example 5-1a; a later, gospel-hymn version shows how decades of popular usage reshaped the tune into the form known best today [Example 5-1b]).

As one can hear in *Hallelujah,* with early nineteenth-century folk hymnody we are back again in the musical world of the Yankee tunesmiths: the parallel fifths of measures 2-3 and 4; the implied modal harmony; the "gapped" melody which makes the tune seem fundamentally pentatonic; the simple, sturdy rhythm. These old style-characteristics are maintained, indeed emphasized, in Wyeth's shape-note hymn collection, which was to be the model for later tunebooks in the developing tradition of Southern spiritual folk songs.

"Spiritual folk song" suggests the better-known term "spiritual." And in facts songs like *Hallelujah* have been termed "white spirituals" by historians beginning with Jackson, who coined the term for his *White*

EXAMPLE 5-1. (a) *Hallelujah, Repository of Sacred Music, Part Second* (2nd ed.; Harrisburg: J. Wyeth, 1820), p. 112; (b) *Come, Thou Fount*, attributed to John Wyeth in *Gospel Hymns. Nos. 1 to 6 Complete* (New York: Biglow & Main Co., 1894), No. 633 (soprano part only).

Spirituals in the Southern Uplands (1933). The complex relationships between such white spirituals and Negro spirituals are not yet wholly clear. What *is* clear is that the Negro spirituals, which were hardly ever discussed in print or transcribed before the Reconstruction period after the

Civil War, arose out of the evangelical song of the great revivals in the American South and West in the period after 1800.[3] These began with the Great Revival of 1800 in Kentucky, which set off a wave of emotional religious revivalism led by the aggressive Methodists, Presbyterians, and Baptists that soon swept across Georgia, the Carolinas, Pennsylvania, Tennessee, and Ohio. The instrument of the revivals was the camp meeting of worshippers who brought tents, bedding, and food for the four- or five-day (and night) marathons of preaching, praying, and singing. Attendance could run in the thousands: at Cane Ridge, Kentucky in 1801, more than 30 ministers preached to a crowd estimated variously to be between 10,000 and 20,000. With meetings of such size, a new kind of religious song inevitably appeared—the revival hymn—simpler even than the traditional hymns and having the text repetitions or verse-and-refrain structure found in many folk cultures. This kind of song was often termed a "spiritual song," as in the title of John C. Totten's pocket-sized book of hymn texts, *A Collection of the Most Admired Hymns and Spiritual Songs, with the choruses affixed, as usually sung at camp-meetings* (New York, 1809). At least one critic of camp-meeting revivalism believed that the repetitive choral refrains of the new type of hymn derived from the Negro: John F. Watson, in a tract of 1819 bemoaning what he called *Methodist Error,* spoke of one

> . . . most exceptionable error, which has the tolerance at least of the rulers of our camp meetings. In the *blacks'* quarter [of the camp ground], the coloured people get together, and sing for hours together, short scraps of disjoined affirmations, pledges, or prayers, lengthened out with repetition choruses. These are all sung in the merry chorus-manner of the southern harvest-field, or husking-frolic method, of the slave blacks.

Watson lamented that "the example has already visibly affected the religious manners of some whites":

> From this cause, I have known in some camp meetings, from 50 to 60 people crowd into one tent, after the public devotions had closed, and there continue the whole night, singing tune after tune . . . scarce one of which were in our hymnbooks. Some of these from their nature, (having very long repetition choruses and short scraps of [text] matter) are actually composed as sung, and are indeed almost endless.[4]

[3] See Nettl, *Folk and Traditional Music of the Western Continents,* pp. 182–85. A brilliant, carefully documented study of the African legacy of the music of black Americans is that of Dena J. Epstein, "African Music in British and French America," *MQ,* LIX (1973), 61–91; Epstein has also given us our most dispassionate and best-documented survey of sources (in a field beclouded by prejudice of various kinds), in "Slave Music in the United States before 1860," *Notes,* XX (1963), 195–212, 377–90.

[4] Quoted in Don Yoder, *Pennsylvania Spirituals* (Lancaster: Pennsylvania Folklife Society, 1961), pp. 27–28.

"Short scraps" of verse, interspersed with "repetition choruses," sung in a "merry chorus-manner," often "actually composed as sung"—this is as good a definition as any of the typical revival hymn. It first appeared in print in pocket songsters, without the music but often with a separate section of "choruses" that could be added to or interpolated in the song leader's chanting of the verses. Wyeth's *Repository . . . Part Second* contained no such revival hymns, but the later Southern tunebooks, which otherwise borrowed so much from Wyeth (Yankee fuging tunes and other pieces, religious ballads, and folk hymns), added revival hymns as well. The most successful such tunebooks were Ananias Davisson's *Kentucky Harmony* (1816) and its *Supplement* (1820); Allen Carden's *Missouri Harmony* (1820); the *Columbian Harmony* (1825) of William Moore from Wilson County, Tennessee; William Caldwell's *Union Harmony* (Maryville, Tennessee, 1837); John Jackson's *Knoxville Harmony* (1838). Especially notable, because so popular, are *The Southern Harmony* of William Walker and *The Sacred Harp* of B. F. White and E. J. King.

"Singin' Billy" Walker (1809–1875) of Spartanburg, South Carolina published *The Southern Harmony* in 1835. In the preface to his *Christian Harmony* (1866; preface reprinted in *ACS*, pp. 67–69) he claimed to have sold 600,000 copies of the earlier work, and he is known to have added proudly to his signature the initials A.S.H. ("author *Southern Harmony*"). The index to the 1854 edition, the last and largest, names 334 pieces, including many new tunes "suitable for revival occasions." Walker's name is attached to forty of the compositions; in his preface to the first edition, he explains that in addition to having "composed several tunes wholly," he also "composed the [accompanying] parts to a great many good airs (which I could not find in any publication, nor in manuscript), and assigned my name as the author." Thus was a popular tune turned into a spiritual folk song. One such tune was *Auld lang syne,* which appears with the title *Plenary* as a setting for an Isaac Watts hymn (*MinA*, No. 99); another, surely an Irish reel in its first incarnation, is *The Good Old Way* (*MinA*, No. 98). Yet another, attributed in *The Southern Harmony* to a David Walker, is *The Hebrew Children,* an infectious hexatonic tune that is known also as a Negro spiritual ("Wonder where is good ole Daniel?"), an Ozark Mountains play-party song ("Where, O where is pretty little Susie?"), and, of later vintage, a college song ("Where, O where are the pea-green freshmen?").[5] The thrice-asked question of each stanza, "Where are the Hebrew children?" (. . . the twelve apostles? . . . the holy Christians? etc.), is answered by the refrain, "Safe in the

---

[5] Walker's *The Hebrew Children* is in *MinA*, No. 97, along with the first stanza of the Negro version, apparently taken from R. Nathaniel Dett, *Religious Folk-Songs of the Negro as Sung at Hampton Institute* (Hampton, Va.: Hampton Institute Press, 1927), p. 73. The play-party version is in Vance Randolph (ed.), *Ozark Folk Songs* (4 vols.; Columbia, Mo.: State Historical Society, 1946–50), III, 364. The college version is part of my own experience.

promised land," in a characteristic form of the verse-with-refrain revival hymn.

Typical of the compilers of Southern folk hymn books, Walker drew tunes that pleased him from no matter what source, transforming them into the rugged, sonorous shape-note style by the addition of two or three surrounding parts. Thus, not only do we find in *The Southern Harmony* borrowings from the eighteenth-century Yankee composers, newly composed pieces by Walker and others, but even Lowell Mason's *Missionary Hymn* and the patriotic song *Hail! Columbia*. The Scottish folk song *Braes o' Balquhidder* is made over into *Lone Pilgrim*, and both *Thorny Desert* and *Something New* sound like folk-hymn variants of Scotch-Irish reels.

Far more lastingly popular than *The Southern Harmony* was *The Sacred Harp* (1844) of Benjamin Franklin White (1800–1879) and his lesser-known co-compiler E. J. King (d. 1844?). As late as 1960, in a revision of 1911 supervised by the Alabama singing-school master S. M. Denson (1854–1936), copies of this tunebook, affirmatively retitled *Original Sacred Harp*, were still rolling off the press of the Sacred Harp Publishing Company of Cullman, Alabama. The Denson Revision consisted mainly in adding alto parts to 327 of the 609 tunes, making four-part songs out of the older three-part ones; otherwise, the twentieth-century *Sacred Harp* preserves the "dispersed harmony" (one part per staff), the four-shape notation (*fa* ◺ , *sol* ○ , *la* □ , *mi* ◇), and the traditional inclusion of an introduction on "The Rudiments of Music." Even the basic "old time" style is fairly well preserved. Example 5-2 shows the beginning of the moving folk hymn *Wondrous Love* in the three-part setting common to both *The Southern Harmony* (see *MinA*, No. 101) and the first edition of *The Sacred Harp*, with Denson's alto part added in cue-sized notes. It can be heard that occasionally the "modern" full triad sound is created by Denson's adding a third to the original's open fifth.

EXAMPLE 5-2. The folk hymn *Wondrous Love*, measures 1–8. Soprano, tenor, and bass parts from W. Walker, *The Southern Harmony* (New Haven, 1835), 1854 ed., p. 252. Alto part composed by S. M. Denson for "Denson Revision" (1911) of *The Sacred Harp* (Philadelphia, 1844); *Sacred Harp* version is whole-tone lower in original.

One of the best-known American spiritual folk songs, *Wayfaring Stranger,* appeared in print for the first time in the 1844 *Sacred Harp.* Its poignant text and mournful pentatonic tune tend to disguise the revival-hymn refrain of the last two lines (Example 5-3a). More characteristic of the lusty vigor of most revival songs is *The Old Ship of Zion,* a tune known in several variants including Negro ones, that of *The Sacred Harp* identified by William Hauser in his tunebook *The Olive Leaf* (see below) as a "North Carolina Version" (Example 5-3b).

EXAMPLE 5-3. Two revival hymns from *The Sacred Harp* (1844). (a) *Wayfaring Stranger* (p. 457 of Denson Revision; tenor part only); (b) *The Old Ship of Zion* (p. 79 of Denson Revision; tenor part only).

Besides the tunebooks cited above, which used the four-shape notation of Little and Smith's *Easy Instructor* based on a *fa, sol, la, mi* solmization system, others appeared in a seven-shape notation that reflected the pressures of the "scientific" school of musical thought to adopt the European *do, re, mi, fa, sol, la, si* (or *ti*) system. The first of these was *The Christian Minstrel* (Philadelphia, 1846), compiled by Jesse Aikin, who showed his respect for Lowell Mason by including 18 of Mason's hymns in the work. Another, destined to be almost as long-lived as *The Sacred Harp*, was the eastern Tennessee tunebook *The Harp of Columbia* (Knoxville, 1848); present-day singers from this book call themselves "Old Harp Singers" as opposed to the "Sacred Harp Singers." One of the last shape-note tunebooks in the traditional style of spiritual folk song, and one which used Aikin's seven shapes, was *The Olive Leaf* (1878), printed at Wadley, Georgia by William Hauser (1812–1880). But this book also reveals the impact of a new style in American vernacular hymnody, that of the gospel hymn.

The gospel hymn, like the earlier revival hymn, was the product of a revival movement. However, unlike the earlier nineteenth-century revival hymn, which arose mainly in the back country and on the frontier, the gospel hymn of the last half of the century was urban. Its musical background was the correct, bland style of Mason and Hastings, but its harmony tended to be more chromatically engorged, its texts more sentimentally swollen. From the earlier revival hymnodists, the gospel-hymn writers, equally intent on engaging large masses in cathartic song-fests, took the idea of repeated refrain-choruses. As Stevenson puts it, in thinly disguised scorn for the genre, "the verse-and-refrain pattern of the revival song joins with Sweet Adeline harmonies to make the gospel song"; Edwin Pierce remarks perceptively on the influence of German secular *Volkslieder* (as they might have become known in the American imitations of the *Männerchöre*).[6]

William B. Bradbury, whom we have met as the composer of *The Lament of the Blind Orphan Girl* (see p. 66), foreshadowed the gospel song's tune in his *Woodworth* of 1849 ("Just as I am, without one plea"). However, the biggest names among gospel-hymn composers (and the Broadway connotation of that terminology is not inappropriate considering the polished publicity and commercial enterprise of the urban revivals) were those of Philip D. Bliss (1838–1876), Ira D. Sankey (1840–1908), and a somewhat lesser light, Rev. Robert Lowry (1826–1899). Lowry's *Beautiful River* ("Shall we gather at the river?") appeared in *The Olive Leaf*; its skipping rhythms entranced generations of Americans and were incorporated in instrumental works by Charles Ives ("Children's Day at the Camp Meeting" violin sonata) and Virgil Thomson (*Variations and Fugues on Sunday School Tunes*). Sankey, fresh from a

[6] Stevenson, *Protestant Church Music in America*, p. 90n; Edwin H. Pierce, "Gospel Hymns," *MQ*, XXVI (1940), 355–64.

two-year revival tour of Great Britain (1873–75) as organist and song-leader for the spellbinding evangelist Dwight L. Moody and immersed in Moody's revival meetings at the Brooklyn Rink in New York City, for which he directed a choir of 250 in addition to playing the organ for his own singing, still found time to see into print a book of *Gospel Hymns* (New York, 1875). Bliss collaborated with him in this hymn book, and in a second enlarged edition the next year; after Bliss's death, Sankey and other collaborators continued to issue enlargements through a sixth cumulative volume, *Gospel Hymns. Nos. 1 to 6 Complete* (1894).

The gospel hymns of Bliss and Sankey are easily denigrated as a "slough of sentimental music-hall sloppiness . . . flabby and futile," as a British observer has put it. But the same historian, shifting critical gears, views them rightly if perhaps unconsciously in the context of an American urban vernacular tradition when he admits that "at its best this music is honestly flamboyant and redolent of the buoyancy of the civilization that created New York and Pittsburgh and Chicago."[7] Bliss's *Pull for the Shore* may have a text as metaphorically exaggerated as a seventeenth-century Italian opera aria and as artfully homespun as the doggerel of Edgar Guest, but its chorus is an almost irresistible march, perfectly suited to its soul-stirring evangelistic purposes (Example 5-4).

EXAMPLE 5-4. P. Bliss, *Pull for the Shore*, No. 51 of *Gospel Hymns. Nos. 1 to 6 Complete* (New York: Biglow & Main Co., 1894), Chorus only.

[7] Erik Routley, *The Music of Christian Hymnody* (London: Independent Press, 1957), p. 166.

The universality of some gospel hymn tunes and text phrases is undeniable. The tune everyone has sung as "How dry I am!" can be found as No. 543 in the 1894 *Gospel Hymns,* beginning "O happy day that fixed my choice/On Thee, my Saviour and my God." Bliss's *Hallelujah, 'tis Done* (No. 2 of the 1883 compilation) became the irreverent parody, "Hallelujah, I'm a bum." Snatches of gospel-hymn texts have become commonplaces in the American vernacular: "Sweet by-and-by" (No. 110, 1894 collection); "Arise and shine" (No. 103); "Throw out the life-line" (No. 441); "Hold the fort" (No. 11); "The old, old story" (No. 28); "Where is my wand'ring boy tonight?" (No. 631); and many others.

I have been speaking, of course, about the major vernacular tradition in American nineteenth-century worship music. Offshoots of this (the Negro spirituals, for instance, or the Pennsylvania Dutch German-language spirituals) deserve and would repay independent attention in a more exhaustive study. Of particular interest would be a study of early published black religious music—e.g., the Allen, Ware, and Garrison *Slave Songs* . . . (1867) and the songs of the celebrated Jubilee Singers of Fisk University, published in J. B. T. Marsh's *The Story of the Jubilee Singers* (revised edition; Boston, 1880)—against the background of revival and gospel hymnody in general. Equally inviting for further study are various other separate, minor vernacular sub-traditions, such as the music (and its unique notation) of the Shakers ("Shaking Quakers"), the California missions, and other minority sects.

BLACKFACE MINSTRELSY

Early in 1854, when Jullien's orchestra was in New York offering "monster concerts for the masses," when the St. Charles Theatre in the Bowery had been presenting German opera for several months, when an Italian opera company producing Donizetti and Bellini was struggling to survive, and when Fry and Bristow were complaining of the New York Philharmonic's neglect of American composers, *Putnam's Monthly* for February called attention to another kind of musical entertainment:

> The only places of Amusement where the entertainments are indigenous are the African Opera Houses, where native American vocalists, with blackened faces, sing national songs, and utter none but native witticisms. These native theatricals . . . are among the best frequented and most profitable places of amusement in New York. While even [the] attempt to establish an Italian Opera here, though originating with the wealthiest and best educated classes, has resulted in bankruptcy, the Ethiopian Opera has flourished like a green bay tree.

This report pinpoints nicely the high point of a kind of American vernacular lyric theater, eschewed perhaps by the "wealthiest and best educated classes" but flourishing among the others. A few months earlier the *Musical World* (October 8, 1853) had noted that "Ethiopian Minstrelsy is on the increase. We now have, in New York, six companies of Minstrels in full blast." The "native theatrical" of blackface minstrelsy was in full flower.

The American minstrel show had crystallized as a form of public entertainment in the early 1840's. Like many other facets of early nineteenth-century American culture, it had British antecedents. In the 1700's it was not uncommon for British dramas to include Negro characters and so-called "Negro songs," usually of an insufferably patronizing and sentimental character. Some British comedians blackened their faces and impersonated Negroes; one of these, Charles Mathews, came to America in 1822. Unfamiliar with American Negroes, he was fascinated by them, especially their dialect and their humor. In New York, at the blacks' own theater, he noted their performance of *Hamlet* and transcribed the song *Opossum up a Gum Tree*. In Philadelphia he heard a black revivalist preacher and tried to reproduce on paper the sermon's dialect. He collected "scraps of songs and malaprops."[8] With such first-hand experience Mathews's skits and mock-lectures, enlivened by dialect songs, tended ever so slightly toward more realistic if still stereotyped parodies of the Negro and helped to stimulate an American style of Negro stage impersonation, which some twenty years later would be the foundation of the minstrel show.

As other Northern comedians exploited the fad for Negro sketches in the 1820's and '30's, two stereotypes tended to crystallize, perhaps first in the skits and songs created by George Washington Dixon in the late 1820's, such as *Coal Black Rose* and *My Long-Tail Blue*. Like the other two early American comic heroes—the shrewd, taciturn Yankee peddler and the lusty, bragging backwoodsman—the two Negro stereotypes were oversimplified exaggerations of real life. One was the plantation hand, a tatterdemalion of low estate but high spirits; the other was the urban dandy with affectedly modish ways and a fashionable "long-tailed blue" dress coat. Jim Crow or Gumbo Chaff, Zip Coon or Dandy Jim—these were the archetypes as sketched by early American blackface comedians like Dixon and Thomas Dartmouth ("Daddy") Rice (1808–1860), who created the internationally famous stage character of Jim Crow, legendarily based on a black stable groom in Louisville, where Rice was playing in 1828.

Bit by bit such comedians, with faces blackened by burnt cork,

[8] *Memoirs of Charles Mathews, Comedian, by Mrs. Mathews* (London, 1839), III, 391.

enlarged their repertory of skits, songs, and dances; gathered into small troupes; and began to develop the format for a whole program. One important milestone was the formation by four star comedians in New York of a minstrel band of instruments associated with the Negro. The *New York Herald* announced their premiere, set for February 6, 1843, as one of the major attractions of the Bowery Circus:

> First Night of the novel, grotesque, original, and surprisingly melodious Ethiopian band, entitled the *Virginia Minstrels*, being an exclusively musical entertainment combining the banjo, violin, bone castanets, and tambourine, and entirely exempt from the vulgarities and other objectionable features which have hitherto characterized negro extravaganzas.

Successful in New York, the four Virginia Minstrels enlarged their act into a full evening's entertainment of songs, dances, and a parody "lecture on locomotives" and opened with it at the Masonic Temple in Boston on March 7; they called it an "Ethiopian Concert." It was the first real minstrel show.

Following the successes of the Virginia Minstrels, other troupes were formed, and the ones already in existence enlarged their shows; soon the Christy Minstrels, Bryant's Minstrels, The Sable Harmonists, The Kentucky Rattlers, The Ethiopian Serenaders, and dozens of others were traveling across the country. Dialect solo songs; satirical stump speeches and dialogues; burlesques; instrumental numbers and dances, either solo or group; and "walk-arounds" (small-scale vernacular *Gesamtkunstwerke* combining solo song, choral song, and dancing to instrumental "symphonies") became the staples of the minstrel shows as the craze for them rose to an early peak in the 1850's. Through them all, at this period, ran a strain of affectionate, good-humored caricature of the Negro, who was portrayed both as jokester and butt of jokes, as comedian and (less often) tragedian. Even if by today's standards the stereotypes and the heavy dialect of the early blackface minstrels are found offensive, they did present the black as a comic hero.[9] The minstrel shows had their villains, but they were of other kinds. Standing up for American popular culture, the minstrels lashed out in stinging parodies and burlesques at the arty and pretentious, the foreign and imported. In the 1850's the "Tyrolean business," mocking the vogue of singing families like the Hutchinsons and the Rainer family, was often to be heard, with such titles as "Tyrolean Solo, displaying a flexibility and volume of voice astonishing and inimitable" and "We Come from the Hills, burlesque à la Rainer family." Italian opera was a favorite target: *Lucia di Lam-*

[9] See Constance Rourke, *American Humor* (New York: Harcourt, Brace & Co., 1931), Chapter III; also her *Roots of American Culture* (New York: Harcourt, Brace & Co., 1942), pp. 262–74.

mermoor was burlesqued as "Lucy Did Lam a Moor." *The New York Clipper* of January 21, 1854 crowed over the Christy Minstrels' satire on Jullien's monster concerts. The virtuosity of visiting violinist Ole Bull and of the fabled Paganini was deprecated by the minstrels, who claimed that

> *Loud de banjo talked away,*
> *An' beat Ole Bull from de Norway;*
> *We'll take de shine from Paganini,*
> *We're de boys from ole Virginny.*

This was an echo of "Daddy" Rice's *Jim Crow* (*MinA*, No. 104), who had boasted about 1828 that

> *I'm a rorer on de fiddle,*
> *And down in ole Virginny*
> *Dey say I play de skientific*
> *Like massa Pagganninny.*

Sometimes the minstrels portrayed the Negro as the same kind of swaggering superman as the frontiersman heroes:

> *My mama was a wolf*
> *My daddy was a tiger,*
> *I am what you call*
> *De Ole Virginny Nigger:*
> *Half fire, half smoke,*
> *A little touch of thunder,*
> *I am what you call*
> *De eighth wonder.*

And sometimes, in transparent disguise, he was shown as a clever out-smarter of authority:

> *A bullfrog dressed in soger's close*
> *Went in de field to shoot some crows,*
> *De crows smell powder an' fly away,*
> *De bullfrog mighty mad dat day.*

The music of the minstrel shows was a mélange of well-known popular songs (even some of the sentimental household type), of adaptations from other sources (even of British and Italian opera airs), of dance tunes and dialect songs. These last two were the mainstays of the shows and had the most remarkable music.

The typical minstrel band of the 1840's was that established by the Virginia Minstrels: banjo, tambourine, bone castanets, and violin, with perhaps also an accordion, a triangle, or a second banjo. All of these except the accordion were instruments associated with the Southern Negro, particularly the banjo, which in fact had African origins. A British minister and lexicographer who had spent many years in Maryland and Virginia wrote of it:

> . . . The favourite and almost only instrument in use among the slaves there was a *bandore;* or, as they pronounced the word, *banjer.* Its body was a large hollow gourd, with a long handle attached to it, strung with catgut, and played on with the fingers.[10]

In the minstrel shows, a singer often accompanied himself on the banjo, tapping his foot in a steady metronomic beat and varying his sung melody on the instrument. Thus *The Boatmen's Dance* (see *AM*, p. 272), claimed by Dan Emmett as his own song but known at least in part on the Ohio River in the 1820's and '30's, might have been played as shown in Example 5-5b. The variation style of short, even running notes is not new: we have met it in the dance music, under English influence, of the late eighteenth and early nineteenth centuries (see above, Example 2-7).

EXAMPLE 5-5. (a) D. Emmett, *De Boatmen's Dance* (Boston: C. H. Keith, 1843), measures 13–16 (air only); and (b) *The Boatman's Dance,* Frank B. Converse, *Frank B. Converse's Banjo Instructor* (New York, 1865), measures 1–4. After *Dan Emmett and the Rise of Early Negro Minstrelsy,* by Hans Nathan. Copyright 1962 by the University of Oklahoma Press.

Much more novel, indeed so fresh as to be a source for the indigenous American rhythms of ragtime and early jazz, are the banjo "jigs" of the minstrel-show dances. Hans Nathan, who first called attention to these remarkable tunes, describes them thus:

[10] Jonathan Boucher, *Boucher's Glossary of Archaic and Provincial Words* . . . (London: Black, Young and Young, 1832), p. BAN; quoted in Dena J. Epstein, "African Music in British and French America," *MQ*, LIX (1973), 61–91. See also Epstein, "Slave Music," *Notes*, XX (1963), 201.

The motion . . . is animated by many irregular stresses: hectic offbeat accentuations projected against the relentless, metrical background of the accompanying taps [of the feet], which change $\frac{2}{4}$ into $\frac{6}{8}$. A large number of accentuations result from sudden, brief rests on one of the four beats in the measure.[11]

A fine example is Emmett's *Pea-Patch Jig*, one of 48 banjo tunes in an early manuscript compiled by Emmett; surprisingly, it also appeared in print in *Kendall's Clarinet Instruction Book* (Boston, 1845). The combinations of triplets and duplets and of even and uneven rhythms in running passages, the repeated notes, and above all the frequent accentuated rests on strong beats contribute to the propulsive, "swinging" character of the music (Example 5-6).

EXAMPLE 5-6. D. Emmett, *Pea-Patch Jig*, first (= closing) strain only. From *Dan Emmett and the Rise of Early Negro Minstrelsy*, by Hans Nathan. Copyright 1962 by the University of Oklahoma Press.

[Sounds an octave lower]

Evidence suggests that although the ultimate source of this style lay in British, especially Scottish and Irish, folk-dance music, the concentration of offbeat accents and other rhythmic shifts derived from the manner in which such music was played by the American Negro, who then provided the direct models for Northern minstrel-show banjoists. As the clarinet instruction book mentioned above shows, the banjo-jig idiom was imitated on other instruments: it crops up not only in Kendall's clarinet book but in violin, fife, and flute manuals as well, and the piano music of early ragtime is clearly indebted to it.

Something of the same buoyant, swingy, chattering spirit enters the dialect songs and the music for walk-arounds of the minstrel shows. The two outstanding composers were Daniel Decatur Emmett (1815–1904) and Stephen Foster. Emmett was the more versatile: banjoist, fiddler, singer, and comedian; author of lyrics, stump speeches, plays for the minstrel stage, and instruction manuals for both fife and drum. He also composed in addition to banjo tunes many songs for the minstrel

[11] Nathan, *Dan Emmett*, p. 195.

shows; about seventy were published. By far the most famous is *Dixie* (*MinA*, No. 109), originally presented by Bryant's Minstrels on April 4, 1859 and announced on the playbill as "Mr. Dan Emmett's new and original song and dance, *Dixie's Land*, introducing the whole troupe in the festival dance." Nathan's description cannot be improved upon:

> The tune is characterized by a heavy, nonchalant, inelegant strut. . . . If music, lyrics, and dance style are taken as an entity, there emerges a special kind of humor that mixes grotesqueness with lustiness and down-to-earth contentment—comparable, to overstate the case, to a blend of Brueghel and Mickey Mouse. . . . "Dixie" indeed is no polite genteel tune. It has a considerable measure of toughness. . . .[12]

Like others of Emmett's walk-arounds, *Dixie* derived from various sources: its "song" and "chorus" melodies can be related to English and Scottish dance tunes as well as to *Gumbo Chaff*, a minstrel song of the 1830's; its closing instrumental "dance" was published in Emmett's *Fife Instructor* with the title "Albany Beef" and is a jig of Irish-Scottish ancestry. Nevertheless, like the best of Emmett's other songs and walk-arounds, *Dixie* integrates these raw materials in a new synthesis. Its rhythmic jolts, related to the banjo-jig syncopations, and its ridiculous homespun humor, common to the minstrel show but originating on the American frontier, make for "a very characteristically national music," as it was described in a Scottish encyclopedia of 1864 in an entry on Negro minstrelsy.

Essentially, although it appeared on the minstrel-show stages of Northern cities, the early minstrel song's earthiness, lustiness, lack of sentimentality, and sinewy vigor came from the world of the frontiersman and the boatman, in those days when the frontier was just over the next range of hills and when rivers and canals were the highways of America. This connection with "primitive" America was certainly one reason why the genteel society of the cities—"the wealthiest and best educated classes," to recall the phrase of *Putnam's Monthly*—looked down their collective noses at the minstrel show and its music. And this is why the other outstanding composer of minstrel-show song, Stephen Foster, had to justify with a fine but defensive show of resolution his decision to move whole-heartedly into the field of minstrel-song composition. In a letter of 1852 to E. P. Christy, leader of Christy's Minstrels, Foster declared: "I have concluded . . . to pursue the Ethiopian business without fear or shame and . . . to establish my name as the best Ethiopian songwriter."[13] By 1852 Foster was a well-known songwriter, both of house-

---

[12] *Ibid.*, pp. 247–48, 250.
[13] The entire text of this interesting letter printed in *AM*, pp. 293–94, and, along with three others letters to Christy, in *ACS*, pp. 54–57.

hold songs and of minstrel-show songs. His comment to Christy shows, however, the lingering doubts he must have had about the propriety and gentility of identifying himself unreservedly with the latter. (He had an economic reason, however, for overcoming those doubts, for his biggest hit, *Old Folks at Home,* had been published under Christy's name as composer; Foster rationalized in the same letter to Christy that "I cannot write at all unless I write for public approbation and get credit for what I write.")

Foster's first songs for the minstrels, four published between 1847 and 1848, were already in the full-fledged indigenous style of the minstrel music of the 1840's. The banjo twang on the afterbeats in the accompaniment to *Lou'siana Belle* and the strumming, rattling rhythm of *Away Down South* (Example 5-7) made those songs immediate successes, like *Uncle Ned* as well. But of the four early songs it was *Oh! Susanna* that was to prove indestructibly vital. *Oh! Susanna (MinA,* No. 107) was prob-

EXAMPLE 5-7. S. Foster, early minstrel songs. (a) *Lou'siana Belle* (Louisville & Cincinnati: Peters, 1847), measures 9–12; (b) *Away Down South* (Louisville & Cincinnati: Peters, 1848), measures 9–16.

ably derived in part from the earlier, anonymous *Gwine 'long Down* (1844), just as Foster's later *Nelly Bly* (1849) seems to come from *Clare de Kitchen* (late 1830's) and his *Camptown Races* (1850) from *Picayune Butler* (1847). But, like Emmett's *Dixie, Oh! Susanna* was a transcendent synthesis of varied elements, not only because of the fine swinging movement of its solo verses and the solid stomp of its five-part chorus (with a potent rhythmic jolt on the last two syllables of "Oh! Su-*san-na*") but because of the deadpan nonsense humor of its text:

> *It rained all night the day I left,*
> *The weather it was dry,*
> *The sun so hot I frose to death,*
> *Susanna don't you cry.*

Between the summers of 1849 and 1850 Foster published nine songs for the minstrel shows, as compared with five for the parlor. Among them were *Nelly Bly*, with its "dulcem melody" rocking along in a heavy-footed two-step rhythm, and *Camptown Races*, with its perfect matching of text and music and its irresistible verve (Example 5-8). Its chorus bears

EXAMPLE 5-8. S. Foster, *Camptown Races* (Baltimore: Benteen, 1850), measures 8–15.

a striking resemblance to that of *Lord, Remember Me*, first printed in the significant collection of Negro songs compiled by Allen, Ware, and Garrison: *Slave Songs of the United States* (1867). Also a product of this period was *Nelly Was a Lady*, its text unusually sympathetic and sweet:

> *Nelly was a lady—*
> *Last night she died;*
> *Toll de bell for Lubly Nell,*
> *My dark Virginny bride.*

In the summer of 1851 appeared the song that would be most completely identified with Foster's name, despite its publication under Christy's: *Old Folks at Home* (*MinA*, No. 108). Wilfrid Mellers was the first to point out[14] that with this song Foster introduced into the minstrel-show context the same nostalgia that pervades his household songs:

> *All up and down the whole creation,*
> *Sadly I roam,*
> *Still longing for the old plantation,*
> *And for de old folks at home.*
>
>   .   .   .
>
> *One little hut among de bushes,*
> *One dat I love,*
> *Still sadly to my mem'ry rushes,*
> *No matter where I rove.*

The same note is heard in the other, later "best-loved" Foster songs issued as "plantation melodies": *My Old Kentucky Home, Good Night* (1853), and *Old Black Joe* (1860). Interestingly, as if conscious of having blurred the distinction between household and minstrel songs, Foster published these two without any Negro dialect spellings.

The reaction of the cultivated-tradition establishment to the fantastic popularity of *Old Folks at Home* was predictable. In its issue of October 2, 1852, *Dwight's Journal of Music* reported with perplexed incredulity on the universal appeal of the song:

> *Old Folks at Home* . . . is on everybody's tongue, and consequently in everybody's mouth. Pianos and guitars groan with it, night and day; sentimental young ladies sing it; sentimental young gentlemen warble it in midnight serenades; volatile young "bucks" hum it in the midst of their business and pleasures; boatmen roar it out . . . all the bands play it.

More than a year later (November 19, 1853) *Dwight's* was forced to an all-out attack—the cultivated against the vernacular tradition:

> We wish to say that such tunes . . . become catching, idle habits, and are not popular in the sense of musically inspiring, but that such and

[14] *Music in a New Found Land* (New York: Alfred A. Knopf, 1965), p. 249.

such a melody *breaks out* every now and then, like a morbid irritation of the skin.

We can see now that Dwight's criticism was silly—like downgrading daisies because they are not orchids. It was also futile: Negro minstrelsy and its "morbid irritations" were on the rise in the 1850's. The genre was to continue through the 1860's as the most vital kind of "native theatrical," with some thirty established non-touring companies and many other traveling companies. From the 1870's on, however, the character of the minstrel show began to change: it tended to become more and more a variety show, foreshadowing vaudeville and burlesque; its integrity was diluted by the introduction of non-Negroid characters and sketches; its format was inflated in a trend to gigantism reflected in the names of such troupes as Haverly's Mastodons, Cleveland's Colossals, and Leavitt's Giganteans. One irony of the minstrel show's declining years was the appearance on the minstrel stage of actual blacks, sometimes even in blackface make-up. One such performer, and the only notable composer of the later period of minstrelsy, was James A. Bland (1854–1911), who wrote some 700 songs, among them *Carry Me Back to Old Virginny* (1878), *In the Evening by the Moonlight* (1880), and *Oh, dem Golden Slippers* (1879).

BANDS AND BAND MUSIC

The vernacular tradition's equivalent to the symphony orchestra was the wind band. By the early twentieth century hardly an American hamlet was without its village band; hardly a public occasion passed without the sound of the brasses, woodwinds, drums, and cymbals of a band; hardly anyone in the Western world was ignorant of at least one American band composer, John Philip Sousa.

The American band developed out of the pre-Revolution British Army regimental bands. Early American bands were often attached to units of the local militia; as well as playing for parades and drills, they sometimes gave concerts. Two early bands whose rosters were exclusively filled with militiamen were the Massachusetts Band, organized in 1783, and the United States Marine Band (1798). In 1800 the Marine Band was made up of two oboes, two clarinets, two horns, a bassoon, and a drum; thus its constitution differed from that of a chamber orchestra only in its lack of stringed instruments. With the invention in Germany about 1815 of valves for cornets, trumpets, and horns, these instruments (admirably suited to the band's outdoor requirements of portability and plenty of sound) gained a new flexibility, hence new popularity. As the bands added brasses to their complements, the woodwinds were first forced out entirely (as, for instance, from New York's City Brass Band, reorganized in 1834 by Thomas Dodworth as an exclusively brass-instrument ensemble) only to be reintroduced, about the middle of the century, in even greater numbers to balance the noisier brass.

Band concerts up to the Civil War, like other concerts, were potpourris inevitably alternating solos by "guest vocal performers" with pieces by the band. Each item was carefully numbered in the printed programs of the day, hence the colloquial use of "number" for a musical composition. The staples of the mid-century band repertory were quicksteps and other marches; dances, especially the popular waltz and polka, with usually a fast $\frac{2}{4}$ galop in conclusion; an occasional overture; and almost always a solo for keyed bugle or the novel valve cornet to amaze the audience with the newly-won agility of the brass instruments. Band music was seldom published as such; because of the lack of a standard band instrumentation each band usually made its own arrangements.

Most prominent among the many nineteenth-century American bandmasters was Patrick Sarsfield Gilmore (1829–1892), who came to the United States via Canada from his native Ireland as a boy of nineteen, already a cornet virtuoso. After leading several bands in the Boston area, in 1859 Gilmore took over the Boston Brigade Band and reorganized it as a professional concert-giving and dance-playing group of thirty-two members known as Gilmore's Grand Boston Band. During the Civil War, Gilmore was for a time in New Orleans, where he organized the first of the gargantuan concerts he became noted for. Like Berlioz, Gottschalk, Jullien, and others, Gilmore dreamed of a monster concert to end monster concerts. Back in Boston after the war, he began organizing such an affair on an unheard-of scale, a National Peace Jubilee to be held in 1869 and to surpass by far the chorus of 5000 and band of 500 (plus supplementary drum and bugle corps) he had mustered in New Orleans. Support for the idea was not easy to come by: Dwight, the Handel and Haydn Society, and other Boston nabobs were shocked at the Barnumesque plan. However, Gilmore cleverly gained the backing of first one, then both the rival directors of the newly established (1867) Boston and New England Conservatories; launched a careful publicity campaign; found building funds for a three-and-a-half-acre Coliseum to house the festival; issued periodic rehearsal orders like a battlefield general to some one hundred choral organizations totaling 10,296 singers; inveigled the great Ole Bull into being concertmaster of 525 orchestra players; commandeered a band of 486 wind and percussion players; and on June 15, 1869, as scheduled, the Jubilee was on. It lasted five days, with a grand opening concert, a second day's "symphony and oratorio" concert, a fourth's "classical" concert, and a final "Children's Day." The third day's concert was called "People's Day"; it featured three overtures, several national and religious songs, a trumpet solo, and two marches. The *pièce de résistance* was the "Anvil Chorus" from Verdi's *Il Trovatore* for the entire massed ensemble plus electrically operated city bells and a dozen cannon, with "the Anvil part performed by One Hundred Members of the Boston Fire Department."

Pleased with the popular (and financial) success of the National Peace Jubilee, Gilmore aimed to outdo it. Termination of the Franco-Prussian War gave him an excuse to try, and in 1872, in a new Coliseum holding an audience of 50,000, he staged a World's Peace Jubilee. A chorus of 20,000 (some from points as remote from Boston as Milwaukee, St. Louis, Iowa City, and San Francisco) and an instrumental assemblage of almost 2000 proved, not surprisingly, unmanageable; the second Jubilee was a monumental failure, although somehow all ten days' concerts were presented.[15] Gilmore attempted no more musical gigantism; nevertheless, having become in 1873 leader of the 22nd Regiment Band of New York, he enlarged it to 66 players, taking it on popular and influential tours throughout the States and, in 1878, Europe.

Gilmore died in 1892, on tour and playing at the St. Louis Exposition. His band settled on a new leader a year later, an Irish-born cellist and composer named Victor Herbert (1859–1924); Herbert was to remain director of the 22nd Regiment Band for seven years. Meanwhile, another bandmaster was rising to prominence: John Philip Sousa (1854–1932).

As a bandmaster, Sousa became internationally renowned. Appointed in 1880 leader of the Marine Band, he made it into a balanced ensemble which by 1891 included 49 players (26 reeds, 20 brass, 3 percussion). Sousa organized his own band in 1892 and with it toured the United States, Canada, Europe, and, in 1910–11, the world. Long-lived, he is the first musician we have encountered in this study to live into the radio-and-recordings era and to help enlarge the popular audience through the new technology of the twentieth century.

As a composer, Sousa essayed many kinds of popular music, notably songs and operettas; the well-known march *El Capitan* was fashioned from two of the songs in an operetta (1896) of that title. But it was as a composer of wind-band marches that Sousa triumphed. He lived at a time when the march was especially popular: not only was it the foundation of the repertory of military and parade bands and of the ubiquitous village bands; it also provided the music for many ballroom dances (e.g., the Two-Step of the 1890's), songs, and hymns. The marches of Sousa were so keenly attuned to his time's temper, so finely honed, such perfect exemplars that Sousa understandably came to be known as "The March King."

The typical Sousa march is a fairly brief work in, of course, duple meter—an even-pulsed $\frac{2}{4}$ or $\frac{2}{2}$ or a galloping $\frac{6}{8}$ —with a number of 16-

---

[15] A historical footnote: concluding the fifth day's program, with the audience requested to sing the last two verses, was the venerable hymn *Coronation* (1793) of the eighteenth-century singing master Oliver Holden (*MinA*, No. 54).

or 32-measure strains preceded by a 4- or 8-measure introduction. Within this conventional framework Sousa was able to achieve remarkable flexibility and variety, particularly in the harmony, which is by no means predictable and is often surprisingly wide-ranging, given the narrow confines of the march form. Sousa's most famous march, *The Stars and Stripes Forever* (1897), is constructed like this: introduction (4 measures); first (16) and second (16) strains, each repeated; Trio (32); "break" (24), unstable, dramatic, and suspensive, leading to a repetition of the Trio, louder and with new piccolo counter-melody; repetition of the "break," leading again to the Trio, with yet another counter-melody in trombones added (see Example 5-9). Typically, although the march begins

EXAMPLE 5-9. J.P. Sousa, *The Stars and Stripes Forever* (1897), after a photostat of the autograph manuscript, Music Division, New York Public Library. (a) Introduction and first-strain theme. (b) Second-strain theme. (c) Trio theme. (d) "Break," beginning.

in E♭, the Trio is in A♭ and the piece ends in the key a fifth lower than its beginning.

Sousa composed about 140 marches, between *The Revival* of 1876 (which appropriately uses for its Trio theme the gospel hymn *In the Sweet By-and-By*) and *The Kansas Wildcats* of 1931. About half are in the skittish $\frac{6}{8}$ meter, including some of the best-known: *Semper Fidelis* (1888), *Washington Post* (1889), and *The Liberty Bell* (1893), *El Capitan combines* $\frac{6}{8}$ and $\frac{2}{4}$, as do several others taken from operettas. Richard Franko Goldman (b. 1910), like his father Edwin Franko Goldman (1878–1956) a prominent bandmaster, has urged more performances of "such magnificent examples as *The Fairest of the Fair* (1908), *Hands Across the Sea* (1899), *The Invincible Eagle* (1901), *The Gallant Seventh* (1922)."[16] Like the earlier favorites, these live up to Sousa's own ideal of a band march: "It must be as free from padding as a marble statue. Every line must be carved with unerring skill. Once padded, it ceases to be a march." Having thus spoken as an artist, Sousa spoke also for the free-and-easy eclecticism of the vernacular tradition:

> The composer must, to be sure, follow accepted harmonization; but that is not enough. He must be gifted with the ability to pick and choose here and there, to throw off the domination of any one tendency. If he is a so-called purist in music, that tendency will rule his marches and will limit their appeal.[17]

Sousa saw himself as a highly skilled and tasteful purveyor of entertainment: true to the vernacular tradition, he was not concerned with elevating his audience but with pleasing it. He unconsciously but sharply distinguished between the thought of the cultivated and vernacular traditions in a reflection made after spending an afternoon with Theodore Thomas:

> Thomas had a highly organized symphony orchestra . . . I a highly organized wind band. . . . Each of us was reaching an end, but through different methods. He gave Wagner, Liszt, and Tchaikowsky, in the belief that he was educating his public; I gave Wagner, Liszt, and Tchaikowsky with the hope that I was entertaining my public.[18]

Mechanical Instruments

A note on mechanical instruments is appropriate here. American technology of the nineteenth century led to a wide variety of them, the

---

[16] "John Philip Sousa," *Hi Fi/Stereo Review*, XIX, No. 1 (July 1967), 35–47.
[17] *Marching Along* (Boston: Hale, Cushman and Flint, 1928), p. 359.
[18] *Ibid.*, p. 132.

so-called nickelodeons of public places and the player-pianos of American living rooms. The former, cheaper in the long run for barrooms, poolrooms, brothels, restaurants, and ballrooms than live musicians, came in all shapes, sizes, and degrees of complexity. The Automatic Harp of the Rudolph Wurlitzer Co. was advertised as "especially desirable where a piano cannot be used, on account of its being too loud." The Violano-Virtuoso of the Mills Novelty Co. was a coin-operated, mechanically played violin with piano accompaniment. The Banjorchestra, when fed a nickel, would produce music from an automatic banjo, with support from piano, triangle, drums, tambourine, and castanets. Orchestrions, basically mechanical pipe organs with extras, ranged in size and cost up to the two Wurlitzer behemoths, the Paganini Violin Orchestra and the Pian-Orchestra. The Seeburg Company's catalogue described the "KT Special" orchestrion as "piano, xylophone, mandolin attachment, bass drum, snare drums, tympani, cymbal, triangle, castanets, tambourines, Chinese block," all encased in a head-high glass-fronted cabinet of rich birdseye maple.

Mechanically operated player-pianos or "pianolas" (the name reflecting the great success of the Aeolian Company's Pianola model) were the domestic counterpart. Activated by foot pedals or electricity, bellows-operated, and fed with perforated music rolls, player-pianos were fabulously popular from the 1890's through the 1920's, when radio, phono-recordings, and ultimately the Great Depression spelled their demise. A later connoisseur and collector, Lewis Graham, claimed that "between 1895 and 1912 there were more player pianos in the United States than bathtubs,"[19] and according to U.S. Department of Commerce statistics some 205,556 of the 347,589 pianos sold in 1923 were player-pianos.

RAGTIME

In 1899 the novelist and musical enthusiast Rupert Hughes (1872–1956) commented:

> . . . If Negro music has its "Go down, Moses" . . . so it had also its hilarious banjo-plucking and its characteristic dances. It is the latter mood that is having a strange renascence and is sweeping the country like a plague of clog-hopping locusts.[20]

Hughes was speaking of the craze for ragtime, which indeed swept the country in the 1890's through the media of piano players, player-pianos,

[19] *The New York Times,* November 3, 1966.
[20] "A Eulogy of Rag-Time," *Musical Record* (Boston), No. 447 (April 1, 1899), pp. 157–59.

dance bands, and commercial sheet music. In the diluted form of the cakewalk march, it was played by Sousa's and other concert bands here and in Europe, where according to a publisher's blurb "the native bands have taken up this peculiar style of distinctly American music, even going so far as to play the *Marseillaise* in rag time."

Many threads of earlier American music came together to form the fabric of the ragtime of the 1890's. Earliest, perhaps, was an emphatic use of syncopation by American blacks, partly derived from African drumming, partly from Afro-Caribbean dance rhythms. Among the few reports we have on secular slave music, several mention the practice of "patting Juba." Reading between the lines of these brief comments, one gets the impression that the practice involved intricate rhythmic patterns played off against a regular beat; syncopation, in short, but of a consistent, insistent kind. Thus, a correspondent of Edgar Allan Poe, likening irregularities in poetic meters to "clapping Juba," described the latter for Poe in a letter of 1835:

> There is no attempt to keep time to *all* the notes, but then it comes so pat & so distinct that the cadence is never lost. . . . Such irregularities are like rests and grace notes. They must be so managed as neither to hasten or retard the beat. The time of the bar must be the same, no matter how many notes are in it.[21]

One source couples the Negro dance-name "Juba" with the English dance-name "jig" and speaks of "patting" as an intricate rhythmic accompaniment to such a "jig"; another, a Mississippi planter discussing in 1851 how to manage a plantation, tells of his slaves' Saturday night dance music: "Charley's fiddle is always accompanied with Ithurod on the triangle and Sam to 'pat.' "[22] A particular *kind* of syncopated rhythm, conceivably one essence of "patting Juba," shows up in two disparate sources of the late 1850's. Gottschalk's *Souvenir de Porto Rico* of 1857 (see above, Example 4-10) opposes a typical $\frac{2}{4}$ *danza* bass rhythm of the Caribbean to a strongly syncopated upper part, emphasizing ♫♩ and ♫♫♩ patterns. In 1859, James Hungerford, of Maryland, published an autobiographical novel, *The Old Plantation*, and in it reproduced a "corn song" one of his slaves had sung on an outing in 1832. Prominent in an otherwise regularly accented $\frac{4}{4}$ meter are the syncopes ♫♩ and, one level higher, ♪♩ ♪ . Even before the 1850's, however, such patterns were well known and were identified with the Negro: they are commonplaces in the songs of the minstrel shows of the 1840's (see above, Example 5-8; cf. the choruses of *Oh! Susanna* and *Dixie, MinA*, Nos. 107, 109), partic-

---

[21] *The Complete Works of Edgar Allan Poe*, ed. James A. Harrison (New York: Thomas Y. Crowell Co., 1902), vol. 17, p. 22.

[22] Both comments quotaed in Epstein, "Slave Music," *Notes*, XX (1963), 383.

ularly the walk-arounds, the dancing for which, in later minstrelsy, was the cakewalk with its prancing kick-steps, bows back and forward, salutes to the spectators. These particular mild syncopes became in fact the hallmarks of the cakewalk Two-Steps played by the Northern bands of the 1890's. Compare, for example, the excerpts in Example 5-10 from the "corn song" transcribed in 1859 by Hungerford and from the "Cake Walk-Two Step" *Bunch o' Blackberries* of 1899, as played by Sousa's band.

EXAMPLE 5-10. Negro slave song and cakewalk rhythms. (a) *Roun' de Corn, Sally!* as transcribed in James Hungerford, *The Old Plantation, and What I Gathered There in an Autumn Month* (New York: Harper & Brothers, 1859), p. 191 (excerpts), (b) Abe Holzmann, *Bunch o' Blackberries* (New York: Feist & Frankenthaler, 1899), Trio (treble melody only), measures 1–8.

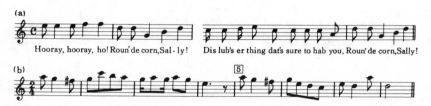

Ragtime included the simple syncopations just cited, plus others. Perhaps the earliest American music to suggest the intricate and fanciful rhythms of ragtime is that of the banjo dances of the early minstrel shows (see above, pp. 110–11). Again, we can relate at least one aspect of these—accentuated rests—to "patting Juba." The poet and musician Sidney Lanier (1842–1881) observed that

> . . . every one who has noticed a Southern Negro's "patting" will have been apt to hear an effect . . . produced by omitting the stroke, of foot or of hand, which the hearer expects to fall on the accented note at the first of the bar, thus:

and similar forms.[23]

The minstrel-show banjo tunes were generally called "jigs." So was early ragtime: until about 1897, when the terms "rag" and "ragtime" gained currency, a pianist or a band that played in the ragtime style was called a "jig pianist" or a "jig band." (Here we see the origin of the malodorous equation of the term "jig" with "Negro.") Thus, in its rhythmic aspects,

---

[23] *The Science of English Verse* (New York: Charles Scribner's Sons, 1880), p. 189.

ragtime derived from the banjo dance-tune style, which may itself be related to "patting Juba."

Ragtime typically involves two layers of rhythmic activity: a regularly accented, even bass and a strongly cross-accented treble. Against the bass, which normally stomps along with a heavy two-beat (♩ ♩) or prances in the band-like oom-pah oom-pah rhythm of ♪♩ ♪♩ , the treble is "ragg'd" by throwing accents onto other, sub-beats. Melodic phrasing of even sixteenths can do it: ♫♫♫♫ or, more common, ♫♫♫♫ (the relationship of the first pattern to the *danza's* ♪·♪♫ is worth noting). Variants of these, throwing an accent on the fourth sixteenth (the bass would come down on the fifth), are many in the early printed rags: ♪♫♩, ♪♫♪, ♪♫♫ and ♫♫♫ all begin the same way. The phrase may run along evenly but bump into an offbeat accent— ♫♫♫, ♫♫♫ —or be drily articulated: ♪𝄽𝄽 ♪ . Accentuating the eighth sixteenth in a measure, usually by anticipating the first note of the next and holding it over the barline, is common also (♫♫♫|♩), especially in patterns borrowing the cakewalk motif (♫♪♫|♩ or ♫♫♫|♩). In Scott Joplin's *Stoptime Rag* (1910) the old banjo-tune technique of accentuated rests is expanded: the composer instructs that ". . . the pianist should stamp the heel of one foot heavily upon the floor, whenever the word 'stomp' appears in the music," which it does on *rests* appearing on normally accented beats.

This brief account of ragtime rhythms has been based only on printed rags. First-hand experience with the playing of ragtime pianists still alive—e.g., Willie ("the Lion") Smith (1897–1973) or James Hubert ("Eubie") Blake (b. 1883)—suggests that, as with most dance music of any era, printed ragtime tends to be a simplified form of the music as performed.

The formal design and the basic meter and tempo of ragtime, as it was first published in the 1890's, came from Euro-American dances (quadrilles, polkas, schottisches) and especially post-Civil War marches, with their several strains, each repeated and one or two dipping into the subdominant key, and their heavy two-beat meter. Joplin's celebrated *Maple Leaf Rag* (1899), the best-known early piano rag to be published, is in $\frac{2}{4}$ marked "Tempo di Marcia"; Joplin elsewhere indicated "Slow March Tempo" and even cautioned performers, "Notice! Don't play this piece fast. It is never right to play 'Ragtime' fast." *Maple Leaf Rag*, from the formal standpoint, might almost be a Sousa march: first strain (16 measures, repeated); second strain (16, repeated); first strain again; "Trio," so named and consisting of a third strain (16, repeated) in the sub-dominant and a fourth strain (16, repeated) back in the tonic.

The interplay of black and white derivations and the intricate racial cross-currents of the minstrel shows which in effect prepared America to go crazy over ragtime make it less surprising that the first published rag so titled, *Mississippi Rag* (January, 1897), was by a white bandmaster, William Krell, who had toured along the Mississippi, while the acknowledged "King of Ragtime" was the black pianist and composer Scott Joplin.

Joplin (1868–1917), originally from Texarkana, Texas, began his career as an itinerant pianst. By 1885 he was in St. Louis, playing in honky-tonks and sporting houses. He went to Chicago briefly (1893) to try his luck in the entertainment halls that had sprung up around the World's Fair, then in 1894 to Sedalia, Missouri, to stay until the turn of the century. His first published rag, *Original Rags*, came out in March, 1899; later the same year appeared *Maple Leaf Rag*, named for a saloon and dance hall in Sedalia. The work was an instant and resounding success, and by the time of his death Joplin had published more than thirty original rags, and other piano pieces, songs, and arrangements as well. He had even larger aims: in 1902 he finished a ballet score called *Rag Time Dance*, and in 1903 the opera *A Guest of Honor*, unpublished and now apparently lost; in 1911 came another opera, *Treemonisha*. The artistic success of these larger works is debatable, but that of Joplin's piano rags is not; they can only be described as elegant, varied, often subtle, and as sharply incised as a cameo. They are the precise American equivalent, in terms of a native style of dance music, of minuets by Mozart, mazurkas by Chopin, or waltzes by Brahms. They can be both lovely and powerful, infectious and moving—depending, of course, on the skill and stylishness of the pianist, for they are not easy music technically and they demand a clean but "swinging" performance. Joplin wrote poignantly of the genre in a brief manual of ragtime exercises that he published in 1908:

That all publications masquerading under the name of ragtime are not the genuine article will be better known when these exercises are studied. That real ragtime of the higher class is rather difficult to play is a painful truth which most pianists have discovered. Syncopations are no indication of light and trashy music. . . .[24]

---

[24] *The School of Ragtime*, reprinted in *The Collected Works of Scott Joplin*, ed. Vera Brodsky Lawrence (New York: The New York Public Library, 1971), I, 283. Some of the comments in this paragraph are adapted from my review (in *Stereo Review*, XXVI, No. 4 [April 1971], 84) of Joshua Rifkin's recording of *Scott Joplin: Piano Rags* (Nonesuch H-71248), which, more than any other single thing, spurred a ragtime revival in the early 1970's.

The earliest published piano rags were a mature kind of music which had merely lacked crystallization in print. They were also a music of metrical precision for all their cross-accents and rhythmic jolts, music for marching or dancing, music that could adequately and accurately be reproduced on the popular player-pianos of the time—which they were, and the wide dissemination of the piano-roll undoubtedly stimulated ragtime's acceptance and popularity. Ragtime on player-piano rolls is thus the very earliest American music we can actually hear in contemporaneous performances.

One such performance is Joplin's of his own *Weeping Willow* (1903), recorded for Connorized player-piano roll No. 10277 (since reissued on a phonorecord). Like most early rags, the form of *Weeping Willow* is built on four different strains plus introduction, played in order Intro-1-2-1-3-4; in Joplin's recorded performance the repetition of each strain finds the treble thrown up an octave to provide new color (Example 5-11). In some later rags, for example the harmonically adven-

EXAMPLE 5-11. S. Joplin, *Weeping Willow* (St. Louis: Val A. Reis Music Co., 1903). (a) First strain, beginning. (b) Second strain, beginning. (c) Third strain, beginning. (d) Fourth strain, beginning.

turesome *Euphonic Sounds* (1909), Joplin turned to a clear-cut rondo form, while in the darkly colored, dense-textured *Magnetic Rag* (1914) the form is a rounded Intro-1-2-3-4-1-Coda. Other ragtime composer-performers modified still other aspects. The New Orleans pianist Ferdinand ("Jelly Roll") Morton (1885–1941) exemplified the Crescent City's style of fairly slow rags with swingier rhythms than the St. Louis manner of Joplin, and with melodic "walking" basses, as in Morton's *King Porter Stomp* (copyrighted 1906; published 1923). The New York pianist James P. Johnson (1894–1955) marks the turn to jazz piano from ragtime: in works like *Caprice Rag* (1914), *Harlem Strut* (1917), and *Carolina Shout* (1925) his striding left hand emphasizes the off-beats and transforms the older two-beat meter into a jazzy four, while his right-hand style dissolves the classic ragtime syncopes into long-breathed runs of even eighths and triplets (Example 5-12).

EXAMPLE 5-12. *Caprice Rag,* measures 5–8 by James P. Johnson. Copyright © 1963 by Mills Music, Inc. Used By Permission.

With this shift in style, the short, happy public career of ragtime was temporarily over, just as the era of the blues was about to begin, at least in the public consciousness of America.

BIBLIOGRAPHICAL NOTES

George Pullen Jackson's books on the shape-note tradition are necessarily the foundation for any further study; following the seminal *White Spirituals in the Southern Uplands* (Chapel Hill: University of North Carolina Press, 1933; reprinted New York: Dover Publications, 1965) appeared *Spiritual Folk-Songs of Early America* (1937; reprinted 1964); *Down East Spirituals and Others* (1939); *White and Negro Spirituals* (1943); *The Story of the Sacred Harp* (1944); and *Another Sheaf of White Spirituals* (1952). In addition to the important articles by Dena J. Epstein cited in footnote 3 above, Harold Courlander's *Negro Folk Music U.S.A.* (New York: Columbia University Press, 1963) is a thoughtful study. One survey of revival hymnody is the dissertation of John Norman Sims, "The Hymnody of the Camp Meeting Tradition" (Union

Theological Seminary, 1960); a complementary study, focusing more on the musical style (of three shape-note hymnbooks: *The Southern Harmony, The Sacred Harp*, and *The New Harp of Columbia*) than the religious or social context, is Dorothy D. Horn's *Sing to Me of Heaven* (Gainesville: University of Florida Press, 1970). Facsimile reprints of Wyeth's *Repository . . . Part Second* (New York: Da Capo Press, 1964), Walker's *Southern Harmony* (Los Angeles: Pro Musicamericana, 1966), an 1860 imprint of the third edition (1859) of *The Sacred Harp* (Nashville: Broadman Press, 1968; includes a reprint of G. P. Jackson's 1944 essay, "The Story of The Sacred Harp, 1844–1944"), and John McCurry's 1855 hymnbook, *The Social Harp* (Athens: University of Georgia Press, 1973) are available, as is the Denson Revision of *The Original Sacred Harp* (Cullman, Ala.: Sacred Harp Publishing Co., 1960).

Edwin H. Pierce has written on "Gospel Hymns," *MQ*, XXVI (1940), and Robert Stevenson on "Ira D. Sankey and Gospel Hymnody," *Religion in Life*, XX, No. 1 (Winter 1950–51). *Gospel Hymns Nos. 1 to 6 Complete* (1894) is reprinted in facsimile in *EAM*, No. 5.

The standard history of the minstrel shows, although virtually silent on their music, is Carl Wittke's *Tambo and Bones* (Durham: Duke University Press, 1930). Hans Nathan's sovereign study, *Dan Emmett and the Rise of Early Negro Minstrelsy* (Norman: University of Oklahoma Press, 1962), is triply valuable as a biography of Emmett, an account of the early period of minstrelsy, and an anthology of minstrel-show music. The chapter on "That Long-Tail'd Blue" in Constance Rourke's *American Humor* (New York: Harcourt, Brace & Co., 1931) is sympathetic and insightful. Four anthologies of music contain minstrel-show sings: Daily Paskman and Sigmund Spaeth, *"Gentlemen, Be Seated!"* (New York: Doubleday, Doran & Co., 1928); S. Foster Damon's facsimile series of *Old American Songs* (Providence: Brown University Library, 1936); Arthur Loesser, *Humor in American Song* (New York: Howell, Soskin, Inc., 1941); and Charles Haywood, *The James A. Bland Album of Outstanding Songs* (New York: E. B. Marks, 1946).

Richard Franko Goldman's *The Wind Band* (Boston: Allyn & Bacon, 1961) has a brief but excellent historical account of American bands and their music. No serious study has been made of Gilmore. Paul E. Bierley's *John Philip Sousa: A Descriptive Catalog of His Works* (Urbana: University of Illinois Press, 1973) is definitive; until Bierley's promised biography of Sousa is published, the best introduction to the March King remains Goldman's article in *Hi Fi/Stereo Review* (see footnote 16). Sousa's autobiographical *Marching Along* (Boston: Hale, Cushman, and Flint, 1928) and his *Through the Year with Sousa* (New York: Thomas Y. Crowell & Co., 1910), a journal-like collection of epigrams, poems, and anecdotes, are primary sources.

Mechanical instruments have been chronicled in Harvey N. Roehl's

Player-Piano Treasury (Vestal, N.Y.: The Vestal Press, 1963) and Q. David Bowers's *Put Another Nickel In* (Vestal: The Vestal Press, 1966).

The most authoritative and carefully documented account of ragtime is *They All Played Ragtime* (4th ed.; New York: Oak Publications, 1971) by Rudi Blesh and Harriet Janis; the music of 16 complete piano rags is included. For data on Joplin's collected works, see footnote 24.

SIX

THE CULTIVATED TRADITION,
1865-1920

American music of the cultivated tradition from the end of the Civil War to the end of World War I was largely dominated by the attitudes, the ideals, and the modes of expression of nineteenth-century Europe, particularly Austria and Germany. Our leading composers almost to a man were initiated into music by first-generation Americans emigrated from Europe; they were trained professionally during sojourns in Europe; and when they came back their music was played by ensembles, choruses, and orchestras led either by Europeans or Europe-trained conductors. Some of their music was even published first in Europe, by Breitkopf & Härtel in Leipzig or by the Leipzig branch of the Boston firm of Arthur P. Schmidt (1846–1921), who in grateful return for an American career (he was German-born) made it a point of conscience to publish American music. In Chapter 3 we examined the sources of this Germanophilia; in Chapter 4 we saw evidences of its rising tide up to the Civil War; in the present chapter we see its highwater mark. However, towards the turn of the twentieth century the work of a few composers reflected other currents: a new interest in American folklore, in developments in French and Russian music, and in topical subject-matter related to the American scene. By the end of the period one remarkable individualist, Charles Ives, had completed most of a body of work which, drawing on both the cultivated and vernacular traditions, offered the possibility of a new synthesis.

It was during the 1860–1920 period that the institutional foundations of the cultivated tradition were firmly consolidated. Music conservatories were founded, among them some still considered pre-eminent: in 1860 the Peabody Institute in Baltimore (its completion delayed by the Civil War and by other problems until 1868); in 1865 the Oberlin Conservatory in Ohio; in 1867 the New England Conservatory in Boston as well as the Cincinnati Conservatory and the Chicago Musical College; in 1904 the Institute of Musical Art in New York, to be merged in 1926 with the Juilliard Foundation; in 1916 New York's Mannes Music School; in 1917 the San Francisco Conservatory. Thanks to Lowell Mason's efforts of the 1830's, music was a part of school curricula across the land; after the Civil War it entered the colleges and universities as well. The first full professorship in music was established at Harvard in 1875, followed closely by the University of Pennsylvania, Yale University, and others. The Music Teachers National Association was founded in 1876, the Music Educators National Conference in 1907 (under the name of Music Supervisors National Conference).

With monies provided not by government but by groups of private citizens spearheaded by individual philanthropists, major concert halls were built: Philadelphia's Academy of Music (1857), Cincinnati's Music Hall (1878), the Auditorium in Chicago (1889; designed by Louis Sullivan); Carnegie Hall in New York (1891); Boston's Symphony Hall (1900). The Metropolitan Opera House in New York was inaugurated in 1883 (razed 1966).

During the entire period New York City was the performance center of the cultivated tradition. But the ideological center was undoubtedly Boston, where John Sullivan Dwight (1813–1893) reigned through his *Journal of Music* (1852–1881) as chief spokesman for the tradition. A Harvardian who had trained for the ministry, Dwight began his career as the first really significant and broadly influential American music critic and arbiter of taste with a series of more than one hundred articles in *The Harbinger,* journal of the Transcendentalist community at Brook Farm from 1845 to 1849. *Dwight's Journal,* which ran through 1,051 issues in its nearly thirty years of publication, was the most substantial and long-lived music periodical America had known (although by no means the first), despite a comparatively small subscription list. It included critical reviews, analyses, reports on concert life in both Europe and the United States, essays on music history and theory, and translations from German and French music treatises, biographies, and journals. Throughout its existence, it was informed with Dwight's unshakably high-minded belief in music—fine-art music, at least—as the language of feeling and of natural religion, whose purpose was "to hallow pleasure, and to naturalize religion" (as he had expressed it in an address to the Harvard Musical Association as early as 1841). In announcing his *Journal,* Dwight promised that "it will insist much on the claims of 'Classical' music . . . because the *enduring* needs always to be held up in contrast with the ephemeral."[1] The *Journal* did so insist, with Dwight of course determining what was to be considered "the enduring."

Among the contributors to *Dwight's Journal* who might appropriately be mentioned in this summary of the "institutional foundations" of the cultivated tradition were America's first musicologist and the first historian of America's music: Alexander Wheelock Thayer (1817–1897), whose *Ludwig van Beethoven's Leben* (Berlin, 1866–1879, with posthumous volumes added by Deiters and Riemann; abridged English translation published 1921) is still the best biography of the great German composer; and the Alsatian-born Frédéric Louis Ritter (1834–1891), whose *Music in America* (New York, 1883) was the first attempt at a comprehensive survey. Ritter relieved himself of any responsibility to treat the vernacular tradition by saying flatly, as he began a last chapter on "The Cultivation of Popular Music," that "the people's song . . . is not to be found among the American people"!

If Dwight and contributors to his journal like Thayer and Ritter were the literary voices of the art-music of the age, a group of New England composers was the musical voice. I shall call them the Second New England School, grouping them together by virtue of their common inheritance, attitudes, and general style much as I grouped the late eighteenth-century composers of the First New England School.

THE SECOND NEW ENGLAND SCHOOL

Oldest of the group, and teacher of many of its younger members, was John Knowles Paine (1839–1906). His first musical studies were with Hermann Kotzschmar, who had come to America in 1848 with the Saxonia Band, an ensemble like the Germanians, and had settled in Paine's home

[1] Quoted in George Willis Cooke, *John Sullivan Dwight* (Boston: Small, Maynard & Co., 1898), p. 147.

town of Portland, Maine. Aiming to become a church organist, Paine went to Germany in 1858 and stayed nearly four years, studying with the Berlin organist Karl August Haupt (as did almost forty younger Americans) and others, and acquiring some reputation as a performer. Back in America in 1861, he got a post as organist in a Boston church. The next year he was appointed instructor at Harvard, to teach a non-credit music course and serve as university organist. By the mid-1870's the university was convinced of the validity of a music curriculum, and the 1875–76 academic year began with Paine as America's first professor of music. He was to remain at Harvard for thirty years, retiring in 1905.

Paine's work as a composer ranged from abstract piano pieces and chamber music to incidental music for plays, overtures, symphonic poems, and full symphonies; from hymns and choral cantatas to an oratorio, a Mass, and a full opera. Most of it cannot be faulted in workmanship, none of it in seriousness of purpose: Paine took very seriously music's mission to "hallow pleasure," and if his music seems somewhat over-aspiring to profundity, hardly daring to relax or smile, this should be ascribed not to incompetence but to his aesthetic attitude and to the difficulty of attempting to emulate the masterworks of Europe's mature cultivated tradition from a base in a still-New World.

Stylistically, most of Paine's music falls within the orbit of the early German Romantics. Mendelssohn is the strongest influence on choral works like the *Centennial Hymn*, Op. 27 (1876; on a text by Whittier), the cantata *Realm of Fancy*, Op. 36 (1882; Keats), the Mass in D, Op. 10 (first performed in Berlin, 1867, Paine conducting), and the oratorio *St. Peter*, Op. 20 (1873), which even includes accompanied chorales in the "German Lutheran custom." Schumann's symphonies are the major models for Paine's First (1876; premiered at Boston by the Theodore Thomas Orchestra) and Second ("Im Frühling"; 1880).

Paine spoke in 1872 in favor of "adherence to the historical forms, as developed by Bach, Händel, Mozart, and Beethoven" as a "healthy reaction" to the "extremely involved and complicated technics of music, like Wagner, Liszt, and their adherents."[2] However, his own style eventually reflected the music of the latter group. An orchestral prelude, part of Paine's choral and instrumental incidental music for Sophocles's *Oedipus Tyrannus*, Op. 35 (1881), is quite Lisztian in its design and its thematic transformations (Example 6-1). And Paine admitted that in his opera *Azara* (1900; libretto by Paine on the medieval legend of Aucassin and Nicolette) he had "followed throughout the connected orchestral rhythmical flow, and truth of dramatic expression characteristic of Wag-

---

[2] Speech at Boston University; quoted in M. A. DeWolfe Howe, "John Knowles Paine," *MQ*, XXV (1939), 257–67.

EXAMPLE 6-1. Thematic transformations in J. Paine, *Oedipus Tyrannus*, Op. 35 (Boston: Arthur P. Schmidt, 1881), Prelude, measures 26–29, 54–57, 78–80.

ner."[3] Nevertheless, Paine's basic musical attitude was conservative; on one of the very few occasions when he permitted himself to turn to a bit of light Americana for source material, he used it as the subject of a fugue unbelievably dry, considering the theme ("Over the fence is out"), given as Example 6-2.

EXAMPLE 6-2. J. Paine, "Fuga Giocosa," *3 Piano Pieces,* Op. 41 (Boston: Arthur P. Schmidt, 1884), No. 3, measures 1–2.

After Paine as unofficial members of the Second New England School came a group of composers about a generation younger: Arthur Foote (1853–1937), George Chadwick (1854–1931), Arthur Whiting (1861–1936), Horatio Parker (1863–1919), Mrs. H. H. A. Beach (1867–1944), and

[3] Letter to Henry T. Finck, May 27, 1900; quoted in Kenneth C. Roberts, Jr., "John Knowles Paine," (unpublished Master's thesis, University of Michigan, 1962), pp. 2–3.

Daniel Gregory Mason (1873–1953). Of these, Chadwick and Parker emerge as the most gifted, or at least the strongest, musical personalities.

Chadwick is notable among the group for his sympathy—reflected unevenly in his works—for the American vernacular tradition's music; for his achievement in approaching a natural declamation in the setting of English texts; and for an earthy humor (occasionally joined to a social consciousness) not common to his rather aristocratic, more isolated peers. A prolific composer, productive from his student days in Leipzig (*Rip Van Winkle* overture, 1879) until the 1920's, he was the most versatile of the New Englanders. His Symphony No. 2 (1886) includes melodies prophetic of the "Negro" themes of Dvořák's much-discussed "New World" Symphony, and a folk-like pentatonicism crops up here and there in works of varied character, as in the opening measures of a Sinfonietta in D (1904) or the "Jubilee" movement of his best-known orchestral work, the *Symphonic Sketches* of 1907 (Example 6-3). Such "American" references are sometimes well assimilated; often, however, they are lodged in a lushly harmonized and orchestrated matrix that contradicts their very nature.

EXAMPLE 6-3. Folk-like themes of Chadwick. (a) Symphony No. 2 (Boston: Arthur P. Schmidt, 1888), 2nd movement, measures 5–8 and rehearsal-letter "M" (accompaniment omitted from both); (b) Sinfonietta in D (New York: G. Schirmer, Inc., 1906), 1st movement, measures 4–13 (violin part only). Quoted by permission; (c) *Symphonic Sketches* (New York: G. Schirmer, Inc., 1907), "Jubilee," measures 58–61 (string parts omitted). Quoted by permission.

One specialist in Chadwick's music has emphasized that the later
works, from about 1907 to 1920, reveal "a gradual discard of the German
conservatory style [and] a more mature musical language, combining
pentatonic melody, subdominant-modal harmony and syncopated rhythmic elements."[4] The "syncopation" is generally limited to the short-long
pattern common to English two-syallable words (cf. "wítching" and "éxile"
in Example 6-5; "slúmber" and the related "lamentátion" in Example 6-6)
but, even so, Chadwick's use of such natural speech rhythms, long a commonplace in songs of the vernacular tradition, sets him apart from Paine,
Parker, and others of the New England school, who tend to set English
as if it were German or Latin. Chadwick transfers this rhythmic motif to
instrumental music as well, as in the "Scherzino" of the Sinfonietta (Example 6-4).

EXAMPLE 6-4. G. Chadwick, Sinfonietta in D (New York: G. Schirmer, Inc.,
1906), "Scherzino," measures 21–28. Quoted by permission.

A song like "Adversity," one of more than a hundred by Chadwick, is in the slow waltz tempo often heard in late nineteenth-century
American ballrooms and even approaches popular song style, transcend-
ing it, however, in a sensitive darkening of the harmony at the last line
(Example 6-5).

Chadwick's stage works, seven operas and operettas, range in
mood and manner from the playful pasticcio *Tabasco* (1894), a "burlesque
opera" (really an operetta) containing galops, marches, hymn tunes,
waltzes, jigs, and a "plantation ballad," to the sobriety, drenched in a Saint-
Saëns-like lyricism and laced with Wagnerian leitmotifs, of *Judith* (1901;

[4] Victor Yellin, "The Life and Operatic Works of George Whitefield Chadwick" (unpublished Ph.D. dissertation, Harvard University, 1957), p. 291.

EXAMPLE 6-5. G. Chadwick, "Adversity," *Six Songs for Mezzo-Soprano or Baritone* (New York: G. Schirmer, Inc., 1902), No. 3, measures 1–11, 28–38. Quoted by permission.

see Example 6-6). Perhaps least deserving of its neglect is *The Padrone* (1912; refused by the Metropolitan Opera Company and not yet per-

EXAMPLE 6-6. G. Chadwick, *Judith* (New York: G. Schirmer, Inc., 1901), Act I, scene 5 ("The Vision of Judith"), measures 54–62. Quoted by permission.

formed). It is a lone example of American turn-of-the-century *verismo*, its subject the exploitation of Italian immigrants in Boston by their dockside guarantors and landlords, the *padroni*.

Chadwick, like Paine, became literally an academician, joining the faculty of the New England Conservatory in 1882 and serving as its director from 1897 until 1930. So too did Horatio Parker, who became professor at Yale University in 1894, after a musical apprenticeship under Chadwick and, from 1882 to 1885, Josef Rheinberger in Munich. Parker's most illustrious student said of him: "I had and have ['great' crossed out] respect and admiration for Parker and most of his music. It was seldom trivial." Charles Ives then went on to pinpoint Parker's strengths and weaknesses:

> His choral works have dignity and depth that many contemporaries, especially in religious and choral compositions, do not have. Parker had ideals that carried him higher than the popular, but he was governed by the "German rule." . . . Parker was a bright man, a good technician, but perfectly willing to be limited by what Rheinberger has taught him.[5]

The major part of Parker's creative output was music for chorus, on medieval or religious subjects, all serious in tone. They range from *a cappella* Latin motets (*Adstant Angelorum Chori*, Op. 45, 1899; on a text by Thomas à Kempis) through occasional pieces (*Hymnos Andron*, ode on a Greek text for the bicentennial of Yale, Op. 53, 1901; *The Spirit of Beauty*, ode for the dedication of the Albright Art Gallery in Buffalo, Op. 61, 1905) to epitomes of the Victorian cantata (*The Dream King and His Love*, Op. 31, 1892) and oratorio for soloists, chorus(es), and orchestra (*The Legend of St. Christopher*, Op. 43 [1898] and *Hora Novissima*, Op. 30 [1892]). The last-named is accounted Parker's masterpiece: an hour-long choral cantata in eleven big movements, it is a setting of a portion (describing the glories of Heaven) of a twelfth-century Latin poem. The spacious work is all the more impressive for its disguising of the rigid tercets of the poem ("Hora novissima/tempora pessima/sunt, vigilemus") through long, leisurely, wide-ranging harmonic sequences, extensive fugues on expansive subjects, and masterly handling of the choral-or-chestral medium. In one aria (No. 3, "Spe modo vivitur") $\frac{4}{4}$ and $\frac{3}{4}$ measures in alternation—something of a novelty for the time—hide the metrical rigidity of the verses. Though its solo movements suggest Italo-French influence, the main atmosphere of *Hora Novissima*, like other choral works of Parker, is that of a German-American hymnic grandeur, rich in sound and powerfully stable in rhythm; this may be suggested by the several fugue subjects given in Example 6-7.

[5] Quoted in Henry Cowell and Sidney Cowell, *Charles Ives and His Music* (New York: Oxford University Press, 1955), pp. 33–34.

EXAMPLE 6-7. Fugue subjects by Horatio Parker. (a) *Hora Novissima* (London & New York: Novello, Ewer and Co., 1893): (1) No. 4, measures 27–31; (2) No. 10, measures 1–5; (3) No. 11, measures 41–44; (b) *Adstant Angelorum Chori* (New York: G. Schirmer, Inc., 1899), measures 88–92; (c) *The Legend of St. Christopher* (London & New York: Novello, Ewer and Co., 1898), p. 134 (Act III, scene 2).

The composers of the Second New England School have been called "the Boston academics" (by Rupert Hughes, writing in 1900) and "the Boston classicists" (by Benjamin Lambord in 1915; most recently by Gilbert Chase in *AM*). But not all of them were academicians nor, if the term "academic" is one of disparagement, were they all or always hidebound. And none of them was a "classicist" except in the sense that Brahms was a classicist: they belonged to that wing of Romanticism that maintained a belief in the viability of the abstract instrumental forms. Like Brahms, and like Beethoven, Schubert, Schumann, and Mendelssohn before him, they wrote symphonies, sonatas, and chamber music; like Brahms, and like Handel, Bach, Mozart, and Beethoven before him, they wrote fugues and contrapuntal choruses. To the late nineteenth century such composers as Paine, Chadwick, and Parker might have seemed "classicists"; our perspective should let us rather see them in context as a group of Romantics of a particular persuasion.

EDWARD MAC DOWELL

To another wing of Romanticism belonged Edward MacDowell (1861–1908). Not for him the abstract traditional forms of symphony and string quartet, nor the semi-abstract forms of orchestral overture or choral cantata. In the tradition of the "New German School" of Liszt and Wagner, MacDowell saw himself as a "tone-poet," trusting in the evocative power of richly colored harmony (especially when the response was directed by a suggestive programmatic title) and narrative, ongoing forms rather than the problem-solving constructivism of imitative counterpoint or the balanced logic of sonata-form. MacDowell believed that Bach was "one of the world's mightiest tone-poets [who] accomplished his mission, not by means of the contrapuntal fashion of his age, but in spite of it," and for him Mozart's instrumental sonatas were "entirely unworthy of the author of *The Magic Flute*."[6] In a climate of aesthetic opinion like that of the later nineteenth century, these attitudes must have seemed truly progressive, truly Romantic, untinged by a "classicistic" bent. Not surprisingly MacDowell was viewed, about the turn of the twentieth century, as America's foremost modern composer by those who shared his aesthetic— which is to say, all but a few.

Of Scotch-Irish descent, MacDowell was born in New York in 1861. In 1876 he was enrolled in the Paris Conservatory but, dissatisfied, he moved to Frankfurt in 1878 for two more years of study as a pianist and composer; a powerful influence on him there was the conservatory's director, the composer Joachim Raff. Except for one trip back to America to get married, MacDowell remained in Germany teaching, composing, and playing piano concerts until 1888, some twelve years after leaving the United States. He then lived in Boston until 1896, when he accepted a newly endowed chair of music at Columbia University. In 1904, after some unfortunately public wrangling with the university administration, MacDowell resigned. Mental illness, exacerbated by a horse-cab accident, prevented his composing any more; he declined more or less steadily until his death.

MacDowell's works were all composed between 1880 (First Modern Suite for piano; First Piano Concerto) and 1902 (*Summer Wind* for women's chorus; *New England Idyls* for piano). They consist mainly of some sixteen collections of *Charakterstücke* for piano, plus four suggestively titled sonatas and two concertos; forty-two songs for solo voice

[6] MacDowell, *Critical and Historical Essays* (Boston: Arthur P. Schmidt, 1912), pp. 265, 194.

and more than twenty for chorus; four symphonic poems; and two orchestral suites. All the favorite themes and images of Romanticism are explored: landscapes and seascapes (*Woodland Sketches; New England Idyls; Sea Pieces*); medieval romances (the symphonic poem *Lancelot and Elaine;* Piano Sonata No. 3 ["Eroica"] on the Arthurian legend); exoticism (Second ["Indian"] Suite for orchestra; *Les Orientales* for piano); reminiscences of childhood ("From Uncle Remus," *Woodland Sketches;* "Of Br'er Rabbit," *Fireside Tales*). Shakespeare inspired the symphonic poem in two parts, *Hamlet and Ophelia;* Romantic poets are interpreted pianistically in *Six Idyls after Goethe* and *Six Poems after Heine.* In the latter collections MacDowell printed the poems at the head of the music; in many others, he indited verses of his own to stand as the "program" of individual pieces.

Considering the brevity of the composer's creative life (comparable to Foster's or Gottschalk's), a lack of stylistic development should not surprise us. More surprising, in view of MacDowell's extraordinary reputation about 1900, is the fact that having begun boldly as a composer of piano concertos of truly Lisztian sweep and breadth, he then tended to produce ever smaller, more rarefied works. After the Second Suite (1896) he wrote no more orchestral music. He never attempted opera. Of the later works, only the Third ("Norse") and Fourth ("Keltic") piano sonatas (1900 and 1901) approach large-scale forms, described by MacDowell as "'bardic' rhapsodies" on their subjects. MacDowell ended up as a composer of concise, evocative genre pieces, surprisingly terse even when their subject-matter is grandiose ("To the Sea," "From a German Forest"); basically very economical and clean of line, even fragile sometimes ("To a Wild Rose," "To a Water Lily," both from *Woodland Sketches*); very precisely fashioned and clearly projected.

MacDowell was himself a competent concert pianist, and some of his most successful piano music demands a virtuoso technique, as in the "Scherzo" of the Second Piano Concerto and various études among the Twelve Virtuoso Studies, notably "March Wind." More of it, however, is relatively easy to play and reveals MacDowell to be a late nineteenth-century composer of "household music." He has also in common with that earlier American music a considerable nostalgia: Mellers has remarked trenchantly that MacDowell's best pieces "are a boy's view of the American past, looked back to from a premature middle age,"[7] as in the song collection *From an Old Garden;* "From an Indian Lodge" and "A Deserted Farm" in *Woodland Sketches;* "From a Log Cabin" and "From Puritan Days" in *New England Idyls.*

The composer's vocabulary, which has often been likened to that

[7] *Music in a New Found Land,* p. 27.

of Edvard Grieg (whom MacDowell admired and to whom he dedicated
the Third and Fourth piano sonatas), shares with Grieg's a remarkable
integrity, homogeneity, and indentifiability. The most characteristic features of MacDowell's style are its Wagnerian chromatic harmony, full of
enharmonic modulations, appoggiatura dissonances, and inversions of
triads, seventh chords, and ninth chords; its texture, which tends to be
thick and fat and, although ranging freely over the entire keyboard, seems
to emphasize the lower registers; and its ebb and flow of rhythmic activity and dynamic contour, both in a state of constant flux. Example 6-8,

EXAMPLE 6-8. E. MacDowell, "In Mid-Ocean," *Sea Pieces,* Op. 55 (Boston,
Leipzig, New York: Arthur P. Schmidt, 1899), No. 8, measures 1–8.

from a piece reported by MacDowell's first biographer to be one of the
composer's own favorites,[8] shows most of these hallmarks of his style. In
another vein, however, are many works which derive, no matter how indirectly, from dance meters, including Mendelssohnian scherzos. These
are lighter in texture, "snappy" in rhythmic shape (often literally so:
MacDowell's Scottish background was strong and "Scotch snap" iambs
appear regularly), and less chromatic in harmony, though never wholly
diatonic. The "Uncle Remus" pieces of *Woodland Sketches* and *Fireside
Tales,* the fifth of the Goethe *Idyls,* the third of the Heine *Poems,*
"Humoreske" and "March" in the Four Pieces, Op. 24, are of this type, as
are the "Love Song" and "In War-Time" movements of the "Indian" Suite
for orchestra. So too is "To a Wild Rose" (MacDowell's best-known single
work), although it is often mistaken for a "poetic" and sentimental piece,

---

[8] Lawrence Gilman, *Edward MacDowell, A Study* (New York: John Lane Co.,
1908), pp. 70–71. Gilman's study has been reprinted with an introduction by Margery
L. Morgan (New York: Da Capo Press, 1969).

played with rubato not even hinted at in the score, and at a tempo considerably slower than that indicated by the composer. Faintly reminiscent of Schumann's "Traümerei" in its design, it moves "with simple tenderness" to a single strategically placed climax and a lone, conclusive iamb (Example 6-9).

EXAMPLE 6-9. E. MacDowell, "To a Wild Rose," *Woodland Sketches* (1896), Op. 51 (Boston, Leipzig, New York: Arthur P. Schmidt, 1899), No. 1, measures 43–51 (conclusion).

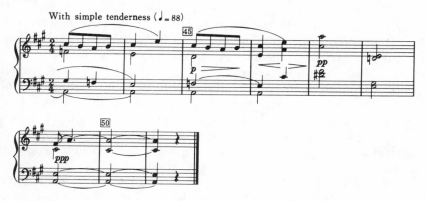

OTHER CURRENTS

Inevitably, a reaction against the predominantly Germanic cast of post-Civil War fine-art music took place. It took two forms: some composers sought to refresh American music with an infusion of folkloristic elements; others turned enthusiastically to the new modes of expression emanating from Russia and France, or to even more exotic sources.

Folklorism was hardly unknown to the European Romantics. A fascination with "primitive" peasant culture or with traditional anonymous folk forms was one manifestation of the Romantics' infatuation with the untrammeled expression of childhood, the "folk" being viewed as national or regional or even racial children. Ultimately Americans came to share this aspect of Romantic thought. The problem for composers was: what was American musical folklore? A few men had given tentative hints of *their* answer to the question: MacDowell, Chadwick, even old Father Heinrich. Others now followed the hint: all too simplistically, they looked to the most "primitive" kinds of music in the nation, the music of the American Indian and the Negro. That there might be other "folkish" music in their past and under their very noses, that the vernacular tradition of popular music might provide a usable stock of invigorating source materials, seems not to have occurred to most of these composers. But then, did not Frédéric Ritter aver that America had no "people's song"? Had not Antonin Dvořák, in a much-discussed and very influential article in *Harper's* (February, 1895), backed up by the example of his "New World" Symphony (New York, 1893), recommended the use of Negro melodies, even claiming that "they are the folk songs of America, and your composers must turn to them"?

Besides their (perhaps unconscious) Romantic interest in "folk" materials, some American composers of the late nineteenth century saw them as a nationalistic instrument as well, as had some Europeans earlier, the "Russian Five," for example. For to the degree that a nation's composers could borrow from indigenous musical sources they were assured a certain national identity; their music would be different from that of other regions or nations. In late nineteenth-century America, and indeed through the first three decades of the twentieth, this aspect of folklorism exerted a strong pull on many composers, who yearned to free themselves from a European musical yoke, hoping to be somehow recognizably "American."

Aggressive steps in this direction were first taken by the Middle Westerner Arthur Farwell (1872–1951). His own turning to Indian music was reflected in a number of works based mainly on Omaha tribal dances and songs. Perhaps even more significant was his enthusiastic championing of new currents in American music through publication by the Wa-Wan Press which he established in 1901. Looking about him, Farwell saw a "quantity of compositions . . . and my own work, all blocked as to publication." He determined to "combine my work with that of these others—we were all in the same boat—and launch a progressive movement for American music, including a definite acceptance of Dvořák's challenge to go after our folk music."[9] When the Wa-Wan Press was sold to the firm of G. Schirmer in 1912, it had published works by thirty-seven composers. Among them were a number with folkloristic interests, especially in Indian and Negro music. Matching Farwell's preoccupation with Indian music was the interest in Negro music of Henry F. B. Gilbert (1868–1928), composer of *Comedy Overture on Negro Themes* (1905) and *The Dance in Place Congo* (1906). Other Wa-Wan Press composers with less selfconsciously "Americanist" aims were men like Arthur Shepherd (1880–1958) and Edward Burlingame Hill (1872–1960).

Hill, who had been a pupil of both Paine and Chadwick, was one

[9] Quoted in Edward Waters, "The Wa-Wan Press: An Adventure in Musical Idealism," *A Birthday Offering to Carl Engel*, ed. Gustave Reese (New York: G. Schirmer, Inc., 1943), pp. 214–33. "Wa-Wan" is an Omaha word identified with a ceremony of peace, fellowship, and song.

of the first Americans to feel the lure of the new French music of the 1890's, reflecting it in his own works and passing on a taste for it to such of his students at Harvard as Walter Piston and Virgil Thomson. In fact, Boston, long the ideological center of American music's Germanophilia, was at last beginning to rebel, beginning to see in the more or less individual styles of Saint-Saëns, D'Indy, Fauré, Debussy, and Ravel a refreshing change. *The Musical Record* of December 1890 quoted approvingly from the *Boston Home Journal:*

> A plea for more French music and less German is demanded. . . . We grope about in German mists . . . and say it is purer and healthier than clear air and a blue sky. We pay American money for the privilege of submitting to German dictation.

Another composer trained at Harvard, John Alden Carpenter (1876–1951), shared Hill's partiality toward French music and showed it in works like the song cycle *Gitanjali* (1913), the orchestral suite *Adventures in a Perambulator* (1915), and a Concertino for piano and orchestra (1916); the Concertino and some later works also included ideas from American popular music.

Charles Martin Loeffler (1861–1935) was a composer so hospitable to French poetry and the *raffinement* of the modern French musical style of the turn of the century that he has often been called a French-American. Actually, although born in Alsace he came of German stock, and his formative years were spent successively in Russia, Hungary, and Switzerland. Trained as a violinist, he came to New York in 1881 but was snatched off to Boston by Major Henry Lee Higginson, patron of the Boston Symphony Orchestra. He sat at the first desk of the orchestra's violin section until 1903, when he resigned to devote himself to composition. An exquisite craftsman, almost obsessively revising his scores again and again, Loeffler published comparatively little; the music he did allow into print is of high polish and a kind of *fin-de-siècle* fastidiousness. Among his orchestral works, *A Pagan Poem*, Op. 14 (1905–06), has proved viable. Many works combine voices and instruments; of these, perhaps the most perfectly realized is a setting of St. Francis of Assisi's *Canticum Fratris Solis* for soprano and chamber ensemble, commissioned for the first concert sponsored by the Elizabeth Sprague Coolidge Foundation at the Library of Congress (October 28, 1925). Typifying Loeffler's interest in unusual instruments and instrumentation are *La Mort de Tintagiles,* Op. 6 (1905), for full orchestra with solo viola d'amore, and two delicate chamber Rhapsodies for oboe, viola, and piano, "L'Etang" and "La Cornemuse" (1905).

Another composer who was susceptible not only to the new French music but also Russian, particularly that of Scriabin, was Charles T.

Griffes (1884–1921). After four years in Germany (1903–07), his early
works were, not surprisingly, Teutonic; among them are some strong
songs of 1909 to poems by Heine, Lenau, Eichendorff, and others. But
Griffes must have considered these works as preliminary to his real beginnings; he later commented: "When I began to write I wrote in the
vein of Debussy and Stravinsky; those particular wide-intervalled dissonances are the natural medium of the composer who writes today's
music."[10] In a number of songs of 1912 to poems by Oscar Wilde, including *Symphony in Yellow* and *La Fuite de la lune*, Debussyesque
harmony predominates, with however a rather firm, chiseled melodic line
close to Ravel's (Example 6-10). Related in style are the *Roman Sketches*
for piano (1915–16), which include the best-known of Griffes's works,
The White Peacock (later to be orchestrated delicately by the composer).

EXAMPLE 6-10. C. Griffes, *Symphony in Yellow,* Op. 3, No. 2 (New York: G.
Schirmer, Inc., 1915), measures 1–8. Quoted by permission.

An interest in Oriental music shows up in *The Pleasure Dome of
Kubla Khan* (piano version 1912; revised and orchestrated 1917). Oriental
flavor is pervasive in a group of songs on pentatonic and hexatonic scales,
Five Poems of Ancient China and Japan; and for a ballet titled *Sho-Jo*
Griffes composed a unique score on Japanese themes, with orchestration

---

[10] Quoted in Edward Maisel, *Charles T. Griffes* (New York: Alfred A. Knopf,
1943), p. 112.

"as Japanese as possible: thin and delicate, and the muted string *points d'orgue* serve as neutral-tinted background, like the empty spaces in a Japanese print. The whole thematic material is given to the flute, clarinet, and oboe—akin to the Japanese reed instruments: the harp suggests the koto."[11] *Sho-Jo* was never published, nor was another unique dance-drama of the same year, *The Kairn of Koridwen* (1917), scored for an eight-piece ensemble of flute, two clarinets, two horns, harp, celesta, and piano. These works, related to Schoenberg's *Pierrot Lunaire* (1912) and Stravinsky's *L'Histoire du soldat* (1918) in their novel chamber-music instrumentation, must have been considered too exotic to be publishable.

In his last year but one, Griffes renounced the delicate shades of the French style and the Orient ("I don't want the reputation of an Orientalist and nothing more") and produced several works of power, even ferocity, that suggested he was approaching a mature synthesis of the several styles in which he had successively immersed himself. The Piano Sonata (Example 6-11), a *Notturno* for orchestra (different from the *Nocturne* transcribed from the Piano Sonata's slow section), the *Poem* for flute and orchestra, and a group of *Three Poems* to texts by Fiona MacLeod (including the shattering song "The Lament of Ian the Proud") reveal Griffes as an American composer on the brink of greatness. The promise of these works was not to be realized, however: Griffes died early in 1921, aged thirty-five.

EXAMPLE 6-11. C. Griffes, Piano Sonata (New York: G. Schirmer, Inc., 1921), concluding measures. Quoted by permission.

[11] Quoted in Maisel, *op. cit.*, p. 206.

BIBLIOGRAPHICAL NOTES

One Hundred Years of Music in America, ed. Paul Henry Lang (New York: G. Schirmer, Inc., 1961), is a collection of essays some of which survey the "institutional foundations" of the cultivated tradition. Dwight's Journal has been reissued in a reprint edition (New York: Arno Press); its predecessors are studied exhaustively in Charles Wunderlich's unpublished Ed.D. dissertation "A History and Bibliography of Early American Music Periodicals" (University of Michigan, 1959), its successors itemized in William J. Weichlein's Checklist of American Music Periodicals, 1850–1900 (Detroit: Information Coordinators, Inc., 1970). Thayer's Life of Beethoven is the title of a new, complete, and thoroughly annotated English-language edition of the work prepared by Elliott Forbes (Princeton: Princeton University Press, 1967).

No extensive studies have been published on the Second New England School or on J. S. Dwight. Various dissertations (on Dwight, Paine, Chadwick, Foote) have been completed; others are in progress. These may be located in the various lists of "Doctoral Dissertations in Musicology," Journal of the American Musicological Society, annually. Parker's daughter, Isabel Parker Semler, published "a memoir for his grandchildren": Horatio Parker (New York: G. P. Putnam's Sons, 1942).

MacDowell's Critical and Historical Essays (Boston: Arthur P. Schmidt, 1912; reprinted New York: Da Capo Press, 1968) reveal his attitudes clearly. Lawrence Gilman's study of 1908 (see footnote 9) remains the most extensive published one. Irving Lowens's "Edward MacDowell," in Hi Fi/Stereo Review, XIX, No. 12 (December 1967), 61–72, is the most definitive biographical account; serious bibliographical and analytic investigation remains to be published.

Reprinted in EAM are Paine's First Symphony (EAM No. 1), Chadwick's Second Symphony (No. 4) and his Judith (No. 3), Parker's Hora Novissima (No. 2), and sets of piano pieces and songs by MacDowell (Nos. 8 and 7).

The entire output of Farwell's Wa-Wan Press has been reprinted in facsimile, with an introductory essay by Gilbert Chase (New York: Arno Press, 1970). An authoritative and sympathetic sketch of Loeffler is Carl Engel's, in Thompson's International Cyclopedia of Music and Musicians. Griffes is the subject of a somewhat gossipy biography by Edward Maisel (see footnote 11); his music still awaits thorough stylistic study, although a definitive catalogue of his works has been written by Donna Kay Anderson: "The Works of Charles T. Griffes: A Descriptive Catalogue" (unpublished Ph.D. dissertation, Indiana University, 1966).

SEVEN

CHARLES E. IVES

The most extraordinary and significant American composer of the late nineteenth and early twentieth centuries was Charles Edward Ives (1874–1954). Because of heart attacks (the first on October 1, 1918) and other serious illness, Ives composed very little after about 1921; ironically, it was only after he had stopped intensive composing and had "cleaned house," as he put it, by printing (at his own expense) the Second ("Concord") Piano Sonata (1920), some *Essays Before a Sonata* (1920), and a volume of *114 Songs* (1922) that his music began to be generally known at all. Acceptance was slow even then: not until the 1940's were many works by Ives performed. Since World War II, however, the number of performances, publications, and phonorecordings has grown steadily, as has Ives's influence on other composers' thought.

Ives grew up in Danbury, Connecticut. In later years he emphasized the importance of his father in shaping his musical thinking. George Ives (1845–1894) was in some ways a typical late nineteenth-century provincial American musician: leader of the Connecticut Heavy Artillery First Brigade Band during the siege of Richmond, he returned after the Civil War to Danbury, where he played the piano for dances and the organ for church services, gave music lessons, organized the Danbury Band, and was in general a musical jack-of-all-trades. He knew academic music theory, was a practical music arranger, and composed a little. Where he differed from other such "town" musicians was in his passionate curiosity about sound, his experimental attitude, and his open-mindedness; all these were to be reflected concretely in his son's music and musical thought. From the age of five, Charles Ives was taught by his father: "Bach and the best of the classical music, and the study of harmony and counterpoint etc., and musical history [and] the use of the ears . . . and the mind to think for themselves and be more independent—in other words, not to be too dependent upon customs and habits."[1] Ives was thus trained in music of the cultivated tradition; he was exposed, through his father's multifarious musical occupations, to both cultivated and vernacular traditions; and he was encouraged toward an open-minded independence of musical thought that could encompass both traditions.

Ives's formal music study was completed at Yale (1894–98) under Horatio Parker, for whom he had a qualified respect (see p. 138). Upon graduation, already aware that his music was "impractical" and sharing his father's view that "a man could keep his music-interest stronger, cleaner, bigger, and freer, if he didn't try to make a living out of it" (*Memos*, p. 131), Ives decided on a business career in life insurance. He pursued it with great success from 1898 until his retirement in 1930. For a time (1898–1902) he was also a practicing musician as organist and choirmaster at the First Presbyterian Church in Bloomfield, New Jersey, then at Central Presbyterian Church in Manhattan; but from 1902 on he limited himself to business and to composing—furiously, at white heat— during evenings and on weekends. He never regretted his double life; in a well-known statement that reveals the New England Transcendentalist strain in his thinking, Ives said:

> . . . The fabric of existence weaves itself whole. You can not set art off in the corner and hope for it to have vitality, reality and substance. There can be nothing *"exclusive"* about a substantial art. It comes di-

[1] *Charles E. Ives: Memos*, ed. John Kirkpatrick (New York: W. W. Norton & Co., Inc., 1972), p. 115. The present discussion of Ives draws mainly, for statements by Ives himself, on four sources: Ives's *Memos*, written and dictated, as their editor puts it, "to answer questions from people curious about his music"; Ives *Essays Before a Sonata and Other Writings*, ed. Howard Boatwright (New York: W. W. Norton & Co., Inc., 1962); John Kirkpatrick, "A Temporary Mimeographed Catalogue of the Music Manuscripts and related materials of Charles Edward Ives" (New Haven: School of Music Library, Yale University, 1960); and Henry and Sidney Cowell, *Charles Ives and His Music* (New York: Oxford University Press, 1955). These will be referred to hereinafter as "*Memos*," "*Essays*," "Kirkpatrick," and "Cowells" respectively.

rectly out of the heart of experience of life and thinking about life and living life. My work in music helped my business and my work in business helped my music.[2]

The demands on his time of business, the non-acceptance of his music, and the lack of direct involvement with the professional music world freed, or forced, Ives to developed his own aesthetic. It was a unique one, and we must understand it if we are to view his music in proper perspective.

IVES'S MUSICAL THOUGHT

Ives prized what he called "substance" rather than "manner" in both music and its performance. "Manner" for Ives approached what others might call "technique," on the part of either composer or performer. "Substance . . . is practically indescribable," admitted Ives, but it "suggests the body of a conviction which has its birth in the spiritual consciousness, whose youth is nourished in the moral consciousness, and whose maturity as a result of all this growth is then represented in a mental image." (*Essays*, p. 75) Common notions of beauty have nothing to do with it; it "has something to do with character. . . . The substance of a tune comes from somewhere near the soul, and the manner comes from—God knows where." (*Essays*, p. 77) On this philosophical ground Ives based some startling concrete ideas. If substance has nothing to do with beauty or manner, then the very sound of music may be insignificant compared to the spirit in which it is produced. The roots of this idea are apparent in an anecdote about Ives's father:

> Once a nice young man . . . said to Father, "How can you stand it to hear old John Bell (the best stone-mason in town) sing?" (as he used to at Camp Meetings) [.] Father said, "He is a supreme musician." The young man . . . was horrified—"Why, he sings off the key, the wrong notes and everything . . . and he bellows out and hits notes no one else does —it's awful!" Father said, ". . . Look into his face and hear the music of the ages. Don't pay too much attention to the sounds—for if you do, you may miss the music." (*Memos*, p. 132)

"The music," the *real* music, resided in the humanity of its producer. This is why Ives could cry out passionately: "My God! What has sound got to do with music!" (*Essays*, p. 84) This is why, in recalling revivalist camp meetings, he could speak with affection of the aberrations in the hymn-sing-

[2] Quoted first in Henry Bellamann, "Charles Ives; the Man and his Music," *MQ*, XIX (1933), 45–58.

ing, and of ". . . the great waves of sound . . . when things like *Beulah Land, Woodworth, Nearer My God to Thee, The Shining Shore, Nettleton, In the Sweet Bye and Bye* and the like were sung by thousands of 'let out' souls. . . . If they threw the poet or the composer around a bit, so much the better for the poetry and the music. There was power and exaltation in these great conclaves of sound from humanity." (*Memos*, pp. 132–33) This is why he could even drive the argument to its logical conclusion and say: "That music must be heard is not essential—what it *sounds* like may not be what it *is*." (*Essays*, p. 84) And this in turn helps to explain a puzzling statement in the "Postface" to *114 Songs:* "Some of the songs in this book . . . cannot be sung,—and if they could perhaps might prefer, if they had a say, to remain as they are,—that is, 'in the leaf.' . . . A song has a few rights the same as other ordinary citizens."

Ives's music often shares the variety, the apparent disorder, the co-existence of seemingly unrelated things of life itself; characteristic is a planar, heterophonic polyphony occasionally so dense that the ear simply cannot distinguish the separate strands. Ives analogized between such co-existent but independent ideas in his music and a game of tennis doubles—"Having four nice different men playing tennis together doesn't always destroy personality" (*Memos*, p. 50)—or the participants in the un-structured discussion and argument of a New England town meeting. In a sketch for the Second String Quartet, whose movements are titled "Dis-cussions," "Arguments," and "The Call of the Mountains," Ives described the work as a "S[tring] Q[uartet] for 4 men—who converse, argue (in re 'Politics'), fight, shake hands [,] shut up—then walk up the mountain side to view the firmament." He seemed to view musical texture sometimes as a microcosm in which the co-existence of disparate elements does not threaten disorder any more than, say, in a forest the co-existence of differ-ent trees, rocks, mosses, flowers, animals, and insects threatens disorder; "disorder," in this instance, is an irrelevant concept, or one too narrowly conceived. Traditional devices for "ordering" musical form (repetitions, periodic phrase structure, classical tonality, and the like) although not al-ways lacking in Ives's music are not by any means always present. Ives could scoff at such devices, questioning for instance "how far repetition is an essential part of clarity and coherence. . . . If nature is not enthusiastic about explanation, why should Tschaikowsky be?" (*Essays*, p. 99) Ives admired quite another order-principle, which he expressed most clearly in his essay on Emerson:

His underlying plan of work seems based on the large unity of a series of particular aspects of a subject rather than on the continuity of its ex-pression. As thoughts surge to his mind, he fills the heavens with them, crowds them in, if necessary, but seldom arranges them along the ground first. (*Essays*, p. 22)

This is a fair description of the tumultuous congeries of materials, and their apparent lack of continuity, in many of Ives's works.

The subject-matter of Ives's music was equally life itself, or "a series of particular aspects" of it. The pages of his manuscripts are studded with verbal comments that particularize the diary-like outpourings of his musical mind. One of the most illuminating examples is found in a manuscript copy of the first movement of the First Piano Sonata, where we read:

> What is it all about—Dan S. asks. Mostly about the outdoor life in Conn[ecticut] villages in the '80s and '90s—impressions, remembrances, & reflections, of country farmers in Conn. farmland.
>
> On page 14 back, Fred's Daddy got so excited that he shouted when Fred hit a home run & the school won the baseball game. But Aunt Sarah was always humming *Where Is My Wandering Boy,* after Fred an' John left for a job in Bridgeport. There was usually a sadness—but not at the Barn Dances, with their jigs, foot jumping, & reels, mostly on winter nights.
>
> In the summer times, the hymns were sung outdoors. Folks sang (as *Old Black. Joe*)—and the Bethel Band (quickstep street marches)—& the people like[d to say] things as they wanted to say, and to do things as they wanted to, in their own way—and many old times . . . there were feelings, and of spiritual fervency! (*Memos,* p. 75)

Thus viewing some of his music as reminiscences, or re-creations in sound, of life experiences, many of which included actual music or were easily associable with specific kinds of music, Ives constantly used musical quotations in his works; they are often the very basis of the musical fabric. Traditional American hymn tunes, marches, and ragtime rhythms are the most commonly quoted, but material from other composers also appears, from Handel, Haydn, Beethoven, and Tchaikowsky to Foster, Mason, Bradbury, and Sankey. Such borrowings had nothing to do with nationalism, folklorism, or mere "local color"; they were a transcendentalist's acceptance of the validity, even divinity, of all the things under God that he had known, felt strongly, and believed to have vitality and "substance." Without naming names, but perhaps referring to Farwell, Ives wrote that the composer born in America and "so interested in 'negro melodies' that he writes a symphony over them [cannot, if he] has not been interested in the 'cause of the Freedmen'," produce something with substance, only with "color." Yet, "if a man finds that the cadences of an Apache war-dance come nearest to his soul," he can use them "fervently, transcendentally, inevitably, furiously, in his symphonies, in his operas, in his whistlings on the way to work [and] his music will be true to itself and incidentally American." (*Essays,* pp. 79–80).

Just as no kind of musical source-material was excluded from the

Ives canon, no kind of performance was either. Ives found the mix-ups
and mistakes, the wrong notes and off-key playing of amateur musicians
just as "substantial" and thus in his view as "musical" as polished perfection, perhaps more so. Some of his music was planned to include such
"mistakes": in a score-sketch for "The Fourth of July," third of his *New
England Holidays,* Ives twice warned his copyist: "Mr. Price: Please
don't try to make things nice! All the wrong notes are *right.* Just copy as
I have—I want it that way. . . . Mr. Price: Band stuff—they didn't always
play right & together & it was as good either way." (Kirkpatrick, p. 11)
Ives wanted performances of his music to have a sense of involvement in
action, of spontaneity and vitality. When *Three Places in New England*
was first played in New York (1931) and conductor Nicolas Slonimsky
apologized for a ragged performance, Ives reassured him: "Just like a
town meeting—every man for himself. Wonderful how it came out!"
(Cowells, p. 106) In some of his scores, Ives offers choices to the performer: a passage in the Second Sonata for violin and piano may be repeated "2 or 3 times decr[escendo] and rit[ardando] gradually," and a
cadenza in the *Scherzo: Over the Pavements* is "to play or not to play! if
played, to be played as not a nice one—but evenly, precise & unmusical as
possible!"

"Nice" meant to Ives something weak, lily-livered, conventional,
effetely genteel. Among his manuscripts is a *Take-off* on the Andante of
Haydn's "Surprise" Symphony, marked "nice little easy sugar plum
sounds," and under some harmonically knotty measures of his *Browning
Overture* Ives wrote: "Browning was too big a man to rest in one nice
little key . . . he walked on the mountains not down a nice proper little
aisle." Ives felt that men's ears and minds could encompass much more
than they thought possible. He equated harmonic complexity with
strength; remembering Thanksgiving as a holiday celebrating the early
American colonists, he noted on one of the sketches for the "Thanksgiving" movement of *New England Holidays* that "our forefathers were
stronger men than can be represented by 'triads' only—these are too easy
sounding." (Kirkpatrick, p. 13)

Persons of a "nice" conformist gentility were epitomized by Ives
with the name "Rollo," borrowed from a mid-nineteenth-century series
of children's books about a boy insufferably priggish, proper, and perfect.[3]
To "Rollo," Ives addressed many sarcastic marginal comments in his
manuscripts: in the Second String Quartet, "too hard to play—so it just
can't be good music—Rollo"; in the *Browning Overture,* "R. B[rowning]'s
mental workmanship is as sound logical & strong as easier plans [which]
Rollo likes."

---

[3] I am indebted to Professor Henry Leland Clarke for clarifying this.

The other side of this ideological coin was Ives's own willingness to try anything musically, his rejection of dogmatic and exclusive musical concepts, and the embodiment of his theoretical speculations not in verbal treatises but in musical works. In an essay that comes closer to being a rounded theoretical statement than anything else he wrote—"Some 'Quarter-tone' Impressions" (1925)—Ives's open-mindedness is trenchantly expressed in two sentences: "Why tonality as such should be thrown out for good, I can't see. Why it should be always present, I can't see." (*Essays*, p. 117)

In sum, Ives believed in substance over manner, in spirit over technique; he believed in music as a re-creation in sound of life itself; he felt that passionate, honest self-expression, by composer and/or performer, would create a "unity" far more significant than traditional order principles; he accepted as source material any sort of musical idea, his own or others', cultivated or vernacular; he identified difficulty with strength; he abhorred the "nice," the easy-sounding, and the genteel; and he was willing to try anything.

IVES'S MUSIC

Ives was a prolific composer. Kirkpatrick's "Temporary Catalogue," the most accurate listing of Ives's works, includes five completed symphonies and two orchestral "sets" (Ives's term for a group of related tone-poems; the First Orchestral Set is better known by its subtitle as *Three Places in New England*), plus other orchestral music. Many pieces for chamber or theater orchestra are yet unpublished; among those published are *The Unanswered Question;* the *Scherzo: Over the Pavements; Central Park in the Dark;* and two pieces called *Tone Roads*. Ives wrote some band music and also chamber music, including two string quartets, six violin-and-piano sonatas, and pieces for various other combinations. The keyboard music includes two piano sonatas (plus a *Three-Page Sonata*), numerous separate pieces for one or two pianos, and some works for organ. Many of the organ and choral works written during Ives's years on the organ bench and left in church libraries have been lost, but a considerable number of choral works remain. Finally, there are songs, almost twice as many as the *114 Songs* published by Ives.

The extraordinary diversity of Ives's music is well seen in his songs. Some sense of the bewilderment with which other composers greeted the book of *114 Songs* when they came upon it is conveyed in Aaron Copland's breathless summary:

> Almost every kind of song imaginable can be found—delicate lyrics, dramatic poems, sentimental ballads, German, French, and Italian songs, war songs, songs of religious sentiment, street songs, humorous songs, hymn tunes, folk tunes, encore songs; songs adapted from orchestral scores, piano works, and violin sonatas; intimate songs, cowboy songs, and mass songs. Songs of every character and description, songs bristling with dissonances, tone clusters, and "elbow chords" next to songs of the most elementary harmonic simplicity.[4]

Clearly, one cannot hope to describe such an oeuvre easily. A close look at one or two songs can, however, suggest some aspects of Ives's music.

Two Little Flowers (1921) is superficially simple, sweet, uncomplicated. The text, written by Ives and his wife, tells of "two little flowers" seen in the backyard on sunny days; other blossoms may be beautiful, but "fairest, rarest of them all are Edith and Susanna" (young Edith Ives and her playmate). The atmosphere of both text and setting is that of the nineteenth-century sentimental household song, and the melody moves predictably along in smooth contours of pitch and rhythm (Example 7-1a). Suddenly, however, three tiny rhythmic jolts occur, at "one in green," "passing fair," and "ever rare"; they point up, in a subtle way, the syntactical divisions of the verses, and they prepare for the wholly original melodic climax with its downward vaulting of an octave and a third (unless the singer can't make it; and Ives offers a simpler alternative) and its suspensive pause on "all," gratefully low in the singer's range (Example 7-1b). The accompaniment has its subtleties, too: initially sounding like a commonplace arpeggiated vamp, it turns out to revolve in groups of seven (not eight) eighth-notes, and rather than outlining a conventional triadic harmony it is quintal, spanning the interval D-E. This whole-tone interval is the basis for the harmonic events through two-thirds of the song, as each of these notes moves outwards in whole-tone motion: D-E, C-F♯, A♯-G♯. Approaching the end, Ives shifts to a V-of-ii, V-of-V, I$^6_4$ pattern, full of harmonic energy (measures 23–24), but returns to the whole-tone idea at the climax: superimposed on the surprising, dark chord at the word "all" is an even more surprising C-E third high in the piano, as if the B♭-D interval were going to move upwards to the E-G of the next measure (through C-E and D-F♯) but couldn't wait. The song ends with chords that sound like ii-V-I, but each contains the critical whole-tone interval: E-D, A-B, D-E.

Even this brief analysis makes the music seem more complicated than it sounds: the total effect of the song is that of simplicity and "familiarity," yet the commonplace is everywhere avoided and we recognize a work in which the familiar is transcended.

[4] Copland, "One Hundred and Fourteen Songs," *MM*, XI (January–February 1934), 59–64.

EXAMPLE 7-1. C. Ives, *Two Little Flowers* (1921). Copyright 1935 Merion Music, Inc.; used by permission. (a) measures 1–10. (b) measures 23–27.

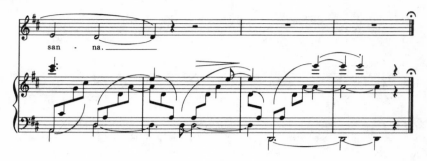

Less traditional by far in melody, harmony, and rhythm is *Cradle Song* (1919), given in its entirety as Example 7-2, although within its tiny nine-measure span it speaks just as evocatively and directly as *Two Little Flowers*. Each of the three phrases of the vocal line comes to rest on G♯, establishing that note as one tonal center, although the scale-basis of the melody might suggest F♯. The accompaniment is less certain about

EXAMPLE 7-2. Ives, *Cradle Song* (1919). Copyright 1935 Merion Music, Inc.; used by permission.

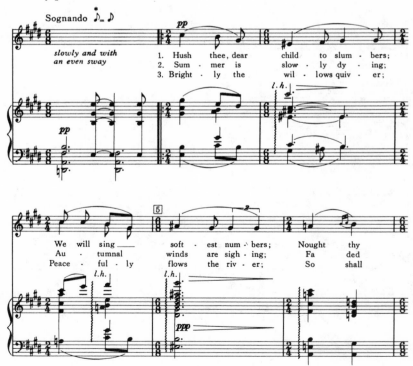

Notes: End song on ⌢ ; This chord may be repeated very quietly at the end of verse sung last.
*It will be observed that a ♩ of the $\frac{2}{4}$ measure is a ♩ of the $\frac{6}{8}$ and not a ♪.

its tonality, finally settling on A (but G♯ appears here, too, linking voice
with accompaniment). No systematic harmony is present, except an *avoid-
ance* of simple triads; there are Debussyesque bichords (measures 1, 9),
added-sixth chords (1, 2, 9), Wagner's *"Tristan* chord" with complications
(5), and other simultaneities inexplicable as single sonorities without
taking into account linear aspects (e.g., the F♯ of measure 4, part of a
treble line moving C♯-E-F♯-G♯). Harmonically, the song seems to "float"
in a void, an effect consonant with the text. The rhythm of the piece con-
firms this effect, as it sways gently between $\frac{2}{4}$ and $\frac{6}{8}$, the $\frac{2}{4}$♩=$\frac{6}{8}$♩ prescrip-
tion precluding any sense of regular meter at all and allowing the rhythm
to float, unmoored to a metric anchor. In measure 8, voice and accompaniment are really in different meters, the voice part ending on a disguised $\frac{2}{4}$ measure, the accompaniment continuing in its broad $\frac{6}{8}$.

One of the lengthiest and most powerful songs, *General William
Booth Enters into Heaven* (1914), on portions of a poem by Vachel
Lindsay, exemplifies Ives's use of "imitative dissonance" and of musical
quotation. The hectic, militant atmosphere of the text, which celebrates
the fanatic revivalism of the first commanding general of the Salvation
Army, leads Ives to begin the song with a typical marching band's drum-
beat: the whack of the snare drums and the thud of the bass drum, lag-
ging a bit behind, are projected in dissonant clusters (Example 7-3a).
Where Lindsay's poem quotes parenthetically (from a Salvation Army
hymn, "Are you washed in the blood of the Lamb?"), so does Ives, though
he uses the revival hymn tune *Cleansing Fountain* ("There is a fountain
filled with blood"). His equivalent to parenthesizing it is to present it in
a key far removed from the tonal sphere of the context. This melody,
redolent of American gospel hymnody in general, is developed in all
kinds of ways in the course of the song; other melodies quoted are the

introduction to James A. Bland's minstrel-show song *Golden Slippers* (responding to the text's mention of a banjo; measures 52–55, piano part) and trumpet-calls (at the mention of trumpets, measures 69–72, and of marching, measures 103–5). One of the most moving passages of the song (Example 7-3b) finds the singer circling "round and round" on a three-note figure, the pianist's right hand circling similarly but in a two-note cycle, while in the middle of the accompaniment, strangely askew, the melody of *Cleansing Fountain* winds its tranquil way. *General William Booth* ends with a haunting, parenthetically off-key statement of *Cleans-*

EXAMPLE 7-3. C. Ives, *General William Booth Enters into Heaven* (1914). Copyright 1935 Merion Music, Inc.; used by permission. (a) measures 1–10. (b) measures 82–91.

ing *Fountain* set to hymn-book harmony, then the drum-beats, lower-pitched as if in the distance, fade—"as a band marching away," wrote Ives in the manuscript.

Other notable songs of Ives, which I can cite but briefly here, are *Charlie Rutlage* (1914 or 1915), a cowboy ballad in which Ives turns to unpitched rhythmic declamation for the climactic measures; *The Circus Band* (1894), with much prancing band music; *Serenity* (1919), to a tranquil poem by Whittier in which a virtually monotonous chant-like vocal line is spun out against an other-wordly, "floating" harmonic oscillation; *Walking* (1902), in which the diffuse, cloudy overtones of church bells are captured subtly, and also the propulsive syncopations of ragtime. In

Majority (originally for chorus and orchestra, 1915; arranged for voice
and piano, 1921), with its perfervid Whitmanesque text, there is an equation between "the Masses" of the poem and massive chords (as many as
fifteen notes) built in clusters of massed seconds; these must be played
either with the forearm or a board, or with the help of a second pianist.
Soliloquy (1907; reprinted in Cowells, p. 158) is subtitled "a study in 7ths
and other things" and systematically explores non-traditional harmonies
and retrograde motion.

A number of the *114 Songs* were originally choral works, but the
bulk of Ives's choral music was for the church: some forty sacred choruses remain. Best-known among these is a setting of *Psalm 67* (1898),
based on a bitonal plan with the men's voices in the sphere of G minor,
the women's in C Major. Most awesome is an eleven-minute setting of
Psalm 90 (1898–1901?) for choir, organ, and bells, underscored throughout by a low C in the organ. Ives's wife heard him say that this was the
only one among his compositions that satisfied him.[5] A number of the
choral works seem to be compositional études; they reveal the speculative vein of Ives's thought, akin to Milhaud's studies in bichords and
Bartók's in scales and intervals. Among these are *Psalm 24* (1897?), which
is based on mirror-image counterpoint and systematic interval-expansion
(Example 7-4a) and the *Processional "Let There Be Light"* (1901), whose
harmonies are based on consistently changing structural intervals; the
chords of its core-passage are abstracted in Example 7-4b (P = perfect;
A = augmented; M = major; m = minor).

Among the secular choral works are *Three Harvest Home Chorales*
(1898, 1902) for chorus, brass ensemble, and organ—"a kind of outdoor
music," according to Ives, in which the tangled yet harmonious co-existence of "the trees, rocks, and men of the mountains in days before ma-
chinery" is expressed through radically independent counterpoint among
the three sound-components.[6] *Lincoln, the Great Commoner* (1912), for
(mostly unison) chorus, orchestra, and piano, exceeds even the *Chorales*
in density of texture and heterophonic polyphony; quotations from *The
Battle Hymn of the Republic, Hail! Columbia, The Red, White & Blue*
("O Columbia, the gem of the ocean"), *The Star-Spangled Banner,
America,* and *The Battle Cry of Freedom* appear in almost cinematic
collage, and more than once the voices split into a tumult of shouted
tone-clusters, a kind of "choral noise" of overwhelming power.

[5] Reported by John Kirkpatrick in his jacket notes for *Charles Ives: Music for
Chorus,* Columbia Records MS 6921; reiterated in the introduction to the published
score of *Psalm 90,* ed. Kirkpatrick and Gregg Smith (Bryn Mawr: Merion Music, Inc.,
1970), p. 3.

[6] The passages quoted are from an Ives letter published in Gertrude Norman
and Miriam Lubell Shrifte (eds.), *Letters of Composers* (New York: Alfred A. Knopf,
1946), pp. 345–46.

EXAMPLE 7-4. "Compositional études" of Ives. (a) *Psalm* 24 (1897?), measures 1–6 (after the manuscript). (b) *Processional "Let There Be Light"* (1901), harmonic plan of measures 9–18 (after the manuscript).

The shorter instrumental works of Ives, like the songs, are remarkable for their diversity and individuality: each seems to create its own expressive world; taken together, they cover an immense range of affective ends, achieved by an equally broad spectrum of technical means.

Among the shorter piano pieces are various Studies (1907–9?), part of an incomplete series of 27 (after Chopin's 27 Etudes?), including *Some South-Paw Pitching,* a showpiece for the left hand under right-hand variants of Foster's *Massa's in de cold cold ground; The Anti-Abolitionist Riots;* and 22 (i.e., twenty-second in the series), in an unusually clear A-B-A-Coda form. Interesting for their relationship to Arnold Schoenberg's much later twelve-tone row technique are *Three Protests* (or *Varied Air &Variations*) of 1914 or 1916: the monophonic theme of the variations, likened by Ives to "the old stone wall around the orchard," is made up of four interlocked, row-like chromatic series—for Ives the musical embodiment of the New England stone fence where none of the stones is exactly the same size or shape. The *Three-*

Page Sonata (1905), actually a substantial eight-minute work, compresses the traditional four-movement form into one, with a dramatic first section, lyric slow section, and last section alternating clangorous march motifs and jerky ragtime rhythms.

Free from the necessity to accommodate his music to conventional performance media, Ives wrote works for an astonishing variety of chamber ensembles, from two pianos tuned a quarter-tone apart (*Three Pieces*, 1923–24) to the combination of strings, brass, and four sets of bells of *From the Steeples* (1901). Many of the chamber works derived from, or were rebuilt into, other pieces. Among those originally conceived as chamber music are two well-known works of 1906 often performed separately but apparently considered by Ives as a pair—*The Unanswered Question* and *Central Park in the Dark in "The Good Old Summer Time"*; the first "A Contemplation of a Serious Matter," the second "A Contemplation of Nothing Serious." *The Unanswered Question*, for trumpet, four flutes, and offstage strings, has an elaborate metaphysical program explaining the three sound-components: the strings represent "the silence of the druids," the trumpet asks "the perennial question of existence," and the flutes—"Fighting Answerers"—attempt to find a satisfactory response. But no explanation is needed for the delicate balance in which the three components are suspended: the strings move slowly and placidly in spacious, diatonic chords from beginning to end; the trumpet occasionally sounds a disturbingly repetitive, atonal phrase from another musical world; and the flutes, increasingly raucous and agitated, provide a dynamic arc for the whole structure. As the Cowells (p. 177) write, "When the dissonant voices disappear, the faint consonant [string] chords continue to hum softly in the distance, like the eternal music of the spheres." No other work by Ives so immediately and movingly brings us in touch with his faith in the harmonious co-existence of disparate elements.[7] *Central Park in the Dark* is for a totally different ensemble (piccolo, flute, oboe, clarinet, bassoon, trumpet, trombone, percussion, two pianos and strings) but similarly juxtaposes quiet sounds with what Ives called "off tunes & sounds."

Ives was capable of musical contemplation not only of cosmically serious matters but of earthily comic ones. *Hallowe'en*, for string quartet and piano with drum *ad libitum*, may have been composed on April 1, 1907. It is a cacophonic spoof combining the humorous surprise of April Fools Day jokes with the crude pranks of Hallowe'en. The first violin plays in the key of C, the second in B, the viola in Db, the cello in D; the piano is atonal. Seldom do accents coincide. Only eighteen mea-

[7] See Eric Salzman's comments on this work, accompanied by a page of the score, in *Twentieth-Century Music: An Introduction* (2nd ed.; Englewood Cliffs: Prentice-Hall, Inc., 1974).

sures long, the piece may be repeated three or four times, omitting or altering various parts each time until the last, when, with a drum adding to the general din, the tempo is to be "as fast as possible without disabling any player or instrument." The *Scherzo: Over the Pavements* (1906–13), which includes the cadenza "to play or not to play," is for piccolo, clarinet, bassoon, trumpet, three trombones, cymbal, drum, and piano. It grew out of a work called *Rube Trying to Walk 2 to 3!!*, which suggests its emphasis on rhythmic counterpoint; this reaches a knotty climax (Example 7-5) in the second section of the A B C cadenza C′ B′ A′ form. Ives has the last laugh on the struggling performers in a comic ending, which sees them all together in an oom-pah, oom-pah vamp on a simple C major triad—a mocking concession to "Rollo."

Ives combined several groups of chamber pieces into "sets." One such set, a three-movement group of which the second is lost, he called *Tone Roads* (1911–15). No. 3, for woodwinds, brass, strings, piano, and chimes, is interesting for its repetitions of sections at varied tempos; its use of quarter-tone inflections; and the "tone road" of the chimes (in

EXAMPLE 7-5. C. Ives, *Scherzo: Over the Pavements* (1906–13), measures 59–61. Copyright 1954 by Peer International Corporation. Used by permission.

all but one section of the work), which approximates a twelve-tone row and is treated at the beginning like a medieval *color*, its pitch-pattern repeated in a varied rhythmic pattern (Example 7-6).

EXAMPLE 7-6. C. Ives, *Tone Roads*, No. 3 (chimes part only), measures 1–12. After a photostat of the manuscript in the Library of Congress.

In more conventional media, and somewhat more conventional forms, are the sonatas for piano and for violin and piano, and the symphonies.

Besides the *Three-Page Sonata*, Ives composed two numbered piano sonatas and began a third, now lost. The Second Sonata ("Concord, Mass., 1840–1860") is a giant four-movement cycle reflecting Ives's admiration for some of the literary participants in the "American Renaissance," as F. O. Matthieson has called it. Howard Boatwright has written, in his edition of the *Essays Before a Sonata* that Ives published in conjunction with the music:

> For some composers, one work, more than any other, may become a channel through which the streams of philosophical concept, musical technique, and style flow in singular unity. For Charles Ives, the Concord Sonata was such a work. It reflects programmatically, and also in deeper, less obvious ways, the influence of the Concord Transcendentalists; it is representative of Ives' highest achievements in richness of harmony and freedom of rhythm. (*Essays*, p. xiii)

Ives himself spoke of the work (*Essays*, p. xxv) more diffidently, saying it was "a group of four pieces, called a sonata for want of a more exact name, as the form, perhaps substance, does not justify it." He described the four movements as "impressionistic pictures of Emerson and Thoreau, a sketch of the Alcotts, and a *scherzo* supposed to reflect a lighter quality which is often found in the fantastic side of Hawthorne." Emerson, for Ives, conjures up a musical portrait of power and density; the first movement, although based on a sonata-form idea, reminds one of Ives's view of Emerson's own "plan of work" (see p. 152). The scherzo on Hawthorne rushes by in a blur except for one quiet, slow passage colored by two-octave-wide cluster-chords vibrating sympathetically high in the treble and another in which Simeon Marsh's hymn *Martyn* appears in a hushed, halting, hymn-book harmony. The Alcotts evoke a gentle variant of *Martyn* (which relates also to the opening motif of Beethoven's Fifth Symphony that appears throughout the "Concord" Sonata) and several of "old Scotch airs," one of *them* related (coincidentally?) to the minstrel-show song *Stop That Knocking at My Door* (1843) of A. F. Winnemore (*MinA*, No. 106). The final movement, "Thoreau," is deceptively calm in spirit; it builds to a single climax, then unwinds in a long denouement synthesizing materials from earlier movements and closing with a hauntingly tentative final gesture. Said Ives of the "Concord" Sonata:

> Every time I play it or turn to it, [it] seems unfinished. . . . Some of the passages now played haven't been written out . . . and I don't know as I ever shall write them out, as it may take away the daily pleasure of playing this music and seeing it grow and feeling that it is not finished. (I may always have the pleasure of not finishing it) . . .[8]

---

[8] *Memos*, pp. 79–80. Ives's own comments on the "Concord" Sonata (in *Essays* and *Memos*) are the best available guides to the work. Both the Cowells (pp. 190–201) and Chase (in *AM*, pp. 418–27) also discuss the sonata at length.

Besides a Pre-First Violin Sonata and a Pre-pre-First Violin Sonata (lost or destroyed), Ives wrote four sonatas for violin and piano between 1903 and 1914–15. More than any other group of Ives's works, the four sonatas seem all of a piece, citizens of the same musical world. All are in three movements; all end with hymn-tune finales; all are characteristically "easy" pieces (by Ives's standards), lacking the tangled thickets of the texture of, say, the first movement of the "Concord" Sonata. Sonatas Nos. 1 and 3 are abstract; Sonata No. 2 offers portraits of "Autumn" and a square dance ("In the Barn") plus a nostalgic view of the mounting intensity of a camp meeting ("The Revival"). Sonata No. 4, entirely based on hymn tunes, is called "Children's Day at the Camp Meeting." "The Revival" movement of Sonata No. 2 is an ingeniously worked piece, a sort of freely unfolding stream of variations on the old hymn tune *Nettleton* (or *Hallelujah;* see p. 98). The ingenuity and freedom with which Ives "re-composed" such borrowed material can be suggested by comparing a passage from "The Revival" (Example 7-7a) with the opening of the third movement of Ives's String Quartet No. 1 (Example 7-7b). In the former, Ives sets the tune as a bitonal canon at the tritone over cloudy pedal points on the tonic and dominant of the respective keys; in the latter, he invents a new ending and sets the tune to a cross between Schubertian and barbershop harmony.

The First String Quartet (1898?) is an assemblage from earlier organ pieces: its last three movements were originally a *Prelude, Offertory,* and *Postlude* composed in 1896 for use in New Haven's Center Church; the first movement derives from a fugue (on Lowell Mason's *Missionary Hymn* [see p. 63], soon combined with Oliver Holden's *Coronation* [see

EXAMPLE 7-7. Two uses of *Nettleton* by Ives. (a) Sonata No. 2 for violin and piano (New York: G. Schirmer, Inc., 1951), 3rd movement, measures 22–23. (b) String Quartet No. 1, 3rd movement, measures 1–4. © Copyright 1961 and 1963 by Peer International Corporation. Used by permission.

p. 118n]) that Ives had written for Horatio Parker. Ives later adapted the fugal movement for use in his Fourth Symphony. The Second Quartet (1911–13; 2nd movement 1907) I have mentioned above (pp. 152, 154); it is a thoroughly mature and "tough" work, one of the most striking examples of Ives's involving the performers in "discussions" and "arguments." The third movement finds the arguments resolved and the participants "viewing the firmament," to material based on the hymn tunes *Nettleton* and *Bethany* (Mason's "Nearer, my God to thee").

As in the violin sonatas. Ives seems in his symphonies to have been mindful of traditional broad formal procedures. Following the early First Symphony (1896–98) in four movements came a Second (1897–1902) in five. Its last movement is the most "Ivesian," with its quotations (*Camptown Races*, another more lyric melody reminiscent of *Old Black Joe*, country-fiddle-style counterpoints, *The Red, White & Blue*, and *Reveille*) and with the magnificent squawk (all twelve tones) of its final chord. The earlier movements seem somewhat labored in their conventionality, particularly the self-proclaiming "developments" of material in the style of European symphonists from Beethoven to Wagner, Brahms, and Dvořák: can Ives have been spoofing? The Third Symphony (1901–12) is characterized by its subtitle, "The Camp Meeting," and is a broad, hymnic three-movement work; both first and last movements betray their origins as earlier organ pieces.

Between the Third Symphony and the completion of the Fourth, Ives wrote three other works of symphonic proportions. *A Symphony: "New England Holidays"* (1904–13) was a gathering of four earlier orchestral movements into a kind of American "Four Seasons": "Washington's Birthday," "Decoration Day," "The Fourth of July," and "Thanksgiving." The First Orchestral Set or *A New England Symphony: "Three Places in New England"* (1903–14) is a three-movement work. Its first movement, "The 'St. Gaudens' in Boston Common," is a brooding piece with some of Ives's most subtle, highly developed use of old melodies. Inspired by the monument of Augustus Saint-Gaudens to Colonel Robert Shaw and the Negro regiment he led during the Civil War, Ives based his music on Foster's *Old Black Joe*, Root's *Battle Cry of Freedom*, and Work's *Marching Through Georgia*. Example 7-8 shows one moment when Ives finds a common denominator (a in the example) between the phrase "I'm coming" of Foster's song and "[Hur]rah! hurrah!" in Work's; combines that material with the chorus ("The Union forever, Hurrah boys, Hurrah!") of *The Battle Cry of Freedom* (b); fashions an ostinato bass (c_1) from a pentatonic motive (c_2) common to the two Civil War songs; and underscores the whole with a traditional military band's drum-cadence (d). The second movement of *Three Places*, "Putnam's Camp," combines the gay, brassy music of a late nineteenth-century

Fourth of July picnic (complete with the village brass band) with a child's vision of the Revolutionary War; the middle section finds the march beat of Example 7-8 (*d*) going along at two different speeds in the proportion 𝅝 = 𝅗𝅥. in a famous example of polytempo. The movement is full of hilarious gaiety and ends in a fine Independence Day burst of pyrotechnical pandemonium and a rather besotted blast of *The Star-Spangled Banner. Three Places* concludes, somewhat like the Fourth Symphony, in murmuring tranquility, with an autumnal portrait of a New England river: "The Housatonic at Stockbridge." A Second Orchestral Set (1912–15), again in three movements ("An Elegy to Our Forefathers," "The Rockstrewn Hills Join in the People's Outdoor Meeting," and "From Hanover Square North, at the End of a Tragic Day, the Voice of the People Again Arose"), completes the roster of Ives's major orchestral works before the Fourth Symphony. A Third Orchestral Set and a *Universe Symphony* (see *Memos,* pp. 106–8, and Cowells, pp. 201–3) were left unfinished.

EXAMPLE 7-8. C. Ives, *Three Places in New England,* 1st movement ("The 'St. Gaudens' in Boston Common"), measures 66–69. Quoted by permission of Mercury Music Corporation.

Ives labored off and on between 1909 and 1916 at his Fourth Symphony, one of the mightiest works in the history of American music. Scored for a huge orchestra and chorus plus a "distant choir" of strings and harps and a special "battery unit" of percussion, it had to wait until April 26, 1965 for its premiere performance (under Leopold Stokowski, assisted by two other conductors). Two movements had been performed in 1927, and program notes for that performance were written by Henry Bellamann, obviously from information supplied by his friend Ives:

This symphony . . . consists of four movements,—a prelude, a majestic fugue, a third movement in comedy vein, and a finale of transcendent spiritual content. [The order of the second and third movements was later reversed.] The aesthetic program of the work is . . . the searching questions of What? and Why? which the spirit of man asks of life. This is particularly the sense of the prelude. The three succeeding movements are the diverse answers in which existence replies. . . . The fugue . . . is an expression of the reaction of life into formalism and ritualism. The succeeding movement [i.e., the movement ultimately made the second] . . . is a comedy in the sense that Hawthorne's Celestial Railroad is a comedy.[9]

Ives added to Bellamann's notes a word on the last movement: ". . . an apothesis of the preceding content, in terms that have something to do with the reality of existence and its religious experience."[10]

The four movements of the Fourth Symphony resolve into two pairs. The Prelude, with its choral inquiry ("Watchman, tell us of the night/What the signs of promise are"), leads to the "comedy" movement, in which nostalgic song-passages are constantly interrupted by strident marches, rags, square-dance tunes, and patriotic ditties—not just separately but sometimes all at once. The fugue, stately, hymnic, suffused with 16- and 32-foot organ pedal color, serves as preparation to the last movement, which is even more complex in texture than the second, but a tapestry of murmurs rather than shouts. It begins mysteriously, like a distant march, with a complex percussion pattern that never ceases, is wholly independent of the rest of the movement's music, and, lingering after the orchestra (with wordless voices) dissolves, fades off in the distance as the symphony ends. For all its growing, then ebbing complexity, the movement breathes a spirit of utter tranquility. Ives wrote no more profoundly conceived and perfectly realized music than this.

Seen against the nineteenth-century background of an American musical culture sharply divided between cultivated and vernacular traditions, Ives's historical position is a unique one. Alone among his contemporaries, he embraced both traditions without reservation: his works emphatically declared that in its vernacular tradition American music had an artistically usable past; they also embodied the highest aspirations of the cultivated tradition. Moreover, Ives's open-mindedness and freshness of musical imagination were to be a continuing challenge to American composers after 1920. Ives is seen by many as the fountainhead of a

[9] Quoted in John Kirkpatrick's extensive preface to the published score (New York: Associated Music Publishers, 1965), p. viii. Kirkpatrick includes a detailed account of the background of the symphony and an authoritative identification of its many musical quotations.
[10] *Ibid.*

new tradition in American music, a basically experimental, pathfinding one. In a few sentences that are rather Ivesian in their bluntness and humor, Virgil Thomson, commenting on "the composer who lives by non-musical work," has remarked:

> [He] makes up his music out of whole cloth at home. He invents his own aesthetic. When his work turns out to be not unplayable technically, it often gives a useful kick in the pants to the professional tradition. The music of . . . Charles Ives did that very vigorously indeed.[11]

It promises to do so for some time to come.

BIBLIOGRAPHICAL NOTES

Besides the basic works cited in this chapter's first footnote, there is surprisingly little substantial work on Ives in print (at present writing; the Ives centennial year of 1974 promises to see considerable activity in the form of festivals, conferences, and writings devoted to him, including, it is to be hoped, publication of Frank Rossiter's fine Princeton University dissertation on "Charles Ives and American Culture").

Peter Yates writes a sympathetic "Introduction to Charles Ives" in his *Twentieth Century Music* (New York: Pantheon Books, 1967). Philip E. Newman has written a dissertation—rather disappointing—on the songs (Ph.D., University of Iowa, 1967). Elliott Carter, who knew Ives well, wrote in 1944 of "Ives Today: His Vision and Challenge," *MM*, XXI, 4 (May–June 1944), 199–202. An article notable for its excellent illustrations (photographs and facsimiles) is David Hall's in *Hi Fi/Stereo Review*, XIII, 3 (September 1964), 41–58. Kurt Stone's "Ives's Fourth Symphony: A Review," *MQ*, LII (1966), 1–16, is an enlightening example of the rather ambiguous and puzzled reaction to Ives's music that must have been common during the composer's creative life (less so today by far). Two studies of Ives's musical quotation practice and of his varied uses of pre-existent music are Sydney Robinson Charles, "The Use of Borrowed Material in Ives' Second Symphony," *Music Review*, XXVIII, 2 (May 1967), 102–111, and Dennis Marshall, "Charles Ives's Quotations: Manner or Substance?" *PNM*, VI, 2 (Spring-Summer 1968), 45–56.

---

[11] *The State of Music*, 2nd rev. ed. (New York: Random House [Vintage Books], 1962), p. 85. In his *American Music Since 1910* (New York: Holt, Rinehart and Winston, 1971), pp. 22–30, Thomson discusses what he calls "The Ives Case" rather less charitably than the quotation above would suggest.

part three

After 1920

EIGHT

THE 1920's

The period surrounding World War I, roughly from about 1910 to the mid-1920's, was a critical one for Western music in general and for American music as part of the larger scene. Many young European composers felt that the main Classic-Romantic tradition had reached a crisis-point and that new means had to be found to renovate it. Various reactions to the tradition, more or less violent, became apparent during this period, which was one of the most turbulent aesthetically and stylistically in the history of Western music. Paris, especially, was a cauldron of ferment; but so was Vienna, for so long a center of the tradition. Composers of other nationalities shared the same sense of crisis as well, partly out of a nationalistic urge for musical independence from Central European domination.

In some works, barbs of satire and ridicule were aimed at the presumed hyperexpressivity and bombast of the tradition. Thus Claude Debussy slyly quoted Wagner's *Tristan und Isolde* in "Gollywog's Cakewalk," the most offhand piece in his *Children's Corner* suite (1906–8),

173

with a tongue-in-cheek instruction to the pianist to play "avec une grande émotion." Erik Satie became virtually a professional musical satirist. The young Darius Milhaud reacted against the inordinate length and grandiloquence of the post-Romantic symphony and opera forms with three-minute symphonies (1917) and *opéras minutes* (1927).

Another kind of reaction was that of an outright rejection of the tradition and an attempt to revolutionize musical expression, especially in media related to the machine age: this was the aim of the Futurist group at first centered in Italy, then in Paris, where concerts of noise instruments—hissers, exploders, cracklers, buzzers, screamers, and the like—were given.

Older, established composers like Ralph Vaughan Williams, Richard Strauss, Gabriel Fauré, and Jean Sibelius, not sharing the sense of crisis of their younger colleagues, more or less unconsciously extended the tradition. But the group of composers in Vienna around Arnold Schoenberg sought *consciously* to extend it beyond past limits, particularly its element of chromaticism. Considering Classic-Romantic tonality a Procrustean bed ill-fitted to the increasingly chromatic vocabularly of melody and harmony, they wrote an ultra-chromatic music that avoided traditional tonality and approached a free atonality. In another sort of evolutionary extension of the tradition, the Czech composer Alois Hába began working with microtones, intervals smaller than the traditional chromatic semitones of the twelve-note tempered scale.

Finally, an immense number of works of the period suggest attempts to revitalize and enlarge the tradition by exotic and atavistic borrowings from musical cultures distant in space, spirit, or time. Thus the primitivistic manner of Igor Stravinsky's *Le Sacre du printemps* (1913) and *Les Noces* (1917–23); the delving into the heart of folk music of Béla Bartók; and the popularesque manner based on urban café music of Milhaud's *Le Boeuf sur le toit* (1920), Arthur Honegger's Concertino for piano and orchestra (1925), and Francis Poulenc's Sonata for piano duet (1918). Related in impulse to these works, which looked to primitive, folk, and popular music for a fresh note, were others that looked back, beyond the Romantic era, to the Classical, Baroque, and even earlier periods in Western music for inspiration: Sergei Prokofiev's "Classical" Symphony (1916–17); Stravinsky's *Pulcinella* (1920) and Octet for wind instruments (1923); Schoenberg's chamber *Serenade*, Op. 24 (1923) and neo-classic Suite for piano, Op. 25 (1924); Maurice Ravel's *Le Tombeau de Couperin* (1914–17); Ottorino Respighi's *Antiche arie e danze* (1916–31) and *Concerto Gregoriano* (1922).

In sum, the atmosphere of European music just before and after the First World War was charged with various currents and cross-currents of progressivism: "New Music" marched under a variety of banners. This atmosphere was characteristic also of the United States, slightly later, between the end of World War I and the economic collapse of 1929. An era of unprecedented prosperity in the U.S.A., the 1920's were notable in American music as years when progressive currents could flourish, and did; years when youthful composers could afford to spurn the achievements of the generation that preceded them, and did.

The older generation, composers in their forties and fifties in the decade after World War I, continued to write in an essentially nineteenth-century manner, to get performances and continued respect. Chadwick, Frederick Converse (1871–1940), Edward Burlingame Hill (1872–1960), Rubin Goldmark (1872–1936), and Daniel Gregory Mason (1873–1953) carried forward the traditionalism, the solid craft if not notable inventiveness, of the Second New England School.

Some slightly younger composers were gaining reputations as the inheritors of the American cultivated-tradition ideal of a music of serious import and large-scale edification—"Americans who work along more or less conservative lines and make no attempt to write anything departing from general types of European music."[1] Among those who were to maintain some prominence during and after the decade of the 1920's was Howard Hanson (b. 1896), a composer of big rhetorical works like the Second ("Romantic") Symphony, the choral cantata *The Lament for Beowulf* (1925), and the opera *Merry Mount* (1933). Hanson was perhaps more lastingly significant as a teacher and as director of the Eastman School of Music (Rochester, N.Y.), where from 1925 he produced annual festivals of American music. Others in this group were Leo Sowerby (1895–1968), an organist-composer who provided much viable music for his instrument, and Randall Thompson (b. 1899), who became as strongly identified with works for chorus as Sowerby with works for organ.

A few other composers leavened their academic heritage with sprinklings of some kind of popular or folk music. John Alden Carpenter's ballet scores *Krazy Kat* (1921) and *Skyscrapers* (1926) were indebted to some rhythmic aspects of American dance music. Charles Wakefield Cadman (1881–1946) took both subject and musical inflections from American Indian music for his opera *Shanewis* (1918). John Powell (1882–1963) delved in Anglo-American folk song, Emerson Whithorne (1884–1958) and Henry Eichheim (1870–1942) in Oriental music. The strains of the jazz-once-removed of white America's ballrooms and dance halls were useful for Louis Gruenberg (1884–1964) in works like *Daniel Jazz* (1925) and *Jazzettes* (1926) and his later successful opera *The Emperor Jones* (1933).

---

[1] Henry Cowell, in an introductory chapter dated January 1933 for *American Composers on American Music* (1933; 2nd ed. New York: Frederick Ungar Publishing Co., 1962), p. 9. It is interesting to compare Cowell's "grouping of composers according to accomplishments and ideals" with that of Aaron Copland written a few years earlier: "America's Young Men of Promise," *MM*, III, 3 (March–April 1926), 13–20.

More notable than these, however, more characteristic of the era of the "Roaring '20's," were younger composers grappling with the new ideas, the new materials, the new approaches to organizing sound that had been proposed by the European leaders of "New Music" (Stravinsky, Schoenberg, the sassy young French composers, the Futurists) and by the new American "urban folk music" of jazz. As Aaron Copland, along with George Gershwin the most prominent young composer of the decade, has written: "Contemporary music as an organized movement in the U.S.A. was born at the end of the First World War."[2]

NADIA BOULANGER; AARON COPLAND

Copland (b. 1900) was one of a large group of American composers to become the student, in Fontainebleau and Paris, of the remarkable musician and teacher Nadia Boulanger (b. 1887). Mlle. Boulanger's unique combination of exacting severity and liberating encouragement (the latter given in exquisitely precise proportion to the pupil's efforts) was to be a magnet for several generations of young Americans; in the 1920's, as one of her pupils of that decade has commented, "What endeared [Boulanger] most to Americans was her conviction that American music was about to 'take off,' just as Russian music had done eighty years before."[3] She was capable of training young composers without dictating one exclusive style: the measure of her phenomenal gifts as a teacher was the variety of personal styles developed in her *atelier*. Nevertheless, the example of Stravinsky was most often set before her students, and certainly Copland's work in the 1920's reveals the impact of Stravinsky more than of any other composer. It also reveals a preoccupation with "Americanism"—with a national identity. The models of Farwell and Gilbert, who had turned to Negro and Indian materials, seemed irrelevant, perhaps especially to Copland, a Brooklyn-born Jew; that of Ives was as yet unknown. Besides, as Copland recalled later:

> Our concern was not with the quotable hymn or spiritual: we wanted to find a music that would speak of universal things in a vernacular of American speech rhythms. We wanted to write music on a level that left popular music far behind—music with a largeness of utterance wholly representative of the country that Whitman had envisaged.[4]

[2] *Our New Music* (New York: McGraw-Hill Book Company, 1941), p. 137.
[3] Virgil Thomson, *Virgil Thomson* (New York: Alfred A. Knopf, 1966), p. 54.
[4] *Music and Imagination: the Charles Eliot Norton Lectures, 1951–1952* (New York: Mentor Books, 1959), p. 111.

In a few works written after his return from three years (1921–
1924) in Paris under Boulanger, Copland seemed to have imagined that
the jazzy rhythms and blue notes of contemporary dance music would
provide sources for the music he sought to write. The first of these works
was *Music for the Theatre* (1925), a twenty-minute suite for small orchestra in five symmetrically ordered movements with a "motto" theme
appearing in each (Example 8-1). The scale of the work, its chamber
medium, its orderly structure, and its crisp unsentimental tone all reflect
the precise anti-Romanticism of Copland's French experience. Its crack-
ling sonorities, bichordal harmonies, and jerky motoric rhythms suggest
Stravinsky and the younger French composers. Its declamatory "motto"
(Example 8-1a), on the other hand, has been related (by fellow-composer
Arthur Berger) to Copland's Jewish backgrounds; and the rhythmic and
pitch inflections especially of the second ("Dance") and fourth ("Burlesque") movements relate to dance music of the 1920's like the Charleston
(Example 8-1c). Rather similar in manner but larger in conception is a

EXAMPLE 8-1. A. Copland, *Music for the Theatre* (1925). (a) "Motto," 1st
movement, measures 2–5 (trumpet part only); (b) 1st movement, measures
14–17; (c) 2nd movement, measures 1–7 (bassoon part only). Copyright 1932
by Cos Cob Press Inc. Renewed 1960 by Aaron Copland. Reprinted by permission of Boosey & Hawkes, Inc. Sole licensees.

Concerto for piano and orchestra of 1927. In later works of the 1920's
Copland gave up the limited expressive range of dance music and turned
to a more abstract, less selfconsciously "American" manner—but one
equally hard, lean, and rhythmically knotty—in a *Dance* Symphony (1929;
three movements adapted from the earlier ballet *Grohg*); a trio, *Vitebsk*
(1929); a *Symphonic Ode* (1930); and a set of *Piano Variations* (1930).

For many, the *Piano Variations* mark the summit of Copland's
achievement. Based on a theme that has a certain hard-edged grandeur
(Example 8-2a), the work, from the outset, treats the piano anti-Roman-
tically as a basically percussive instrument, with hammers (which of
course it is). The continuous set of twenty close-knit, mainly clangorous
variations culminates in an overwhelmingly resonant coda. Certain variations suggest that Copland had by this time absorbed the principle of
Schoenberg's tone-row technique, perhaps unconsciously, into his own
lucid, often brittle, and generally rhythm-dominated style (Example

EXAMPLE 8-2. A. Copland, *Piano Variations* (1930). (a) Theme, measures
1–11; (b) Variation 2, measures 21–24. Copyright 1932 by Aaron Copland,
Renewed 1959. Reprinted by permission of Aaron Copland, Copyright Owner,
and Boosey & Hawkes, Inc., Sole Publishers and Licensees.

8-2b).[5] The *Variations* seem to mark a synthesis by Copland of his American background, his French training, and a range of expression and means of tonal organization related to the Viennese School; they come very close to achieving Copland's ideal in the 1920's of a music that would "speak of universal things . . . with a largeness of utterance wholly representative of the country."

Many other young composers hied themselves off to Boulanger's studio in the 1920's: Virgil Thomson, Roy Harris, Walter Piston, Elliott Carter, Robert Russell Bennett, Marc Blitzstein, and others. These, however, did not gain the early prominence of Copland; their works belong more to the story of American music after the 1920's, and I shall refer to them in later chapters.

EDGARD VARÈSE

The "organized movement" in contemporary music in the 1920's spoken of by Copland was reflected in the many groups founded to give concerts of new music, like the series produced between 1928 and 1931 by Copland and Roger Sessions; in the contributions of some major conductors who performed new works, notably Serge Koussevitzky (1874–1951), conductor of the Boston Symphony Orchestra from 1924, and Leopold Stokowski (b. 1882), conductor of the Philadelphia Orchestra from 1912 to 1938; and in the formation of composers' groups, especially the League of Composers (which sponsored the important journal *Modern Music*, 1924–46), the International Composers' Guild (1921–27), and the Pan American Association of Composers (founded 1928; dissolved early 1930's).

Founder of both the Guild and the P.A.A.C., and in the vanguard of American music in the 1920's (and again in the 1950's), was the Paris-born composer Edgard Varèse (1883–1965), who came permanently to New York City late in 1915. In the 1920's Varèse founded no school of composers, but with his first American work, purposely and meaningfully titled *Amériques* (1918–22), he offered a challenge to musical tradition that was reiterated with each of his important compositions of the 1920's (*Offrandes, Hyperprism, Octandre, Intégrales, Arcana*) and the celebrated all-percussion piece *Ionisation* (1930–31). Perhaps because of the last-named work and the high proportion of percussion instruments he called for in others, Varèse's name has sometimes been linked with the Futurists and their *bruitisme*. Actually, Varèse stood alone: he was uninterested in

[5] In this connection, one might note that Copland transcribed the *Piano Variations* for orchestra in the 1960's, after he had adopted the twelve-tone technique whole-heartedly.

a revolutionary "noise music" or a "machine music" as such; he believed, however, in the legitimacy of *any* sound as a vehicle for musical expression, and (as he put it in an unpublished lecture at Princeton University, September 4, 1959) he became a sort of diabolic Parsifal looking not for a Holy Grail but for a bomb that would blow wide open the musical world and let in sound—all sounds, [including those] at that time, and sometimes even today, called 'noise.' " As early as 1917 he was writing of a "dream of instruments obedient to my thought, and which with their contribution of a blossoming of unsuspected timbres will . . . bend to the demands of my inner rhythm."[6] That dream was to be realized, but only in the electronic era of the 1950's; in the 1920's Varèse had to content himself with conventional instruments, assembled, however, in unusual groupings and supplemented with a large number of so-called percussion instruments, some not so conventional. Important among the latter were sirens, whose arching curves of sound embodied and projected one of Varèse's most important concepts: that of music as a spatial art, as "moving bodies of sound in space." Not only are sirens employed in *Amériques* but in *Hyperprism* (1922) and *Ionisation* as well. Their use, and that of an inexhaustible variety of drums, cymbals, gongs, tam-tams, bells, chimes, wood-blocks and castanets, slapsticks and rattles, chains and anvils, bespoke Varèse's definition of music simply as "organized sound" limited in no way to traditional notions of "musical tone" as against "noise."

Varèse's music of the 1920's is marked especially by an emphasis on sheer sonority, often achieved by multiple repetitions of notes or aggregates of them, by writing at the extremes of an instrument's range, or by spacing of "chords" in unconventional ways and by dispersing their notes through a huge registral spectrum. Stridency of sound is characteristic: the performance-indication "hurlant" (yelling) is not uncommon. Traditional formations of harmonies do not typically appear, yet neither is the music organized by anything like Schoenberg's chromatic tone-rows. Individual sounds, pulsating with a life of varied intensities and changing timbres, are important, as at the opening of *Hyperprism*, where a C♯ introduced by a trombone is variously mutated, first by different attacks and approaches, then by coloration in horn, then by dynamic, timbral, and articulative shifts among three horns (Example 8-3a). That single note and the D-C♯ interval formed when the bass trombone enters are examples of what Varèse called "sound-masses":

> There is an idea, the basis of an internal structure, expanded and split into different shapes or groups of sound, constantly changing in shape, direction, and speed, attracted and repulsed by various forces. The form of the work is the consequence of this interaction. (Princeton lecture)

[6] My translation from *391*, No. 5 (New York, June 1917).

EXAMPLE 8-3. E. Varèse, *Hyperprism* (1922); (a) measures 1–6 (percussion parts omitted); (b) measures 11–13 (percussion parts omitted). © 1924 by Edgard Varèse & assigned to Colfranc Music Publishing Corp., New York. By permission of the Publisher.

Varèse likened such "an idea, the basis of an internal structure," to a crystal, which although restricted in internal form can appear in limitless external forms. In *Hyperprism* the most important such "crystal" would seem to be the major seventh interval (or its inversion, a semitone): this interval appears in innumerable aggregates. The sonority of measures 12–13, for instance, is a "splitting" of the C♯ sound (measure 11) into a four-note aggregate composed of two pairs of sevenths: flute C and clarinet D♭, and trumpet C♯ and trombone C (Example 8-3b). These sevenths relate back, of course, to the first interval heard in the work, the D–C♯ of measure 5 (see Example 8-3a); and the final sonority of the entire piece is a nine-note aggregate made up of the following transpositions of that interval: C–B, B♭–A, G–F♯, E–E♭, F♯–F. (To be noted, especially in view of some procedures in *Intégrales,* is that the initial D–C♯ is specifically omitted at the close.)

"Thematic" material in a traditional sense is not characteristic of Varèse's music: "sound-masses," whether based on pitch, timbre, or rhythm replace it. These are then varied, developed, interlocked, or super-imposed somewhat the way themes might be. Ironically, in view of the furor that attended its early hearings, *Ionisation* contains a very im-portant idea (presented by the *tambour militaire* in measures 8–13) that approximates the periodic organization of a "theme," with its mid-point signaled by an isolated *sforzando* bang (Example 8-4). To follow this idea through the entire work, in which there is no melody or harmony in the traditional sense, only rhythms and an extraordinary variety of timbres produced by thirteen players on about forty instruments, is a fruitful ap-proach to Varèse's concept of musical crystals, the variety of external forms they may assume, and their "attraction and repulsion" by various forces. Another idea in *Ionisation* interesting to trace through its various manifestations is the cloudy metallic sonority of gong, high tam-tam, and low tam-tam first announced in measure 1.

EXAMPLE 8-4. E. Varèse, *Ionisation* (1930–31), measures 8–13 (*tambour militaire* part only). © 1934 by Edgard Varèse & assigned to Colfranc Music Publishing Corp., New York. By permission of the Publisher.

Both *Hyperprism* and *Ionisation* lead to massive single climaxes near their conclusion, *Hyperprism* on an *hurlant* sonority at top volume (measures 72–75), *Ionisation* on an all-metal crash (measure 65). This procedure links Varèse with earlier composers, indeed with the post-Romantics, who loved the quasi-dramatic plan of a build-up to a single climax. *Intégrales,* a larger work of 1924 for woodwinds, brass, and per-cussion, is organized in three broad sections, each with charcteristic sound-mass material; it too climaxes toward its close (measures 153–54).[7]

HENRY COWELL

Another composer who embodied the progressivism of American music of the 1920's in his own music, in his support of new trends, and in his writings was Henry Cowell (1897–1965). Cowell was a Californian, a fact of significance in its suggestion of the end of the American frontier

[7] An authoritative approach to an analysis of *Intégrales* is offered by Varèse's former pupil Chou Wen-chung in "Varèse: A Sketch of the Man and His Music," *MQ,* LII (1966), 151–70.

and the broadening of America's musical base to encompass the entire continent, also in its reminder that though American composers had traditionally looked eastward across the Atlantic to European cultural models, they could also look westward across the Pacific to the Orient. In a long career as aesthetic gadfly of American music, Cowell sought to find a context in *world* music for that of America, interesting himself in traditional and folk music of the entire world's peoples.

In the 1920's Cowell became notorious for novel uses of the pianoforte, including "tone-clusters," for extensions of the rhythmic range of music, and for many other explorations into *New Musical Resources,* as the title of his 1919 book (published 1930) put it. His fertile musical imagination first addressed itself to the piano and its untapped reservoir of sound-possibilities: in March, 1912, at the age of fifteen, Cowell amazed a San Francisco audience with pieces like *The Tides of Manaunaun* (1911), which superimposes MacDowellesque thematic material over deep oceanic roars produced by playing the lowest notes of the piano with the flat of the left hand or with the forearm. *Advertisement* (1915) finds fistfuls of tone-clusters cascading frantically from top to bottom of the keyboard, in a satiric evocation of the repetitious raucousness of advertisers. Besides his use of tone-clusters of massed seconds on the keyboard, Cowell achieved other new sonorities by playing directly on the piano strings. In *The Banshee* (1925) the lower bass strings (which are wrapped in metal coils) are stroked along their length; this produces sounds four octaves above the keyboard tones, with a curious and even terrifying wailing effect. In *Sinister Resonance* (1935) Cowell applied to the piano strings techniques of stopping, muting at the bridge, and producing harmonics, theretofore used only for such stringed instruments as violins.

As early as 1914, Cowell began working with textures fashioned of melodic strands in independent rhythms: the piano piece *Fabric,* for instance, begins with a three-voice texture in which the relationship of beats between the voices in the first measure is as 8 to 6 to 5, in the second measure 9 to 7 to 5, etc. Believing that human limitations precluded the realization of the full range of polyrhythms he envisioned, Cowell developed (in cooperation with the musical-instrument inventor Leon Theremin) the Rhythmicon, an instrument capable of producing very complex combinations of beat-patterns; it was combined with orchestra in a work of 1931 titled *Rhythmicana* and in several others.

Cowell was a fighter for other's new music as well as his own. In 1927 he founded a quarterly publication of innovative scores, *New Music.* In an introductory note to Volume I, Number 1, he commented on the dilemma of progressive composers, even in an era of "modernism":

. . . There are very few opportunities at present for the modern American composer to publish his works, as publishers cannot afford to risk losing money in such publications, with the result that many of the finest works ever written in America remain unpublished. When modern works are published in America, few copies are sold. The work is therefore not distributed, and the composer gains no financial profit. . . .

As editor of *New Music* until 1936, Cowell bravely and selflessly sought to change that situation. The first issue (October 1927) consisted of a piece for small orchestra, *Men and Mountains*, by Carl Ruggles (1876–1971), an older New England composer rather like Charles Ives in his disdain for popular success, his alternation of composing and non-musical activity (painting, in Ruggles's case), and his forging of a unique personal style. Never a prolific composer, Ruggles produced a handful of tough, dense-textured, contrapuntal works of a uncompromising integrity and a very high incidence of secundal dissonance. (On his studio wall hung the motto, "Dissonant chords should have talismanic ecstasy.") His major composition is the symphonic work *Sun-treader,* begun in 1926 and completed in 1931; other important ones are *Angels* (1920; originally the middle movement of *Men and Angels*), *Portals* (1925), and *Organum* (1944–47) for orchestra; and *Evocations* (1935–43; revised 1954) for piano.

Besides his support for Ruggles (and for Ives as well) through publishing their works in *New Music,* Cowell furthered the careers of a number of other composers who seemed poised on the leading edge of musical practice during the 1920's: George Antheil (1900–1959), Wallingford Riegger (1885–1961), John J. Becker (1886–1961), Adolph Weiss (1891–1971), and Ruth Crawford Seeger (1901–1953).

POPULAR MUSIC AND MUSICAL COMEDY

The 1920's also saw major developments in popular music. Some of the most important were technological: the establishment of commercial, public radio stations and the development of the electrical recording process (with disc recordings as its product), the public address system, and the sound track for film. All used the microphone and the sound amplifier, with significant impact on the nature of orchestration and popular vocal style, hence on the ideas of performers, arrangers, and even songwriters. All tended to broaden the audience—in a sense to nationalize it—for popular music, but at the same time to make it a more passive one, an audience of listeners rather than participants. This tended to heighten the importance of professionalism and sophistication among both performers and arrangers; it also tended to increase commercialism in the transmission (the "distribution") of popular music to its audience. Thus the era of the American popular-music *industry* was born—an inevitable concomitant of the electronic age's "mass media" (though the term was yet uncoined).

New York City was the power-center of the popular-music industry during the 1920's: it had Broadway and Shubert Alley, center of American popular lyric theater (the declining operetta and the developing musical comedy), and it had Tin Pan Alley, center of the songwriting business and the still-powerful sheet-music publishers. The recording studios and the radio networks were also based in New York. But recordings and radio opened up possibilities for a striking new development: they made available, to any who cared to listen, kinds of popular music heard previously only in limited geographical areas or by specific ethnic and social groups—especially the blues, gospel songs, and jazz of black Americans (at whom a sub-section of the recording industry aimed so-called "race records") and the traditional music of the southern Appalachians and other rural areas of the South and West ("hillbilly music," as a term coined in this period defined it). The latter music was not to affect the mainstream of American popular music until much later, but the former influenced American popular music of the 1920's in many ways; novelist Scott Fitzgerald could even call the era "The Jazz Age"— which, although an exaggeration, reflected the inroads of black-American musical influence on the consciousness of the nation at large.

Out of the popular mania for ragtime at the turn of the century had come an American craze for dancing. By the second decade, however, the older waltz, two-step, and cakewalk gave way—especially under the influence of the smooth, elegant models of Irene and Vernon Castle, the foremost dance team of the time—to a brisk but modest four-four dance for couples: the fox-trot. With many variants, it was to be the basic step in "ballroom dancing" for decades, relieved occasionally by more exotic ones like the tango, the rumba, and the maxixe. But another dance is even more strongly identified with the 1920's (and especially with the New American Woman of the 1920's, now a legal voter and thought to be emancipated in various other ways over her Victorian mother and grandmother). This was the athletic Charleston, which, despite its name and its anything but langorous tempo, probably derived musically from Latin sources: its basic rhythm ($\frac{4}{4}$ ♩. ♩. ♪ | ♩. ♩. ♪ |), like that of the tango, was related to the Spanish *habanera*.

Responding to the new popularity of dancing two-by-two (and also, as Irving Berlin's song of 1935 put it, "cheek-to-cheek"), dance-bands proliferated in the 1920's. But in retrospect the period seems more notable for an explosion of songs and songwriters than for instrumental music and composers of it (except in jazz). Individual songs were published in great numbers; some were immensely popular, like the ballad (a term connoting, in popular music, not a story-telling song but a slow

love-song) *Star Dust* (1929) by Hoagy Carmichael (b. 1899), which originated as a piano piece but was furnished with lyrics by Mitchell Parish.
But the most successful songs, in every sense, came out of the newly
popular form of American lyric theater, the musical comedy (or just
"musical"). The combination of a play with interpolated songs and dances
was not new: as we have seen, it had been part of the American tradition
from the eighteenth century and, after minstrel-show interlude, had re-
gained popularity, in the form of operetta, late in the nineteenth. But the
musicals of the 1920's had a different style and feeling from those of
operetta: they tended to avoid the sentimentality and the slightly aristocratic tone (which came out of Viennese operetta); they were more brash
and brassy, lively and spicy, colloquial and earthy; they incorporated
more identifiably American elements of dance and music; and they
mirrored faithfully the optimism and hedonism, the motoric energy, and
the devil-may-care attitudes of the postwar boom era.

The American musical has been likened to a latter-day ballad
opera, but the balance and inter-relationship of its components are vastly
different. The ballad opera had been basically a play dotted with occasional songs; the musical, at least that of the 1920's, was essentially a
garland of songs and dances strung on a thin plot-line, with occasional
spectacular "production numbers" planned at strategic points. Least important, perhaps, in a musical comedy of the period was the "comedy"—
the drama. The success of a musical depended essentially on three things:
the quality of the actor-singers and dancers (and of the director who
guided them); the quality of the songs themselves; and a delicate balance
between the music and the other components of the whole work. It was
the necessity for the latter, perhaps more than anything else, which resulted in the inevitable out-of-town tryouts (i.e., in other places than
New York) during which songs were shuffled about, rewritten, replaced,
or dropped entirely until, hopefully, a "hit" was assured. The *ad hoc* and
ad hominem attitudes that went into the making of a musical, whereby
its components were all separable from each other, ready to be reassembled into various shapes and orders, meant that never was such a
work subject to the singleminded vision or the unique control of one
individual; all kinds of "specialists" were involved—producer, director,
author, lyricist, composer, arranger, conductor, choreographer, and various
associates and assistants (not to mention those performers who would
actually project the work across the footlights). This splintering of authority over a musico-dramatic work, even greater than in the mounting of
an opera, was and remains one of the greatest problems of musical
comedy.[8]

[8] A fascinating account emphasizing this is Don Dunn, *The Making of No,
No, Nanette* (New York: Dell Publishing Co., Inc., 1972), which is a chronicle of the
1970 revival of a 1924 musical.

The major songwriters of the 1920's who dominated the field of the musical were Jerome Kern, Irving Berlin, Richard Rodgers, and George Gershwin.

Jerome Kern (1885–1945), after beginnings in the shadow of Victor Herbert, turned to a slightly more colloquial, popular American manner at about age 30; more than one critic of American popular song dates the shift at 1914, with the poignant *They Didn't Believe Me*, from the show *The Girl From Utah*.[9] Over a long career, with more than sixty works for the stage to his credit, Kern achieved many hits with a song style that tended to be gentle, lyrical, and virtually untouched by elements of blues or jazz. In fact, many of his songs border on an operetta-like theatricality (*Ol' Man River* and *Bill*, from *Show Boat* of 1927, considered by many Kern's masterpiece) or "artiness" (*Yesterdays* and *Smoke Gets in Your Eyes*, from *Roberta* of 1933; *All The Things You Are*, from *Very Warm For May* of 1939, his last musical). The harmonic scheme of *All The Things You Are* suggests how rapidly American popular songwriters had developed in sophistication of harmonic thought. In less than a half-century, a basic vocabulary of little more than tonic, dominant, and subdominant chords, seldom in any but the tonic key, had increased immensely, to include major sevenths as consonances (measures 4, 12), enharmonic changes (23–24), sudden changes of mode (8–9), and altered chords (30); and tonal sensibility had been refined to allow for such uncertain, floating tonality as we hear in this song—until it ends declaratively in A♭, we cannot be certain whether it is in the key of F minor, A♭ major, C major, C minor, E♭ major, G major, or E major.

Irving Berlin (b. 1888) has survived several major shifts in American popular musical taste and until the rock revolution, at least, went on writing songs at an incredible pace: as late as 1969 his publishing company listed 899 songs as being in print; many others have gone out of print or were never published.[10] Berlin's first great popular hit was *Alexander's Ragtime Band* (1911), which ironically is lacking in any shred of rag rhythm. In the 1920's he was associated with Flo Ziegfeld, the extraordinary producer of super-spectacular "revues," and wrote songs for a number of the periodic *Ziegfeld Follies* beginning with that of 1919 (which included *A Pretty Girl is Like a Melody*). Later, his knack for pouring essentially old familiar musical wine into slightly different bottles and having it come out seeming fresh and beguiling led to some apparently timeless songs: *Always* (1925), *Blue Skies* (1927), *How Deep is the Ocean* (1932), *The Girl That I Marry* and *I Got the Sun in the Morning* (both from the musical *Annie Get Your Gun* of 1946) are a few. In a special class altogether are two other songs by Berlin—*White Christ-*

[9] See Alec Wilder, *American Popular Song: The Great Innovators, 1900–1950* (New York: Oxford University Press, 1972), pp. 32, 34–36.

[10] *Ibid.*, p. 92.

mas (from the 1942 film *Holiday Inn*), which with its yearning lyrics matched by a surprisingly sensuous chromatic line has become virtually a popular hymn; and *God Bless America* (instantly popularized by singer Kate Smith in 1939 although it had lain unused since 1917), which has become a sort of unofficial national anthem.

A few extremely effective collaborations between musical-comedy songwriters and lyricists arose in the 1920's. Among them was the team of Richard Rodgers (b. 1902) and Lorenz Hart (1895–1943), who worked together from 1919 (when Rodgers was only sixteen) until 1940. Most of Rodgers's more than 250 songs were composed for the stage; an unusual number of them became hits. More than either Kern or Berlin, Rodgers picked up from popular dance music rhythmic devices it had in turn derived from jazz; they appear in the opening "verse" and following "chorus" of both *The Blue Room* (from the very successful musical, *The Girl Friend*, of 1926) and *Thou Swell* (1927; from *A Connecticut Yankee*). Less colloquial, more "arty," are others, like the top hit of 1929 by Rodgers and Hart, *With a Song in My Heart*. Almost all—and this can be said of the overwhelming majority of American popular songs after about 1925 and for the following quarter-century—share certain formal characteristics. An opening "verse," apt to be somewhat tentative and suspensive musically, and frequently declamatory in vocal style, is followed by a "chorus" (by which the entire song is generally identified, at least by all but pop-song connoisseurs). The "chorus" is more shapely and memorable from the musical standpoint; it is typically 32 measures long, in 8-measure phrases, in an A A B A form (or variants of it). The "B" phrase is called for no good reason whatsoever the "release"—a real misnomer, for it usually wanders afield harmonically and the tensions thus created are not released until the return of the "A" material. The over-all bipartite form (verse/chorus) resembles, and may well have derived from, the recitative/aria form of opera and operetta.

Another brilliant collaboration of the 1920's was that between George Gershwin (1898–1937) and his brother Ira (b. 1896). Together, they wrote some of the gayest musical-comedy scores of the decade, especially *Lady, Be Good* (1924), *Oh, Kay!* (1926), and *Funny Face* (1927), all seeming in retrospect to be preparation for the political satire *Of Thee I Sing* (1931), the first musical to weld together so firmly plot, dialogue, and music that it received the Pulitzer Prize for drama. Gershwin's later *Porgy and Bess* (1935), which he characterized as "folk opera—opera for the [popular] theatre, with drama, humor, song, and dance," was a more pretentious but hardly more artistically successful contribution. It relied mainly on some memorable songs (*Summertime, I Got Plenty o' Nuttin', It Ain't Necessarily So*) which displayed the same special characteristics as Gershwin's earlier show songs: beguiling rhythms (as in *Fascinating Rhythm,* 1923); unusual form (*Embraceable You,* 1928); and harmonic materials richer than those of most American popular songs (*The Man I Love,* 1924; *Liza,* 1929; *So Are You,* 1929).

That the boundary between cultivated- and vernacular-tradition American music was becoming blurred once again is suggested not only by the sophistication and artistry, albeit on a small scale, of many of the songs mentioned in the preceding paragraphs, together with their undeniable popular mass appeal, but by such a phenomenon as Gershwin's moving back and forth from popular to "serious" music, or the critical success of his musical comedy *Of Thee I Sing* alongside the popular success of his full-scale opera *Porgy and Bess.* More than a decade before the latter work, in fact, Gershwin had successfully introduced the idioms of Tin Pan Alley into the concert hall, first with *Rhapsody in Blue* (1924), a concerto-like work for piano and dance-band (later orchestrated more fully) that achieved unparalleled popularity. Belatedly, Gershwin conscientiously sought to learn some techniques of "classical" composition—the *Rhapsody* had been scored not by the composer but by Ferde Grofé (1892–1972)—and produced several other concert works, among them a Concerto in F (1925) for piano and orchestra and *An American in Paris* (1928) for orchestra alone. Three Preludes for piano (1926), smaller in scale and better controlled than the orchestral works, are unpretentious but charming trifles, among the very best "household music" of the 1920's.

CITY BLUES AND JAZZ

For many people, Americans and others alike, the most significant American music of the 1920's, the most indigenous and unprecedented, was jazz. Jazz had existed long before the 1920's, as had the special vocal styles and forms of blues, but only as an exclusively Negroid music unknown to the larger American community. What had been a music of and for Southern Negroes began to be diffused thanks to the earliest phonograph recordings (sporadically from 1917, then in greater numbers from 1923); the First World War (which found Negroes, jazz performers among them, spread over both North America and Europe);[11] commercial radio stations (from 1920); and the increased mobility of southern blacks, particularly in the direction of northern cities like Chicago, Detroit, and

---

[11] The best-known example is the 369th U.S. Infantry Jazz Band led by Lieutenant James Reese Europe (1881–1919) in France and briefly after the war in New York. Before the war, in New York, Europe had directed dance bands (Europe's Society Orchestra) and even concert groups like the Clef Club Symphony Orchestra (150 strong, including 50 mandolins, 30 harp-guitars, 10 banjos, and a saxophone along with other more conventional components of a "symphony" orchestra).

New York. In New York, especially, a massive influx of blacks and their concentration in the Harlem area of upper Manhattan was important in the development of jazz and its diffusion out to the white community. Harlem night-spots, with blues singers and jazz groups, were active inter-racial entertainment centers. A whole series of "black musicals" appeared "downtown," just off Broadway; important among them were the collaborations of Eubie Blake and Noble Sissle (b. 1889) in such shows as *Shuffle Along* (1921), *The Chocolate Dandies* (1924), and *Shuffle Along of 1933* (December, 1932 opening).

The surest sign of the impact of jazz on America at large was the appearance in the popular entertainment world of pseudo-jazz, like that of Paul Whiteman (1890–1967) and innumerable other dance-band leaders, and the characterization of the entire decade as "The Jazz Age." The end of the 1920's saw jazz recognized as a national phenomenon, though centered in the Negro ghettoes of Northern cities, notably Kansas City, Chicago, Detroit, and New York (besides, of course, Southern centers like New Orleans and Memphis). It saw the faithful emulation of black jazz musicians by whites, not just the diluted strains of "symphonic jazz"; it saw a whole new sub-industry of the phonorecording business ("race records"—jazz and blues recordings initially produced for and distributed to the American Negro community); it saw the beginnings of world interest in jazz as a new music; and it saw the first major shift in jazz style itself, from the small "combo" of early jazz to the "big band."

Early jazz was a synthesis of the march/dance beat and overlaid syncopations of ragtime; other kinds of syncopated dance rhythms of Afro-Caribbean origin; a rudimentary but dynamic harmony rooted in the Euro-American traditions of dance music and revival hymnody; and the expressive, flexible vocal style of various branches of American Negro song, such as the repetitive, chant-like, and usually responsorial work-song, the solitary field holler, the religious spiritual, and (hardly different from the last-named in musical style) the secular blues.

In the formally standardized, instrumentally accompanied form of "city blues" (as opposed to the formally unstandardized and earlier "country blues")[12] the blues was to become one of the two major foundations of 1920's jazz (the other being rags). Such city blues, as recorded by the "classic" female blues singers like Mamie Smith, Ma Rainey, Bessie Smith, and Ida Cox, tended to be strophic songs with a characteristic pattern to the text of each strophe, the succession of its accompanying harmonies, and the over-all musical form. Jazz musicians appropriated the *musical* design of such blues; from then on, "blues," whether with

---

[12] Some specific meanings for these two terms, so often used loosely, are given by Charles Keil, *Urban Blues* (Chicago: University of Chicago Press, 1966); see especially Chapter II and Appendix C.

text or not, was to mean that design. Basically, blues design is one of a twelve-measure pattern ("12-bar blues") divided into three four-measure phrases, with the harmonic progressions indicated below:

$$\begin{array}{c} 4 \\ 4 \end{array} \quad \begin{array}{cccc} \overline{1 \quad 2 \quad 3 \quad 4} & \overline{5 \quad 6 \quad 7 \quad 8} & \overline{9 \quad 10 \quad 11 \quad 12} \\ \text{I} \underline{\hspace{2cm}} & \text{IV} \underline{\hspace{0.3cm}} \text{I} \underline{\hspace{0.3cm}} & \text{V} \quad (\text{IV}) \quad \text{I} \underline{\hspace{0.5cm}} \end{array}$$

Other lengths than twelve measures are found, and elaborations of the basic harmonies are legion; I have indicated in measure 10 one of the most common in the 1920's; after that time, the general tendency was to add more and more elaborative variants to the scheme of harmonies, preserving however the twelve-measure structure and the principal harmonic pillars.

In vocal blues, the three phrases of song per stanza are super-imposed on this basic structure. Each phrase of the singer typically lasts for three measures of the four-measure unit, leaving a "hole" until the beginning of the next unit; this hole is filled, in a responsorial way per-haps going back to primordial call-and-response techniques, by some sort of instrumental or hummed or spoken response to the singer's phrase. The whole combination, then, might be suggested this way:

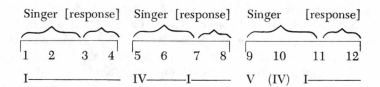

One particularly clear example (available in both a recording and a notated transcription)[13] among many that might be cited is the perfor-mance by Ferdinand "Jelly Roll" Morton (1885–1941) of *Mamie's Blues.* In an introduction to the music, spoken as he begins to play, Morton ex-plains that this is "no doubt the first blues [he] ever knew," which (if we can believe his memory) would place it back around the turn of the century.

If blues contributed to jazz one of its most common formal struc-tures, it contributed even more importantly to its instrumental style. Early blues *vocal* style was one of great variety and flexibility of intona-tion, mode of attack, tone color, vibrato, degree of nasality, regular

[13] Commodore Records album FL 30,000 (*New Orleans Memories*); Alan Lomax, *Mister Jelly Lord* (New York: Grosset and Dunlap [The Universal Library], 1950), pp. 269–71.

rhythm or rubato. These freedoms (from the viewpoint of a singer trained in the Euro-American cultivated tradition of art-song or opera) were partly inherent in the folkish lack of "sophistication" of the country blues singers, partly the result of vestiges of the primordial African style concepts of the American Negro. Significant for jazz in the vocalism of the blues was the transfer from voice to instrument of this blues style: the jazz instrumentalist, unbound by notions of "correct" performance on a trumpet, a trombone, a banjo or guitar, used his instrument as a substitute for, or an extension of, his voice, bringing to it the same broad range of expression as that of the blues singer's voice. The various narrowly prescriptive attempts that have been made to categorize the "blue notes" of jazz (usually vastly oversimplified as the flatted third and seventh of the major scale) arise from a preconception, dominated by the cultivated tradition's ideas of the musical scale and of instrumental performance technique, as to what is and what is not "basic" or "natural" in musical structure and style.

Rags were the other major source of the repertory of jazz in the 1920's, thanks to the broad popularity of ragtime as a kind of marching and dancing music early in the century. The historic first recordings of jazz, ironically made by the all-white performers of the Original Dixieland Jass (*sic*) Band (1917), included blues and rags in about equal measure, like *Livery Stable Blues* and *That Teasin' Rag.* So did the musically more significant recordings, from the middle 1920's, of the bands of Joseph "King" Oliver (1885–1938), Louis Armstrong (1900–1971), and Morton, such as the 1923 recordings by Oliver's Creole Jazz Band of *Dippermouth Blues* and *Snake Rag*, the 1925–26 recordings by Armstrong's Hot Five of *Royal Garden Blues* and *Muskrat Ramble* (the latter a rag composed by trombonist Edward "Kid" Ory [1886–1972]), and the 1926 recordings by Morton's Red Hot Peppers of *Jelly Roll Blues* and *Black Bottom Stomp.*

Jazz instrumentalists brought to the performance of ragtime the same flexible, vocalistic nuances of pitch and rhythm that they brought to the blues; thus, in performance style the two types of early jazz were equivalent. Within the frameworks of blues or ragtime forms, early jazz performances were built on a principle of improvisatory variation; in terms of the broad Euro-American Western tradition, the result was close to the Baroque era's "strophic variations," a chain of varied repetitions of a basic "tune." In jazz, the "tune" was more a matter of the underlying harmonies of an original piece than its melody, and virtually any music could *become* jazz, by adoption of its "tune" as the basis for improvisatorily varied repetitions in jazz style. Most of the early jazz recordings were made by New Orleans musicians, and despite attempts to challenge the legendary primacy of the Crescent City as the sole birth-

place of jazz, it remains important as the first major center. The New
Orleans jazz bands were typically small groups (combos) made up mainly
of clarinet, cornet, trombone, and drums, deriving from the military and
civic marching bands of the post-Civil War period. They played outdoors
for parades and funerals and, seated in placarded wagons, for advertising; indoors, in brothels, barrelhouses, and dance halls, with perhaps a
ragtime piano and a banjo or guitar added, for dancing. The ensemble
style, as heard typically in the first chorus (stanza) and the last, "ride-
out" chorus(es) of a piece, was a roughly contrapuntal music with the
powerful cornet projecting the main melodic voice, the clarinet weaving
a treble counter-melody, the trombone providing a solid but melodic bass,
and the drums and other instruments supplying the basic beat against
which raggy syncopations could work. Between first and last choruses,
individual musicians would play one or more improvisatory solo choruses
in succession.

Example 8-5 shows the improvisatory melodic style of such New
Orleans jazz, taken from a later recording (1947) by Louis Armstrong;
the example is chosen partly to suggest the absorption by jazz, as the
1920's closed, of a third formal pattern in addition to those of ragtime
and blues: that of the 32-measure chorus, in AABA design, of the popular songs of Tin Pan Alley. In Example 8-5, (a) is the original melody of
the pop song *Black and Blue* (1929), with its harmonies indicated. The
transcription of Armstrong's cornet melody (b) does not attempt to show
the nuances of pitch and tone-quality in his solo; it does however attempt to show rhythmic nuances, as Armstrong plays slightly earlier (+)
or later (−) the notes as indicated in the notated version.

EXAMPLE 8-5. (WHAT DID I DO TO BE SO) BLACK & BLUE by Andy Razaf,
Thomas Waller, and Harry Brooks. Copyright © 1929 by Mills Music, Inc.
Copyright renewed © 1957 by Mills Music, Inc. Used By Permission. (a) as
published; (b) as played by Louis Armstrong on the recording *Satchmo at
Symphony Hall* (Decca DL 8037); my transcription.

The 1920's saw the appearance of the first important non-Negro jazz musicians, beginning with the New Orleans Rhythm Kings, who went to Chicago in 1920. Later in the decade came Leon "Bix" Beider-becke (1903–1931) and the Wolverine band, and a number of Chicago musicians who, playing together from schoolboy days, have been called the "Austin High School gang." Among them were Bud Freeman and Frank Teschemacher (1906–1932), both players of the saxophone, an instrument which although not commonly used in New Orleans jazz was to become indispensable in later jazz groups. Other instruments assuming new importance in jazz of the late 1920's were the trumpet, replacing the more mellow but less brazen cornet; the guitar, replacing the earlier banjo; and the string bass, replacing the tuba of the brass bands.

Another important development in jazz of the 1920's was the formation of "big bands" rather than small "combos." Any group larger than, say, a half-dozen players needed some kind of musical arrangement, a plan of action, whether sketched out in notation or worked out empirically through rehearsals; it could not rely on the collective improvisation within the spare, linear contrapuntal texture of the small group. Early examples of such "arranged" jazz, which required a real composer or at least a dominant director and organizer, are the 1926 recordings of Jelly Roll Morton and his Red Hot Peppers. Even in their earliest works as a seven-man group (*Black Bottom Stomp, The Stomp,* and *Grandpa's Spells;* all recorded in 1926), it is clear (and there is documentary evidence to prove it) that the music was prepared with careful rehearsals. By 1929, Morton had enlarged his recording group to eleven (with results not so strikingly successful, however).

Three other pianists, each with a different orientation from Morton's (which was, of course, that of New Orleans jazz), were to prove themselves even more skilful leaders of big-band jazz in the 1920's. One was Fletcher Henderson (1898–1952), whose background was that of the New York dance-bands and Harlem jazz. Henderson's group was dominated by the ideas of saxophonist-arranger Don Redman, a conservatory graduate who developed a technique of scoring for the brass, reed, and rhythm sections of a big band that gave it the feeling of freedom, mobility, and relaxation of a small combo. He treated each section like a single voice and maintained an improvisatory style even in the most carefully worked-out arrangements; and individuals could still improvise freely over the arranged backgrounds of many choruses. Famous recorded examples of Henderson's early style are *Copenhagen* (1924) and *Sugar Foot Stomp* (1925), the latter based on King Oliver's *Dippermouth Blues;* in both performances, Louis Armstrong figures prominently. After Redman left the Henderson band in 1927 to become co-leader of a Detroit group (McKinney's Cotton Pickers), and after its leader was injured in an automobile accident in 1928, the Henderson group went into

decline. But, in the 1930's, its arrangements picked up by Benny Goodman and nationally popularized, it was to have a triumphant vindication.

Another pianist important in the development of successful big-
band style was Bennie Moten (1894–1935), whose six-piece group became
the most popular jazz combo in Kansas City in the early 1920's. Reflecting the Southwest origins and popularity of ragtime, Moten's band (as
heard on recordings from 1923 on) played very differently from either
the New Orleans or New York schools: it emphasized a heavy   beat,
even eighth-note rhythms, and frequent blues patterns. By 1926 Moten
was recording with a ten-piece band and had developed both an earthy,
rocking beat (*Kansas City Breakdown*) and a "pushy" rhythmic drive
based on the motoric ostinato cycles of boogie-woogie piano (*New Tulsa
Blues*). Out of this style was to develop the powerful "Kansas City"
swing style of the 1930's.

The last of the three progressive big-band pianist-leaders of the
1920's to be cited here—and, quite simply, one of America's greatest
composers—is Edward Kennedy ("Duke") Ellington (1899-1974). Initially
a leader of dance-bands in Washington, D.C., Ellington went to New York
in 1922. In 1924 he settled into the Kentucky Club with his band, the
Washingtonians; in the late 1920's and early 1930's he embellished (and
made famous) the Cotton Club. Ellington cut his first electrical recordings in 1926, with a twelve-piece band. An important element in roughen-
ing and individualizing the otherwise rather sweet, "white" dance-band
sound of the group was the plunger-mute technique and raspy "growl-
ing" of trumpeters James ("Bubber") Miley (1903–1932) and Joe ("Tricky
Sam") Nanton (1900–1946). Miley's original compositions and his ideas
on arranging for the band were also important in the crystallization of
the "Ellington sound," which, emphasizing at first so-called "jungle"
effects, was documented in the three major early works to be recorded:
East St. Louis Toodle-Oo, Black and Tan Fantasy, and *Creole Love Call*
(late 1926–early 1927). The last of these broadened even further the
group's sonorous palette by employing a wordless voice—that of Adelaide
Hall—as an extra instrument (as does *The Mooche* of 1928). Besides his
"jungle" pieces, Ellington also explored new jazz sonorities in bluesy
"mood" compositions like *Misty Mornin'* and *Awful Sad* (both recorded
1928), which seem in retrospect to have been precursors of the most famous such composition, *Mood Indigo* (1930). Ellington also sought rest-
lessly to expand and vary the conventional forms of jazz—which, at least
on recordings, were necessarily limited to the brief time-span (three
minutes and ten seconds) of a ten-inch, 78-revolutions-per-minute disc.
This search culminated first with the double-side composition *Creole
Rhapsody* (two versions completed by 1931); the stage was set for the
even larger and more complex works of later decades.

BIBLIOGRAPHICAL NOTES

A book that communicates vividly the sense of ferment in European music and the other arts in the period 1885–1918 is Roger Shattuck's *The Banquet Years* (Garden City: Doubleday Anchor Books, 1961). The most comprehensive general survey of early twentieth-century music is William Austin's *Music in the 20th Century* (New York: W. W. Norton and Company, Inc., 1966), although Eric Salzman's *Twentieth-Century Music: An Introduction* (2nd ed.; Englewood Cliffs: Prentice-Hall, Inc., 1974), written from a composer's standpoint, is more insightful on matters of style and musical thought.

Arthur Berger has written a sympathetic study of Copland's music (New York: Oxford University Press, 1953); Copland's own view of his early career is expressed in an autobiographical essay in *Our New Music* (see footnote 2), a book later revised and issued under the rather too-pretentious title *The New Music 1900–1960* (New York: W. W. Norton and Company, Inc., 1968). A useful bibliography of writings by and about Copland (and many others) is *Some Twentieth Century American Composers*, compiled by John Edmunds and Gordon Boelzner (2 vols.; New York: New York Public Library, 1959–60).

An authoritative biography of Varèse will be, when completed, that by his wife Louise: *Varèse: A Looking-Glass Diary* (New York: W. W. Norton and Company, Inc.); Volume I was published in 1972; it covers the years 1883–1928. Besides the article cited in footnote 7, Chou Wen-chung has published two brief but important articles on Varèse in *PNM*, V, 1 (Fall–Winter 1966); see also Milton Babbitt's "Edgard Varèse: A Few Observations of His Music," *PNM*, IV, 2 (Spring–Summer 1966). Robert P. Morgan draws startling parallels between Ives and Varèse and proposes that they "represent the true center of twentieth-century music" in his "Rewriting Music History: Second Thoughts on Ives and Varèse," *Musical Newsletter*, III, 1 and 2 (January and April 1973).

All too little of substance has been written on the history of musical comedy. One attempt, by now very much out of date, is Cecil Smith's *Musical Comedy in America* (New York: Theatre Arts Books, 1950); another is Lehman Engel's *The American Musical Theater; A Consideration* (New York: The Macmillan Company, 1967). Alec Wilder's *American Popular Song . . . 1900–1950* (see footnote 9) is unique in being the first book on the subject to deal exclusively—analytically and critically—with the music itself.

The best biographical account of Gershwin is Edward Jablonski and Lawrence D. Stewart, *The Gershwin Years* (Garden City: Doubleday and Company, Inc., 1958; many illustrations and facsimiles); a new edition is promised for 1974. One of the few insightful and serious attempts to discuss Gershwin's music is a little-known article by Frank C. Campbell, "The Musical Scores of George Gershwin," *Library of Congress Quarterly Journal of Current Acquisitions*, XI, 3 (May 1954), 127–39. Leonard Bernstein's "Why Don't You Run Upstairs and Write a Nice Gershwin Tune," reprinted from *The Atlantic Monthly* of April 1955 in *The Joy of Music* (New York: Simon and Schuster, 1959), is deceptively off-hand.

Robert Kimball and William Bolcom treat the lives of two leaders of the black musicals of the 1920's (whose careers also involved ragtime and jazz) in *Reminiscing with Sissle and Blake* (New York: The Viking Press, 1973); it is lavishly documented with photographs and facsimiles. Urban blues is discussed in an excellent book of that title by Charles Keil (Chicago: University of Chicago Press, 1966).

By far the best book on the stylistic development of jazz, with many transcriptions notated from recordings, is Gunther Schuller's *Early Jazz: Its Roots and Musical Development* (New York: Oxford University Press, 1968), the first volume in a two-volume study. Still valuable, in a field marked by great unevenness of bibliography, are Marshall Stearns's *The Story of Jazz* (New York: Oxford University Press, 1956; reissued as a Mentor paperback); Rudi Blesh's *Shining Trumpets* (2nd ed.; New York: Alfred A. Knopf, 1958); and André Hodeir's *Jazz: Its Evolution and Essence* (New York: Grove Press, 1956).

NINE

THE 1930's AND EARLY 1940's

The 1930's in American music were a complete contrast to the 1920's. The optimistic, progressive, strident voices of the 1920's were muted in the decade of the Great Depression. As Virgil Thomson wrote later in his autobiography, "The time was not for novelty." Copland, in a famous statment about the trend to simplicity in his own works of the 1930's, said:

> The old "special" public of the modern music concerts had fallen away, and the conventional concert public continued apathetic or indifferent to anything but the established classics. . . . I felt that it was worth the effort to see if I couldn't say what I had to say in the simplest possible terms.[1]

A characteristic gesture of the concert-music establishment was that of the Philadelphia Orchestra's management in announcing just before

---

[1] *Our New Music,* p. 229.

the 1932 season opened that "debatable" new music would be avoided on the orchestra's programs. Even the lusty voice of jazz was stilled after the stock market crash of 1929; with a few notable exceptions, it was not heard again for about six years, and then it spoke differently from before. This musical atmosphere of conservatism, probably due in largest part to the impact of the Great Depression, seems not to have been broken until after the end of World War II (1946); thus "the 1930's" as an era in American musical history actually extended to the mid-1940's.

THEMES OF THE PERIOD

Even if the most characteristic atmosphere of the period was one of a broad conservatism, the music of the Depression Era revealed several new and distinctive trends. Perhaps the strongest was a historical or regional Americanism. This was certainly related to the political and social thought of the era, its populist and collectivist temperament and its tendency to an American isolationism; the latter was reflected musically in a suspicious attitude toward the "Europe-ness" of the international new-music movement of the 1920's. One might speak of an "American Wave" in music of the 1930's as the art historians do of painters like Charles Burchfield, Edward Hopper, Thomas Hart Benton, and Grant Wood.

Closely related to this trend was a new and persistent preoccupation of composers with their relationship to the broad musical community and to society at large. The century's new mass media of communication (radio, phonorecordings, sound films, and [from late in the 1930's] television) had created a vast new potential audience for music, but a different one from the concert audiences of the past; many composers saw these media as a challenge to their ability to communicate on a broad scale. At the same time, conflicting impulses of individualism and integrity beset them; the role of the composer in an industrial society, wishing both to serve and be served by it, was an issue. As one major figure of American music of the 1930's, Roy Harris, put it: "How to serve society as a composer, how to become economically and socially recognized as a worth-contributing citizen, how to establish durable human contacts with individuals or groups is a harassing problem."[2]

One common way in the 1930's to become "economically recognized" was of course through trade-union organization; and in place of the idealistic and music-minded modern-music societies of the 1920's,

---

[2] "Problems of American Composers," in Henry Cowell (ed.), *American Composers on American Music* (1933; 2nd ed. New York: Frederick Ungar Publishing Co., 1962), p. 164; the entire essay reprinted in *ACS*, pp. 147–60.

composers of the 1930's banded together in hard-headed, economics-minded protective associations. In addition to the theretofore practically monopolistic American Society of Composers, Authors, and Publishers (ASCAP; organized 1914), the period saw the formation of the American Composers Alliance (ACA; organized 1937) and Broadcast Music. Inc. (BMI; organized 1939). Performers too became more solidly organized: the American Federation of Musicians (organized 1895) became ever more aggressively protective under its president, James C. Petrillo; the American Guild of Musical Artists (AGMA), organized in 1936, watched over the fortunes especially of singers, both soloists and choristers. Some aid to both composers and performers, during the depths of the Depression, was forthcoming from the government via the Federal Music Project of the Works Progress Administration. Created in 1935, by 1938 the Project was providing work for about 10,000 persons. Project-supported concerts, music lending libraries, and music education programs in rural and congested urban areas helped to broaden the American audience; programs of collecting folk and ethnic music stimulated interest in these fields. Composers were not, however, subsidized for free musical composition (as were painters under the Federal Art Project of the W.P.A.); they were assigned musical task of various sorts, with a few asked to supply music for documentary films.

The major works written by Aaron Copland during this 1930–1945 period reflect the themes I have cited: a conservative trend, a historical or regional Americanism, and a search to reach a broader public. Abstract music with the ferocity and astringency of the *Piano Variations* or *Vitebsk*, from the late '20's, was replaced with gentler, smoother, and generally more accessible works, virtually all of them on regional or topical themes.[3] The orchestral tone-poem *El Salón México* (1936) was based on popular-song material from south of the border. The ballet scores for *Billy the Kid* (1938) and *Rodeo* (1942) evoked the spirit of the Far West and included some skillfully re-composed cowboy tunes, while *Appalachian Spring* (1944) dealt with early nineteenth-century Pennsylvania rural life, expressed in country-fiddle-style tunes and hymn-like cantilenas and climaxing with some lucid variations on the Shaker-sect song *Simple Gifts*. In a cheerfully utilitarian spirit, Copland wrote works for amateur and school ensembles, like the high school play-opera *The Second Hurricane* (1937) and *An Outdoor Overture* (1938) for orchestra. For the new mass media he composed works like *Music for Radio* (1937; subtitled *A Saga of the Prairie*) and film scores for *The City* (1939), *Of Mice and Men* (1939), *Our Town* (1940), and *The Red Pony* (1948). The entry of the United States into World War II evoked several frankly

---

[3] The exceptions that proved the rule were two abstract sonatas, for piano (1939–41) and for violin and piano (1943), and *Statements* (1933–35) for orchestra, in which something of the acid bite of the *Piano Variations* is to be heard.

patriotic works from him, among them *Lincoln Portrait* (1942), which mingled Stephen Foster song-fragments and folk songs (notably *On Springfield Mountain*) with narrated excerpts from speeches of the Civil War president, and *Fanfare for the Common Man* (1942). The latter's wide-intervalled, jagged diatonic theme typified Copland's new melodic manner, one that somehow was inevitably associated with the broad plains and rugged mountains of the country, though it came from the pen of an urbane New York composer (Example 9-1).

EXAMPLE 9-1. A. Copland, *Fanfare for the Common Man* (1942), measures 1–16 (percussion omitted). Copyright 1943 by Aaron Copland. Reprinted by permission of Aaron Copland, Copyright Owner, and Boosey & Hawkes, Inc., Sole Publishers and Licensees.

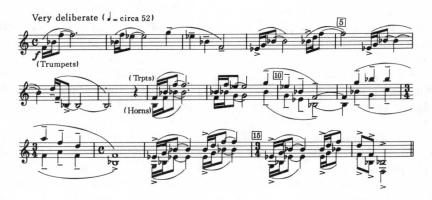

Most of these works were not only aimed at the broad new American audience; they drew from a wide spectrum of the American experience for subject matter and from the American past for musical materials. Indeed, the American musical past was generally viewed with new interest and re-evaluation during the period. In 1931 appeared the first really comprehensive history of American cultivated-tradition music, *Our American Music*, by John Tasker Howard (1890–1964). By 1946, so much new research had been done that Howard had to revise the book completely. Especially notable was the rediscovery (perhaps it would be more accurate to say the "discovery") of the music of Charles Ives—pianist John Kirkpatrick's 1939 performance of the "Concord" Sonata was a landmark—and of earlier American music, especially the eighteenth-century New England singing-school music and American folk music in general. These rediscoveries were reflected in the form of innumerable "Hoedowns," "Hayrides," "Square Dances," and the like, in a variety of media. Ross Lee Finney (b. 1906), a Middle Westerner trained under

Nadia Boulanger and Alban Berg in Europe, found inspiration in Colonial music for his choral work *Pilgrim Psalms* (1945), which drew on melodies from Ainsworth's psalter, and in Federal-era music for his orchestral *Hymn, Fuguing and Holiday* (1943), which went back to the Yankee tunesmiths, as did the *Prelude to a Hymn Tune (after William Billings)* (1937) of Otto Luening. Henry Cowell began a series of works titled *Hymn and Fuguing Tune* (1943–47). William Schuman (b. 1910) made use of an ubiquitous American children's call (phoneticized by him as "wee-awk-eee") in *American Festival Overture* (1939); his *William Billings Overture* (1943) drew from three singing-school pieces of the early Boston composer.

THOMSON, HARRIS, AND BLITZSTEIN

Three composers who shared a common background of study in the 1920's with Boulanger and who participated in the musical "American Wave" were Virgil Thomson, Roy Harris, and Marc Blitzstein. The first two were interested in America's musical past, Blitzstein in certain aspects of the present. Of Harris and Thomson, both Middle Westerners, Harris was the more aggressively "Americanist," but Thomson's music suggested an equally profound immersion in, and sympathy for, the American musical heritage; and his uses of it, which went back to the late 1920's, antedated other composers'.

Thomson once wrote a quotably succinct autobiographical note:

> I was born November 25, 1896 in Kansas City, Missouri, grew up there and went to war from there. That was the other war. Then I was educated some more in Boston and Paris. In composition I was a pupil of Nadia Boulanger. While I was still young I taught music at Harvard and played the organ at King's Chapel, Boston. Then I returned to Paris and lived there for many years, till the Germans came, in fact. Now I live in New York, where I am Music Critic of the *Herald Tribune* [from which he resigned in 1954].[4]

Thomson has called his *Sonata da Chiesa* (1926) for clarinet, trumpet, viola, horn, and trombone in three dissonant, neo-Baroque movements (Chorale, Tango, Fugue) a "bang-up graduation piece" from Boulanger's studio, but the inclusion of the popular dance rhythms of a tango suggests the impact of Satie and the younger French composers, as had

[4] Quoted in Peggy Glanville-Hicks, "Virgil Thomson," *MQ*, XXXV (1949), 210.

Two Sentimental Tangos (1923) and *Synthetic Waltzes* (1925). As early as 1926, however, Thomson, a Protestant and an organist, began to turn to American hymnody. One important result was a *Symphony on a Hymn Tune* (two movements sketched 1926; completed 1928). At about the same time he composed some pointedly irreverent and very funny *Variations and Fugues on Sunday School Tunes* (1927) for organ, and settings of several texts by Gertrude Stein, who had accepted Thomson as an artistically fastidious, amusing, and courageous fellow-expatriate in Paris (*Susie Asado*, 1926; *Capital, Capitals*, 1927). Thomson's Francophilia, his sophisticated, pseudo-innocent way with American hymn-book harmony, his respect for language, his wit, and his close relation with Stein were to result in one of the most extraordinary works of American music: the opera *Four Saints in Three Acts*, first produced by the Friends and Enemies of Modern Music of Hartford, Connecticut in 1934. Stein's own account of the genesis of the work runs like this:

> Virgil Thomson had asked Gertrude Stein to write an opera for him. Among the saints there were two saints whom she had always liked better than any others, Saint Theresa of Avila and Ignatius Loyola, and she said she would write him an opera about these two saints. She began this and worked very hard at it all that spring [1927] and finally finished Four Saints and gave it to Virgil Thomson to put to music. He did. And it is a completely interesting opera both as to words and music.[5]

Four Saints is a work of fantasy, liveliness, and inexplicable charm. Impossible to interpret literally, equally impossible to dismiss as meaningless, it offers a child-like, surrealistic procession of tableaux about saints (many more than four) doing what we suppose saints do: receiving visitors, posing for earthly reproductions, discussing human problems and saintly ones too, loving Christ, rejoicing. Thomson's setting is similarly child-like: "With meanings already abstracted, or absent, or so multiplied that choice among them was impossible . . . you could make a setting for sound and syntax only, then add, if needed, an accompaniment equally functional," he said;[6] and he composed deceptively simple music which both supports discreetly and projects impeccably the verses of Stein. The original chamber orchestration of nineteen players is dominated by the sound of an accordion, which gives a pungent reediness to the successions of plain chords that characterize the harmony. The very beginning of the Prologue establishes the tone of affected yet effective simplicity, with a waltz vamp underlying a metrically variable

---

[5] *The Autobiography of Alice B. Toklas* (New York: Harcourt, Brace & Co., 1933), p. 281.
[6] Thomson, *Virgil Thomson* (New York: Alfred A. Knopf, 1966), p. 90.

exhortation by the chorus, in crystal-clear octaves, to "prepare for [four?] saints" (Example 9-2). Saint Theresa is introduced with affectionate

EXAMPLE 9-2. V. Thomson, *Four Saints in Three Acts* (1934), measures 1–8. Quoted by permission of Beekman Music. Inc.

malice as one who pontificates repetitiously about the obvious ("There are a great many persons and places near together"); Thomson's music leads to a neo-Handelian climax marked "Grandioso (liberamente)." A celebrated Vision of the Holy Ghost ("Pigeons on the grass alas") begets strangely moving music. A Saints' Procession finds Thomson retiring almost completely into the background, allowing Stein's leaden processional ("In wed in dead/in dead wed led/in led wed dead") to plod solemnly across the stage, over sustained chords. Ultimately the work defies description and perhaps analysis; as John Cage has sensitively written: "To enjoy it, one must leap into that irrational world from which it sprang, the world in which the matter-of-fact and the irrational are one, where mirth and metaphysics marry to beget comedy."[7]

Historically, *Four Saints* more than any other single work offered a model for the new simplicity in American music of the 1930's and suggested how the triadic harmony of the American past could be used with fresh incisiveness: as Thomson commented in his saucy survey of

[7] Kathleen Hoover and John Cage, *Virgil Thomson: His Life and Music* (New York: T. Yoseloff, 1959), p. 157.

The State of Music in 1939, it had music that was "simple, melodic, and harmonious . . . after twenty years of everybody's trying to make music just a little bit louder and more unmitigated and more complex than anybody else's." A similar artful simplicity pervades the later Stein-Thomson collaboration, *The Mother of Us All* (1947), although that opera is "fatter" than *Four Saints* in almost every respect.

Thomson was the first major American composer of concert music to write for films. But he did not enter the highly specialized and, for a concert-music composer, infinitely frustrating musical wing of the Hollywood industry; he wrote instead scores for several government-sponsored documentary films: two produced by Pare Lorentz, *The Plow that Broke the Plains* (1936) and *The River* (1937), and a wartime propaganda film for the Office of War Information, *Tuesday in November* (1945). His best-known film score, for Robert Flaherty's *Louisiana Story* (1948), was similarly composed for a documentary, produced by the Standard Oil Company. In all these, Thomson's sympathy for American folk and vernacular-tradition music was apparent: *The Plow* draws on cowboy songs; *The River* on white spirituals from *Southern Harmony* and *The Sacred Harp; Tuesday in November* on waltzes, hymns, and *Yankee Doodle; Louisiana Story* on the Acadian ("Cajun") songs and dances of the bayou country.

Roy Harris (b. 1898) was another of the early pupils of Boulanger (1926–29). A prolific composer, by the early 1940's he had produced a vast number of works in almost all media except opera. From his Op. 1, a Piano Sonata (1928–29), Harris's style seemed firmly and idiosyncratically established: it was marked by expansive, rolling melodies, often modal but equally often chromatic; bichordal harmony of an immediately recognizable sort; contrapuntal textures and devices of all kinds; and a sense of form that avoided the neo-Classic types popular in the 1930's with many composers, but did include neo-Baroque principles like fugue, ostinato, and passacaglia. Harris displayed his Americanist interests in works like the *Folksong Symphony*, No. 4 (1940); the orchestral overture *When Johnny Comes Marching Home* (1934), based on a Civil War song and divided precisely in two halves to fit the sides of a 78-revolutions-per-minute phonorecord; *Gettysburg Address Symphony*, No. 6 (1944); *Railroad Man's Ballad* (1941) for chorus and orchestra; and *American Ballads* (1942) for piano. Many works, however, were musically abstract, like the two which some still consider, almost four decades later, to be his most masterly: the Quintet for Piano and Strings (1936) and the Third Symphony in One Movement (1938). Characteristic of the long-breathed melodic line of Harris is the theme of the second ("lyric") section of the symphony: very chromatic, uncertainly focused on any single tonic note; fluid in tempo, phrase-length, meter, and dynamics but even-paced in rhythm, it seems boundless, a grand rhetorical prose-like utterance (Example 9-3a). In sharp contrast is the terse, motive-filled, energetic yet asymmetrical subject of the fugal section of the symphony; not identifiably related to anyone else's music, its internal cross-rhythms and ambiguous meter nevertheless stamp it as "Made in the U.S.A." (Example 9-3b). The "pastoral" section of the Third Symphony is justly famous for

EXAMPLE 9-3. R. Harris, *Third Symphony in One Movement* (New York: G. Schirmer, Inc., 1939). Quoted by permission. (a) "Lyric" theme (measures 60–97). (b) "Fugue" subject (measures 416–21).

its "seemingly endless succession of spun-out melodies" (the phrase is Copland's); few seem to have noticed its basis in a bellows-like ostinato figure, expanding and contracting in the bass, or its carefully planned polychordal harmony, gradually increasing in density, resonance, and tension until it bursts into the resolute fugue. The Piano Quintet is less originally shaped; it represents the more retrospective, contrapuntal turn of Harris's mind with its three movements, Passacaglia, Cadenza, and (triple) Fugue.

If works like Thomson's *Hymn Tune Symphony* and Harris's *Folksong Symphony* posited a new rapprochement between concert music and the music of America's older vernacular and folk traditions, several works for the lyric theater by Marc Blitzstein (1905–1964) did the same for contemporaneous popular music. Especially in *The Cradle Will Rock* (1937) and *No For an Answer* (1941), Blitzstein, taking a cue from the musico-dramatic style of works by Berthold Brecht and Kurt Weill, particularly *Die Dreigroschenoper* (which Blitzstein later translated), raised the Broadway musical to an exquisitely calculated level of harsh refinement. Both works were morality plays written from the leftist, trade-unionist viewpoint; both might be seen as modern ballad operas based on the style of the American pop song and the speech of the American streets; both were deceptively "easy" works; and neither could have been composed by anybody without the thorough training (both with Schoenberg in Berlin and Boulanger in Paris) and high intelligence of Blitzstein. Preferring to call these works "plays with music," Blitzstein cunningly built up substantial scenes with a unique combination of spoken dialogue, precisely rhythmic speech (notated in score), and song; take any of these elements away, and much of the peculiar power of their blend is lost. "Penny Candy," from *No For an Answer*, is a murderous satire on a do-gooder's morbid curiosity about addiction; without its preliminary monologue, spoken over a sparse, dry accompaniment, the song itself seems only silly. Yet even the briefest excerpt of "Honolulu," from *The Cradle Will Rock*, can suggest Blitzstein's subtle transformation of popular song style: the clichés of the vocal line are cancelled out by the freshness of the accompaniment, with its irregular texture underlying the first four phrases; its hint of Hawaiian steel guitars under "-lulu" and "banned"; its offbeat accentuation of the bass under the raucous refrain; and its acrid inversion of a dominant ninth under "isle" (Example 9-4).

Blitzstein was committed to an ideal of moral persuasion in his art. One of the songs in *The Cradle Will Rock* summarizes his scorn for other ideals:

> *Art for Art's sake,*
> *It's smart, for Art's sake,*
> *To part, for Art's sake,*
> *With your mind, for Art's sake,*
> *Be blind, for Art's sake,*
> *And deaf, for Art's sake,*
> *And dumb, for Art's sake,*
> *Until, for Art's sake,*
> *They kill, for Art's sake,*
> *All the Art for Art's sake.*[8]

This was a point of view common enough among socially conscious, leftist artists of the 1930's. But periodic revivals of *The Cradle Will Rock*

[8] Quoted by permission of the Estate of Marc Blitzstein.

as well as the success of his later (and more elaborate) opera *Regina* (1949) and his powerful translation and adaptation of the Brecht-Weill *Three Penny Opera* (1952) suggest that it was not so much the message as the music that was significant in Blitzstein's art.

EXAMPLE 9-4. Blitzstein, "Honolulu," *The Cradle Will Rock* (1937), measures 1–13. Quoted by permission of the Estate of Marc Blitzstein.

THE COMPOSER-PROFESSORS

Reflective of a new approach to the education of musicians (and, more profoundly, of the fact that few composers could make a living by composing), many of the most highly esteemed composers of the period occupied professorial chairs in American universities. Roger Sessions (b. 1896) was at Princeton and then at the University of California at Berkeley (later to return to Princeton). His early studies at Harvard and Yale linked him with the academic tradition of the Second New England School, but more significant in his development were two years (1919–21) with the Swiss-American composer Ernest Bloch (1880–1959). In the 1930–1945 period, Sessions's style was moving from the diatonic neo-Classicism of his First Symphony (1927) and First Piano Sonata (1930), through the more chromatic and expressionistic manner of a Violin Concerto (1935) and a First String Quartet (1936), to the highly chromatic, long-lined, dense-textured, and almost serialized Second Piano Sonata (1946) and Second Symphony (1946). Walter Piston (b. 1894) was at Harvard (from which he retired in 1960), writing an elegant if icy neo-Classic music mostly in abstract, traditional instrumental forms. A some-time pupil of Boulanger (1924–26), he reinterpreted her French scholastic pedagogy in several influential textbooks: *Principles of Harmonic Analysis* (1933), *Harmony* (1941), *Counterpoint* (1947), and *Orchestration* (1955). Roy Harris moved from institution to institution. Quincy Porter (1897–1966) taught at Vassar and the New England Conservatory, then (1946) returned to Yale, where he had begun as a pupil of Horatio Parker. He was emphatically a composer of chamber music, e.g., ten string quartets, in an international style. Douglas Moore (1893–1969) was at Columbia and well into a career emphasizing operas on American subjects: *The Headless Horseman* (1936) and *The Devil and Daniel Webster* (1939) were to be followed after World War II by the highly successful, musically nostalgic opera *The Ballad of Baby Doe* (1956) and another, *Carry Nation* (1966). William Schuman was at Sarah Lawrence College, Ross Lee Finney at Smith College.

The presence on college and university campuses of these and other eminent composers reflected the fact that, especially in institutions beyond the eastern seaboard, the professional training of young musicians, formerly limited typically, as in Europe, to the conservatories, was being taken up by academic institutions. The major conservatories in the U.S.A., such as the Juilliard School in New York, Peabody Conservatory in Baltimore, the Curtis Institute in Philadelphia, and the New England Conservatory in Boston, still offered the most thorough professional training. But more and more the colleges and universities, better endowed than the small conservatories, assumed the function of training ground for musicians. This was to have broad ramifications in the post-World War II years in the development of college instrumental ensembles and opera workshops of remarkably high calibre, and the establishment of professional performing groups, soloists, and composers "in residence." But before the war, the picture was dominated by the composer-professors, attempting to maintain their integrity as composers while employed as full-time professors.[9]

To many colleges and universities in the 1930's, furthermore, came refugees from Europe during the Nazi and Fascist regimes. The 1940's opened with such composers in America as Stravinsky, Schoenberg, Hindemith, Bartók, Weill, Krenek, Martinu, Wolpe, and Milhaud, most of whom

[9] Sessions has offered some sober speculations on the composer as professor in a "Conversation With Roger Sessions," *PNM*, IV, 2 (Spring–Summer 1966), 29–46. Twenty-three American composers confront the matter, in as many essays, in "The Composer in Academia: Reflections on a Theme of Stravinsky," *College Music Symposium,* X (1970), 55–98.

were soon attached to college music departments. Their very presence contributed to a breakdown of the American tendency of the period to a musical isolationism and ultimately to a new role for the United States after World War II as international leader of progressive trends in Western music. Among other side-effects of the emigration of European musicians to America was the stimulus it provided for the establishment of musicology as an accepted discipline in American universities: although a chair of musicology had been created in 1930 for Otto Kinkeldey (1878–1966) at Cornell, it was really the impact of such newly-arrived European musicologists of the stature of Alfred Einstein, Curt Sachs, Hans David, Karl Geiringer, Leo Schrade, and others that led to a rapid development of musicological curricula in American universities and to the consolidation of the American Musicological Society (established 1934) and the Music Library Association (1931).

YOUNGER COMPOSERS OF THE PERIOD

If the composer-professors typified the basic conservatism of the 1930–1945 period, so did the rise to prominence of fundamentally conservative young composers as opposed to vanguardists. The acknowledged young leaders were probably Samuel Barber, Gian-Carlo Menotti, William Schuman, and an "Eastman School group."

Barber (b. 1910) demonstrated a conservative lyricism in his earlist works: songs and choral pieces, and an impassioned setting for voice and string quartet of Matthew Arnold's *Dover Beach* (1933). He adapted an easy, cantabile vocal line to instrumental works like the Sonata for Violoncello and Piano (1932) and to two orchestral pieces that achieved a *succès d'estime* when, alone among American compositions, they were performed by the ultra-conservative Arturo Toscanini and the NBC Symphony Orchestra: *Essay for Orchestra*, No. 1, and A*dagio for Strings* (both 1938; the *Adagio* arranged from an earlier string quartet). Despite some absorption of Stravinskyan textures in a work like *Capricorn Concerto* (1944) and of Schoenbergian chromaticism in a Piano Sonata (1949), Barber's style continued along a neo-Romantic, "expressive" path. One of the most poignant exemplars of that style, partly because of the warm nostalgia of its text by James Agee, is *Knoxville: Summer of 1915* (1948) for voice and orchestra, in a characteristically accessible rondo-like form.

A close associate of Barber from their days together as students at the Curtis Institute was Gian-Carlo Menotti (he was to be the librettist for Barber's elaborately Victorian opera *Vanessa* [1958] and the chamber opera *A Hand of Bridge* [1959]). By the mid-1940's Menotti (b. 1911 in

Italy; to America 1927) had successfully bridged the gap between the opera house and Broadway: after modest successes with *Amelia al Ballo* (produced in 1937 in English translation) and *The Old Maid and the Thief* (1939), his intense and spooky short opera *The Medium* (1946), preceded by a curtain-raising skit, *The Telephone,* began in 1947 a durable career as competitor to the spoken dramas of the Broadway playhouses. Menotti combined the theatrical sense of a popular playwright and a Pucciniesque musical vocabulary with an Italianate love of liquid language and a humane interest in characters as real human beings; the result was opera more accessible than anyone else's at the time. Writing his own librettos, Menotti had a knack for choosing timeless themes of human conflict in topical settings: two later operas, both cannily full of *coups de théâtre, The Consul* (1950) based on the frustrations of life under a bureaucracy, and a Christmastide fantasy, *Amahl and the Night Visitors* (1951; commissioned for television performance), were to become even greater popular successes than *The Medium.*

William Schuman was mentioned earlier (p. 203) as a participant in the "American Wave" of the 1930's. *American Festival Overture* was followed by other works on American themes, such as the baseball opera *The Mighty Casey* (1953) and the cantata after Walt Whitman, *A Free Song* (1943). Schuman also wrote several big works for wind band, among them *Newsreel (in Five Shots)* (1941) and *George Washington Bridge* (1950). These were a response to the immense proliferation of bands in schools and colleges across the land. The marching band, most often in evidence between the halves of intercollegiate football games, had once again become a major voice of American vernacular-tradition music. This revival of the band's popularity was accompanied, however, by cultivated-tradition ideals of polished performance. An old problem of bands, their uncertain instrumentation, was disappearing as a more or less standardized instrumentation emerged. After the football season the marching bands, often retitled "symphonic wind ensembles," became concert-giving organizations. Good contemporary music was needed for them. Schuman was not alone in helping to fill the demand: among others, Thomson contributed *A Solemn Music* and *At the Beach* (both 1949); Harris the overture *Cimarron* (1941), *Take the Sun and Keep the Stars* (1944), and *Fruit of Gold* (1949); Barber a *Commando March* (1943).

More important in Schuman's output were orchestral symphonies, string quartets, and choral works. A pupil of Harris, Schuman shared with him a fondness for either rhapsodic or ostinato forms, long chromatic slow themes, and polychordal harmony. Schuman's rhythms, however, tended to be more nervously athletic than Harris's, more clearly related to pop-music origins, and his orchestration brighter, more sharp-edged with brass and metal-percussion instruments. Two excerpts from his

Symphony for Strings (1943), the first also a part of his *Three-Score Set* for piano (1943), can suggest respectively Schuman's resonant bichordal harmony and his energetic, stuttering fast-movement rhythms (Example 9-5).

EXAMPLE 9-5. W. Schuman, *Symphony for Strings* (New York: G. Schirmer, Inc., 1943). Quoted by permission. (a) 2nd movement, measures 1–4. (b) 3rd movement, measures 1–11 (1st violin part only).

Several other younger composers of promise in the late 1930's and early '40's were graduates of the Eastman School of Music at the University of Rochester, under Howard Hanson's direction; they had studied either with Hanson or with Bernard Rogers (1893–1968). This "Eastman Group" included Robert Palmer (b. 1915), Robert Ward (b. 1917), William Bergsma (b. 1921), and Peter Mennin (b. 1923). All shared the relatively conservative, evolutionary attitudes of their mentors; all seemed to share an aim to write the Great American Symphony by way of the Depression-era Overture, a one-movement piece ten minutes in length or less, with at least one section of broadly arching, wide-intervalled, mostly diatonic melody supported by slow-moving, rich harmony. The latter, although functional and directive, avoided structures like dominant sevenths or ninths and diminished-seventh chords; non-tertial sonorities replaced them, as did sometimes triads or added-tone chords derived from diatonic (but not major) modes.

Related to these Eastman composers in his general style, but possessing the lyric gifts of a Barber as well, was Norman Dello Joio (b. 1913), a prolific composer on whose works was stamped the impress of his Italianate background and of his training under Paul Hindemith. Also related to the Eastman School (if only as a sometime student there) is David Diamond (b. 1915), whose first major orchestral work, *Symphony in One Movement* (1931), was premiered at Eastman while he was a special student of violin there. Diamond left the school after a year's study with Rodgers (1933–34) to seek a more progressive atmosphere. He worked with both Sessions and Boulanger and lived for many years in Florence, Italy (1953–65). A prolific, professional composer with eight symphonies, ten string quartets, and many other works in all media to his credit, Diamond gained many performances of works like *Psalm* (1936) for orchestra, *Elegy in Memory of Maurice Ravel* (1938–39), and—his most frequently performed piece—*Rounds* (1944) for string orchestra, all in a lyrical, but intense, and finely crafted personal style.

The only strong avant-garde impulse during the period was felt on the West Coast: there, carrying on where Henry Cowell had begun, younger composers like John Cage and Lou Harrison (b. 1917) interested themselves in percussion music, non-Western scales, and new means of formal organization; an older one, Harry Partch (1901-1974), pursued a lonely path to a whole new theory of music based on division of the octave into 43 tones. Partch codified his theory in detail in the book *Genesis of a New Music* (1949).

Cage (b. 1912) studied with both Cowell and Schoenberg. In a foreword to a catalogue of his works, he summarized "the various paths my musical thought has taken"; those of the period before World War II were:

> . . . chromatic composition dealing with the problem of keeping repetitions of individual tones as far apart as possible (1933–34); composition with fixed rhythmic patterns or tone-row fragments (1935–38); composition for the dance, film and theatre (1935–   ); composition within rhythmic structures (the whole having as many parts as each unit has small parts, and these, large and small, in the same proportion) (1939–56); intentionally expressive composition (1938–51). . . .[10]

Few people in the period were aware of Cage as an early exponent of Schoenberg's tone-row technique, or as a composer who applied rather similar principles to the organization of rhythm. Many more were familiar with Cage's "prepared piano." "Preparation" meant the alteration of the instrument's tonal quality by inserting between the strings various bits of material; the preparation varied depending on the expressive aim. The sonorous result was not unlike an Indonesian orchestra of gongs and delicate percussion. "The need to change the sound of the instrument arose

[10] *John Cage* (New York: Henmar Press Inc., 1962), p. 5.

through the desire to make an accompaniment, without employing percussion instruments, suitable for the dance . . . for which it was to be composed," is Cage's comment on the first prepared-piano piece, *Bacchanale* (1938).[11] Cage's most extended work for prepared piano, the seventy-minute *Sonatas and Interludes* (1946-48), aims to express the various "permanent emotions" of (East) Indian tradition; his interest in the Orient, later to be decisive in his musical thought, was already apparent. Two movements for prepared piano flank two all-percussion trios in *Amores* (1943), and Cage's interest in what Varèse had called "sound—any sound" led him to write a number of all percussion pieces, adding to the more or less conventional instruments such new sound-sources as recordings of constant and variable pitch-frequency, sound-generator whines, and other mechanical and electronic devices (*Imaginary Landscape No. 1;* 1939).

JAZZ: SWING AND BOP

Jazz of the 1930's underwent a major change in style from that of the 1920's. For most of the pre-World War II period, in fact, the very term "jazz" implied the earlier style, the "hot jazz" of the '20's. The newer style was called "swing," the word perhaps derived from a 1932 recording of Duke Ellington's band with singer Ivy Anderson: *It Don't Mean a Thing if It Ain't Got That Swing.* The swing style was materializing in the late 1920's and early '30's, but most Americans did not hear it until about 1935. In the intervening years, between the financial crash and the mid-1930's, the strident, earthy music of New Orleans jazz was out of fashion: America in crisis seemed to want rather to be lulled by the soothing sounds of radio crooners, like Rudy Vallee (b. 1901) and Bing Crosby (b. 1904), and of non-jazz dance-bands like Guy Lombardo's and Wayne King's. Some bands, however, found a way to compromise between the large, euphonious, popular dance-band and the improvisatory, "swinging" manner of jazz: thus did the new jazz reach the ears of the public (partly through several popular late-evening radio programs, like "Let's Dance" and "The Camel Caravan," the former sponsored by a cracker-manufacturing corporation, the latter by a cigarette company).

The main vehicle for swing was the big band—even bigger than those developed in the later 1920's. As Benny Goodman (b. 1909), the clarinetist whose band more than any other helped to popularize swing, explains it in his autobiography:

[11] *Ibid.,* p. 15.

It was about this time [1934], or maybe just a little earlier, that large bands became standardized with five brass, four saxes, and four rhythm. . . . Ten men . . . used to be considered the limit of even a large dance orchestra.[12]

In the new big-band style, the individual voices of earlier jazz combos were replaced by three "sections," one of brass instruments (trumpets and trombones), one of reeds (saxes, doubling occasionally on clarinets), and one of rhythm instruments (typically guitar, double bass, piano, and drums). Too unwieldy to permit either the casual approach to form or the collective improvisation of early jazz, the big swing band of the 1930's relied on written arrangements. Increasingly, jazz improvisation became a matter of solos set off against an arranged background music. Models for such arrangements were found in the earlier work of Fletcher Henderson and Duke Ellington, and in the arrangements for Jimmy Lunceford's band made by Sy Oliver between 1933 and 1939. These men could simulate an improvisatory style in their written-out, repetitive "riffs" for full band. Moreover, the sections did not play the notes exactly as written; through many rehearsals they shaped the written arrangements into an even more improvisatory, swinging style.[13] Partly because of the new necessity to be able to read music, partly because of the richly harmonized ensemble arrangements, and partly because the swing band had to play not only the older jazz "standards" but also the harmonically more sophisticated popular songs, the chordal vocabulary of jazz musicians expanded. This was reflected in more adventurously chromatic solo improvisations.

The rhythmic basis of swing was a strong, even $\frac{4}{4}$ ("solid" was a favorite adjective of the period) as opposed to the tendency of earlier jazz to march along in $\frac{2}{2}$. Swing drummers typically overlaid the regular thumping four-beats-to-the-measure of the bass drum with a slight emphasis on beats 2 and 4 through a conventional pattern (♩ ♪♪ ♩♩ ♪♪♩ | ♩) played with drumstick or wire brush on a high-hat cymbal, with totally different effect from the accents on beats 1 and 3 of early jazz. One of the first drummers to establish this convention was Chick Webb (1902–1939), but it was more closely identified with the "Kansas City style" of jazz as played by the bands of Bennie Moten and his successor, William "Count" Basie (b. 1904). Basie's band, along with Ellington's, was probably the most influential of all in establishing the swing style, but nation-

[12] *The Kingdom of Swing* (Harrisburg: Stackpole Sons, 1939), p. 138.
[13] The use of "square" as a term of opprobrium came into existence during the era as a precise description of the way swing was *not* to be played. To the degree that soloists and even whole sections did not round off notated rhythms and pitches in an improvisatory, feelingful way, they were "square."

ally the style was diffused by the bands of white leaders like Goodman, Tommy Dorsey (1905–1956), Artie Shaw (b. 1910), and Glenn Miller (1904–1944), perhaps mainly because discriminatory practices made it difficult for the Negro bands to get the same degree of exposure to the mass audience.

The swing style bred virtuosos, stars who improvised brilliantly over the background riffs of the big bands' "sidemen." Some of the misplaced values of any star system were evident in the development of swing, as the star players seemed to be trying to play as fast or as high, or both, as possible. The so-called "screech trumpet" of a Maynard Ferguson, star soloist with the huge, colorful band of Stan Kenton (b. 1912), was symptomatic, as was the dazzling piano virtuosity of Art Tatum (1910–1956). Typical of a trend to choose ever faster tempos for fast pieces, Benny Goodman's trio (which included Negro pianist Teddy Wilson [b. 1912] and thus helped initiate a breakdown of "segregated" jazz) recorded *After You've Gone* in 1944 at $\downarrow = 165$, thereby shortening the first chorus by ten seconds compared to their 1935 recording of the same piece at $\downarrow = 120$. With such virtuosity, and with a transcontinental popularity bred in radio stations, recording studios, and on the stages of movie houses (where swing bands appeared increasingly "in person"), jazz began to be more than just a functional music to dance to or to drink to: it became a concert music as well. In 1938, Goodman's band appeared in concert at New York's Carnegie Hall; since that time, jazz as concert music has become commonplace and the balance between its use as utilitarian music and as a new kind of art-music has swung increasingly toward the latter.

In the early 1940's, several further developments took place. All can be viewed as reactions to certain aspects of jazz in the '30's, especially the very "bigness" of the big swing bands and the pressures on such bands to cater to public and commercial taste. The development of a concert culture for jazz meant a broadening of its base of patronage; but, just as in the development of a concert culture in art-music a century or more earlier, one result was a growing lag between the musical thought of the advanced performer and of his public. After-hours "jam sessions," in which jazz musicians played for each other rather than for the public, became important proving grounds for new jazz expression. The style of "bebop" (or simply "bop"), which emerged in New York early in the 1940's, owed its origin to such exclusive and selfconsciously progressive music-making.

Among the leaders in the crystallization of the bop style were saxophonist Charles ("Bird") Parker (1920–1955)—along with Armstrong and Ellington one of the three most significant inventors in the history

of jazz—trumpeter John ("Dizzy") Gillespie (b. 1917), and drummer
Kenny Clarke (b. 1914). Parker, especially, evolved a melodic style that
was asymmetrically phrased, chromatic, and built up by surprising combinations of the briefest ejaculatory motifs and very long, very fast, looping lines. Bop drummers like Clarke and Max Roach (b. 1925) gave up the
incessant four-beat thudding bass drum of the swing style, reserving the
instrument for occasional "bombs" dropped irregularly into a new, top-
cymbal-dominated, shimmering background beat. One of the most common conceits of bop musicians was to base a piece on the harmonies of
a well-known song, but to substitute for its original melody a new one in
bop style and then to retitle the work. Thus, only the really knowledge-
able would recognize Gillespie and Parker's *Anthropology* as a reworking
of Gershwin's *I Got Rhythm*, or Gillespie's *Groovin' High* as the old
popular song *Whispering* (1920) without the original melody. Example
9-6 shows the beginning of *Whispering* and of its bop derivative, *Groovin'
High*, transcribed from the 1945 recording of Gillespie and Parker. The
curt two-note figure that opens *Groovin' High* is a characteristic bop motif;
some say that the term "bebop" originated as an imitation of such figures.

EXAMPLE 9-6. A bop-style melody and its source. (a) W/M John Schon-
berger, Richard Coburn, and Vincent Rose. Copyright 1920 MILLER MUSIC
CORPORATION, New York, N.Y. Copyright renewal 1948 MILLER MUSIC COR-
PORATION and Fred Fisher Music Co., Inc. for the United States and Canada.
Rights throughout the rest of the world controlled by MILLER MUSIC CORPORA-
TION. Used by Permission. (b) Dizzy Gillespie, *Groovin' High*. After a transcrip-
tion of Rondolette recording A-11 by Frank Tirro.

Note: In Gillespie's performance, ♩♩ = approximately ♪♪, more precisely ♪♪

Also in the 1940's occurred a revival of the Dixieland style of early jazz. This was first noticeable on the West Coast, where the Yerba Buena band of Lu Watters (b. 1911) made some recordings in faithful imitation of the early discs of Louis Armstrong. Actually, the New Orleans jazz revival was but one of many signs of a growing American nostalgia for the 1920's: before long, young Americans were once again dancing the Charleston and getting their parents raccoon coats out of mothballs, aggressively acting out their rosy imaginings of life in the prosperous, "secure" 1920's.

MUSICAL COMEDY AND POPULAR SONG

With the rapid rise of sound films, during the 1930's, to a favored position among public entertainment media, the Broadway musical was threatened by the film musical of Hollywood, which could lavish more money on a single show and thus produce even more star-studded, eye-popping, mind-boggling spectaculars than Ziegfeld had offered in his Follies. Musically, however, the Hollywood musical offered nothing new. Nor did the theater musical of the 1930's immediately strike out on any new paths. Nevertheless, it tended to give increasing emphasis to the dramatic element and to span, in its songs, a greater range of emotional and psychological expression. And, now and then, some of the social preoccupations of other American arts (and music) were visible in it, as in Harold Rome's *Pins and Needles* (1937), the opening number of which (*Sing Me a Song of Social Significance*) ushered onstage a cast drawn entirely from theater classes of the International Ladies' Garment Workers Union.

Among the musical comedy figures to be lured to Hollywood were the Gershwins, who left New York for California after *Porgy and Bess* (see p. 188). They seemed on the way to a series of successful film musicals (beginning with *Shall We Dance* and *A Damsel in Distress;* both 1937) when the composer died of a brain tumor at the age of thirty-eight. (*The Goldwyn Follies,* for which Gershwin had planned to compose a full-scale ballet under the working title of *The Swing Symphony,* was released posthumously in 1938; it included four Gershwin songs, among them the ineffably sweet *Love Walked In.*)

The other top musical comedy team, Rodgers and Hart, maintained their successful collaboration. They began the decade with a score for *Simple Simon* (1930) which included the poignant *Ten Cents A Dance,* about a dime-a-dance "hostess" in a Depression-era public ballroom. Later musicals by them that were outstanding for their songs were *Babes in Arms* (1937), *The Boys From Syracuse* (1938), and—outstanding also for its unwonted dramatic weight and development of character (that of a "perfect heel")—*Pal Joey* (1940).

The 1930–45 period saw the major successes in the lyric theater of Cole Porter (1892–1964). Unlike Gershwin or Rodgers, Porter wrote both the lyrics and music of his songs. A Yale University graduate (and later a student of music at both Harvard and the Schola Cantorum in Paris), a *bon vivant* with an independent income and a fondness for residence in both Paris and Venice, Porter wrote songs with mordantly witty lyrics married to music of often brittle and always sophisticated charm. He was an ironic, sometimes caustic spokesman for the pre-jet-set, *New Yorker*-reading, up-to-the-minute urbanites who knew a good *double entendre* when they heard one—whether verbal (*Let's Do It,* from the show *Paris* of 1928; *Katie Went to Haiti,* from *Du Barry Was a Lady* of 1939) or both verbal and musical (*But In the Morning, No,* also from *Du Barry;* the song is a gavotte, with a wicked quotation of a musical phrase from *The Star-Spangled Banner*). Blues inflections, in Porter's earlier songs (*What Is This Thing Called Love?* of 1929), are cast in swing-style rhythms in the later ones (*It's De-Lovely,* from *Red, Hot and Blue* of 1936; *Most Gentlemen Don't Like Love,* from *Leave It to Me* of 1938).

Porter's thorough musical training shows up in various ways in his songs. To point only to his two most famous ones: in *Begin the Beguine* (from *Jubilee;* 1935) it allows him to control a song of extraordinary length (108 measures) and unique form; in *Night and Day* (from *The Gay Divorce;* 1932) it lies behind the unusual chromaticism and tonal plan, the unconventional form, and the cleverly offset repeated-note monotony.[14] At another level, that of the musical as a whole, Porter was to reveal this thorough musical knowledge, along with his innately elegant and witty personality, in his later (and perhaps greatest) musical, *Kiss Me, Kate* (1948), based on Shakespeare—even though its individual songs did not become classics of the popular genre.

[14] Pianist-composer Leo Smit has noted the resemblance between the chorus theme of *Night and Day* and Schumann's song *Die Lotosblume* (and similar echoes of European art music in other Porter songs) in a provocative little essay on "The Classic Cole Porter," *Saturday Review,* December 25, 1971. I am grateful to Ms. Lynn Siebert for calling my attention to this essay.

A few other composers deserve mention here as writers of songs or musicals that are striking in one way or another. Harold Arlen (b. 1905) is considered by some critics to be in every way the peer of Gershwin.[15] *Stormy Weather* (1933) suggests the flexibility of Arlen's phrase-lengths (in a field tyrannized by four-measure fragments); *Over the Rainbow* (from the film *The Wizard of Oz* of 1939) seemed to be tailor-made for the wide-eyed yearning innocence of the young Judy Garland; *Blues in the Night* (from the movie of the same title; 1941) and *That Old Black Magic* (1942) each have unique qualities. Vincent Youmans (1898–1946) has proved to have remarkable staying power: his 1924 hit musical, *No, No, Nanette,* had a successful revival in the early 1970's (see p. 186, footnote 8); *Tea For Two* was its top song. Kurt Weill (1900–1950), who had come to the United States as a refugee in the mid-1930's, put his experience in German musical theater to good use in several Broadway musicals, most notably *Lady in the Dark* (1941) and the virtually operatic *Street Scene* (1947). But *Street Scene*—and, no less, a work like Porter's *Kiss Me, Kate*—might never have been possible without a musical of 1943 that set a new standard for the genre. This was *Oklahoma!,* a collaboration between Richard Rodgers and his second partner, Oscar Hammerstein II. It had excitingly original choreography by Agnes de Mille that synthesized ballet movement and square-dance figures. The artfully folkish work brought plot, music, and dance into such a tightly-knit whole that some believed themselves witnessing a new form of American vernacular opera.

One other composer identified with musicals of the 1930's (and both earlier and later) must be mentioned here, although he never wrote one. This is Robert Russell Bennett (b. 1894), one of the early students of Nadia Boulanger. Bennett dominated the field of orchestral arrangements of the scores of musicals from 1927 (*Show Boat*) through 1960 (*Camelot*); among many others for which he provided adroit orchestrations that set the highest of standards were *Of Thee I Sing, Oklahoma!, Kiss Me, Kate, South Pacific* (1949), and *My Fair Lady.*

BIBLIOGRAPHICAL NOTES

Eric Salzman's "*Modern Music* in Retrospect," *PNM,* II, 2 (Spring–Summer 1964), 14–20, analyzes the American musical mood of 1924–46 as revealed in the pages of *Modern Music.* Copland's *Our New Music* (see Chapter 8, footnote 2) remains valuable as a view of things looking back from 1941; Cowell (ed.), *American Composers on American Music* (see

---

[15] See Wilder, *American Popular Song,* p. 253.

footnote 2), as a view looking forward from 1933. Thomson's *The State of Music* (1939; 2nd ed. New York: Vintage Books, 1962) is concerned with both the aesthetic and economic ways and means of the American composer.

Thomson's *Virgil Thomson* (see footnote 6) is a deliciously written autobiography which supersedes the biographical half of Kathleen Hoover and John Cage's *Virgil Thomson* (see footnote 7); in the latter, Cage's incisive analysis of the music is masterly.

Mellers's *Music in a New Found Land*, Chapter X, is sympathetic to both the art and ideology of Blitzstein; since both are revealing of a major theme of the 1930's, Mellers's discussion is especially valuable.

Nathan Broder's *Samuel Barber* and F. R. Schreiber and Vincent Persichetti's *William Schuman* (both New York: G. Schirmer, Inc., 1954) include analyses but should be read with caution as a publisher's self-serving products.

Sessions's *Questions About Music* (Cambridge: Harvard University Press, 1970), based on his Charles Eliot Norton lectures at Harvard in 1968–69, is an important distillation of the composer's musical credo. Walter Piston's life and work are surveyed by Klaus George Roy in "Walter Piston," *Stereo Review*, XXIV, 4 (April 1970), 57–67; Piston himself speaks in Peter Westergaard's "Conversation with Walter Piston," *PNM*, VII, 1 (Fall–Winter 1968), 3–17.

The literature on jazz of the 1930–45 period is voluminous but very uneven; the best bibliographical guide to it is Robert Reisner's *The Literature of Jazz; A Selective Bibliography* (2nd ed.; New York: New York Public Library, 1959). Two volumes in the Macmillan Jazz Masters Series, edited expertly by Martin Williams, are relevant: Rex Stewart's *Jazz Masters of the Thirties* (1972) and Ira Gitler's *Jazz Masters of the Forties* (1966). Ross Russell's *Bird Lives! The High Life and Hard Times of Charlie (Yardbird) Parker* (New York: Charterhouse, 1973) is strong on the biographical facts and on the general jazz scene of the 1930's and '40's, less so on the nature of the music itself. Russell is also the author of *Jazz in Kansas City and the Southwest* (Berkeley: University of California Press, 1971).

The authoritative documentary book on Cole Porter's life and the lyrics of his songs (not the music, which is hardly mentioned) is Robert Kimball's *Cole* (New York: Holt, Rinehart and Winston, 1971). George Eells's *The Life That Late He Led* (New York: G. P. Putnam's Sons, 1967) is a journalistic but detailed biography.

TEN

AFTER WORLD WAR II

The period after World War II, like that after World War I, was one of marked progressivism and rapid development in American music, due partly to a rising prosperity which increased the sources of patronage and the audience for music. With the introduction in 1948 of the long-playing microgroove phonorecording, the cost of records diminished, sales boomed; the phonorecord became almost as important a medium for new music as the concert (more, for some). Giant industrial and philanthropic foundations, most notably the Ford and Rockefeller Foundations, as well as state, county, municipal, and (by 1965) federal organizations in support of the arts provided new money for composers' commissions and per-formance organizations. The audience grew spectacularly: a favorite statistic of the 1950's was one demonstrating that more Americans went to concerts than to baseball games. By the early 1960's, arts centers were being constructed in city after city, the most extensive being Lincoln Center for the Performing Arts in New York, a giant complex of buildings housing a major concert hall and several smaller ones; two theaters for drama, ballet, musical comedy, and even opera; a library-museum; and a huge opera house. Despite the advent of television, radio continued to appeal to a large audience, and a 1965 survey revealed that about 1,000 radio stations broadcast a weekly total of 13,795 hours of "concert music" (i.e., neither jazz nor pop music), an average of about fourteen hours per week per station. The number of composers increased dramatically. So did the number of performance organizations: one survey[1] reported that whereas in 1939 there had been about 600 symphony orchestras in the U.S.A., by 1967 there were 1,436, more than half of the world's 2,000 such orchestras; there were 918 opera-producing groups; there were, in American schools, some 68,000 instrumental music organizations (of which 50,000 were wind bands).

This lively, developing scene in the musical culture at large was reflected in musical composition as well. The post-war period saw various trends of widely diverging character, in rapid evolution.

TWELVE-TONE COMPOSITION AND RELATED METHODS; ELLIOTT CARTER

One striking development was the triumph of the twelve-tone technique of composition. Viewed before the war as the more or less private method of composers associated directly at one time or another with Schoenberg, the technique of organizing music on the basis of a row or series of the twelve chromatic tones was now being used by a majority of younger American composers (like their European contemporaries). Some older ones as well, composers who before the war had not practiced row-technique at all, began to do so in the late 1940's.

Reflecting this trend was the belated recognition of a composer like Wallingford Riegger (1885–1961), who had long utilized serial technique but had to wait until its general adoption before gaining the esteem of the musical community, as embodied in the New York Music Critics Circle prize awarded his Third Symphony (1948). As was typical of the Americans who had grown into twelve-tone technique from other directions than tutelage by Schoenberg, Riegger's application of it, from his earliest example (*Dichotomy*, 1932), was anything but doctrinaire. In the Third Symphony, a twelve-tone row is the main source of the first movement's thematic material (Example 10-1; the oboe theme—"b" in the example—exposes the entire row), but the development section of the

---

[1] *Concert Music USA, 1968* (New York: Broadcast Music, Inc., 1968).

quasi-sonata-form structure abandons the row, reverting to chromatic clusters of a sort found in many of Riegger's other works, e.g. his *Music for Brass Choir* (1948–49). The second movement of the Third Symphony is not row-based at all, and the last movement's passacaglia and fugue subjects are both seven-tone themes, not twelve-note (although they are ultra-chromatic).

EXAMPLE 10-1. W. Riegger, Symphony No. 3, first-movement row-based themes. Copyright 1949 Associated Music Publishers, Inc. Used by permission. (a) "Motto," measures 1–4. (b) First-group theme, first statement, measures 4–6. (c) First-group theme, climax, measures 64–68. (d) Recapitulation, "Quasi fugato," measures 213–16.

Two older European-born composers with twelve-tone experience also rose to prominence shortly after World War II: Ernest Krenek (b. 1900) and Stefan Wolpe (1902–1972). Though a prolific composer, Krenek's impact on American music was felt more through his teaching and his didactic works, especially the books *Music Here and Now* (originally *Über neue Musik;* English translation published 1939) and *Studies in Counterpoint Based on the Twelve-Tone Technique* (1940). Wolpe, in America from 1938, was rather to influence a number of young Americans through his music per se, which proposed many new extensions of the tone-row technique. His music, like that of Webern (with whom he had worked briefly in 1933), invited a whole new method of listening based on the perception of intervals rather than melodic "themes" or harmonic "chords," let alone larger-dimension relationships between chords.

Among the mature Americans who gradually came to incorporate dodecaphonic principles in their music were Roger Sessions, Aaron Copland, Ross Lee Finney, a whole "Stravinsky school," and Hugo Weisgall.

Sessions's increasingly chromatic style of the 1930's and '40's had led him to the brink of row usage. In the most natural way, he began viewing his ideas as susceptible to tone-row abstraction: "As a result of the fact that the opening theme [of the Sonata for Violin Solo, 1953] contained twelve different tones, and seemed to go naturally on that basis, I caught myself using the twelve-tone system."[2] Thus Sessions's twelve-tone music *sounded* hardly different from his pre-twelve-tone music. It retained the dense texture, the proliferation of contrapuntal filigree-work, the lengthy, non-repetitive and usually non-sequential melodic line, and the Classic-Romantic traditional expressive gestures of his earlier music.

Copland first essayed serial technique, tentatively and not without a certain stiffness of effect, in his Piano Quartet (1950), more masterfully in his Piano Fantasy (1955–57). In the Fantasy a ten-note row is the basis; the other two chromatic notes (E, G$\sharp$) are reserved for special use as a kind of cadence-interval. In fact, the work may be heard tonally as being in or about E major. Neither the Fantasy nor the Quartet, nor the later *Connotations* for orchestra (1962), make use of folk or popular materials; even so, they are transparently the work of the composer of *Appalachian Spring* and *Rodeo*. In this connection, Copland had some sensible things to say about the impact (or lack of it) of twelve-tone usage on a composer's style and the expressive content of his music: "To describe a composer as a twelve-toner these days is much too vague. . . . Twelve-tonism is nothing more than an angle of vision. Like fugal treatment, it is a stimulus that enlivens musical thinking. . . . It is a method, not a style."[3]

Finney had been a student not only of Nadia Boulanger (1927–28) but of Alban Berg (1931–32); not until about 1950, however, did he interest himself in serial technique. I have mentioned above (see pp. 202–3) his interest in the American musical past; this was expressed through a forceful, masculine style in a music distinctly tonal, rhythmically energetic, and neo-Classic in formal principles. With his String Quartet No. 6 (1950) Finney began to work with tone-rows, but with the explicit aim of reconciling them with larger plans of tonal organization, such as architectonic design of tonal centers and aspects of functional directive harmony. Another of his concerns in the 1950's was with arch forms and

[2] Cone, "Conversation with Roger Sessions," *PNM*, IV, 2 (Spring–Summer 1966), 40.

[3] Copland, "Fantasy for Piano," *New York Times*, October 20, 1957.

other symmetrical or circular plans, as in the Sixth and Seventh Quartets. The latter (1955) he thought of as resembling a figure-eight:

> Like a skater, the first movement starts at the mid-point, then circles out, returning to the beginning, using the pitches in reverse order but making different music with them. The second [final] movement accomplishes figuratively the opposite sweep, and the quartet ends in the center with the theme.[4]

Such "spatial" visions of music, deriving from the various reversible and invertible, horizontal (linear) and vertical (harmonic) points of view in twelve-tone method, were becoming increasingly common during the 1950's.

Among other mature composers who, after many years of lack of interest in Schoenberg's method, adopted it suddenly and absorbed it into their individual styles were some identified as a "Stravinsky school." These were mainly former pupils of Boulanger and included Louise Talma (b. 1906), Arthur Berger (b. 1912), Ingolf Dahl (1912–1970), and Irving Fine (1914–1962). At the same time that Stravinsky approached row-composition (via Renaissance counterpoint) in his *Cantata* (1952) and turned definitively to dodecaphony in the mid-1950's, these composers began to espouse the twelve-tone idea. As with Sessions and Copland, its use by them hardly affected their personal idioms although it distinctly reduced their tendency to neo-Classic formal structures.

Twelve-tone procedures and a style akin to the Viennese expressionists were heard in several operas of the 1950's and '60's by Hugo Weisgall (b. 1912), a former pupil of Sessions. A cultivated litterateur, Weisgall found libretto material in plays by Wedekind (*The Tenor,* 1950), Strindberg (*The Stronger,* 1952), Pirandello (*Six Characters in Search of an Author,* 1956), Yeats (*Purgatory,* 1959), and Racine (*Athaliah,* 1964). All are intense, densely packed works musically; *Six Characters,* leavened by wit and melodrama, has the most subtle and penetrating characterization, sensitive balancing of voices and orchestra, and theatrical presence.

Related to the intense, near-expressionist atmosphere of Weisgall's operas is the music of three other composers, all of whom felt the impact of Schoenberg's ideas or his music in significant ways. Leon Kirchner (b. 1919) actually studied with both Schoenberg and Sessions and, although he did not adopt the twelve-tone method of organization, his music carries on their highly expressive, ultra-chromatic manner.

[4] The description is by Leslie Bassett (b. 1923), a former pupil and later colleague of Finney's and a Pulitzer Prize-winning composer in his own right, writing in the program booklet for The University of Michigan School of Music's 1966 Festival of Contemporary Music.

George Rochberg (b. 1918) has tended to move with the vanguard sty-listically: after works of the 1940's in various neo-tonal manners, the *Twelve Bagatelles* were Rochberg's first twelve-tone pieces; dedicated to the Italian composer Luigi Dallapiccola, they reflect his lyrical and finely-ordered style. Ben Weber (b. 1916) also writes a music of lyric grace; characteristic is his Symphony in Four Movements, for baritone and orchestra (1954), on poems of William Blake. The work of all three composers suggests that for them the anti-Romantic struggle is over, its issues dead. As Rochberg put it in 1963: "Now that the question arises on all sides: after abstractionism, what next? the answer rings out clearly: the 'new romanticism.'"[5]

By about 1960, the composer whose music, though not twelve-tone, seemed most sovereignly to embody these attitudes of an urgent expressivity, also of high seriousness and even "monumentality," was Elliott Carter (b. 1908). Carter was a "second-generation" pupil of Bou-langer (from 1932 to 1935) after working under Piston at Harvard. More important ultimately in his development were his close association with Ives and Ives's music; certain procedures in Debussy's music which sug-gested to him unusual modes of "musical logic"—change, process, evolu-tion; and his unshaken belief in the musical work as *communication* between composer and listener. Writing slowly and fastidiously, Carter first achieved in his Piano Sonata (1945–46) that sense of a work's being *sui generis* that has been typical of every later composition. The sonata is in every way a work for pianoforte; no transcription is imaginable, nor is any aspect of the piece derived from other instrumental idioms. Even the harmonic materials grow from the piano's special qualities of resonance and its sostenuto-pedal effects. Rhythmic complexities abound; at the time of the sonata's composition, Carter believed these realizable only in a soloist's work, but later he was to find the means to make them play-able by ensembles. In two big, subdivided movements, the Piano Sonata is cyclic but ever-developmental; various ideas announced in the intro-duction (Example 10-2)—the conflict between B and A$\sharp$, the material in thirds, the rising arpeggio figure—are re-presented, but in constant flux. The scope of the work sonorously, developmentally, and formally is very grand, and no other American piano sonata succeeds as well in realizing to the fullest the ideas it proposes.

With each of his later major works Carter's musical conception has seemed to grow larger, his mode of expression more commanding. The Sonata for Cello and Piano (1948), the three string quartets (1951, 1959, 1972), the Sonata for Flute, Oboe, Cello, and Harpsichord (1952), the Variations for Orchestra (1955–56), the Double Concerto for Piano and Harpsichord (1961), the Piano Concerto (1965) are all "masterworks"

[5] Quoted in Alexander Ringer, "The Music of George Rochberg," *MQ*, LII (1966), 414.

EXAMPLE 10-2. E. Carter, Piano Sonata (New York: Mercury Music Corporation, 1948), measures 1–7. Quoted by permission.

in concept, aims, and realization. Carter takes a long time to write a piece of music—there were no works premiered between the last two just mentioned, for instance—but each piece is a major event.

Since the late 1940's, Carter's music has been marked by an increasing richness of texture, an increasing "personalization" of instrumental voices, and an increasing complexity of rhythmic procedures. The Piano Concerto has passages with as many as seventy-two different parts proceeding simultaneously (a degree of density the composer refers to as "swamping"); what a leap from the movement in the earlier *Eight Etudes and a Fantasy* (1949), for woodwind quartet, that is written on one note only (although of course that was only a witty conceit)!

Carter's "personalization" or "personification" of instruments is in line with his view that his scores are "scenarios, auditory scenarios, for performers to act out with their instruments"; in the Second Quartet, each instrument "is like a character in an opera made up primarily of 'quartets.' The individuals of this group are related to each other in what might be metaphorically termed three forms of responsiveness: discipleship, companionship, and confrontation"; in the Piano Concerto, the solo piano "is in dialogue with the orchestral crowd, with seven mediators—a concertino of flute, English horn, bass clarinet, solo violin, viola, cello, and bass"[6]—who serve as a kind of soothing Greek chorus between the sassy piano and the square orchestra.

[6] The three quotations of Carter's words are from, respectively, "Shop Talk by an American Composer," *MQ*, XLVI (1960), 189–201; jacket notes written by Carter for the Composers Quartet recording of his First and Second String Quartets (Nonesuch H-71249); and an essay written for *The Orchestral Composer's Point of View*, ed. R. S. Hines (Norman; University of Oklahoma Press, 1970), pp. 39–61. In the last essay, Carter offers some very revealing explanations of his techniques, as of the 1960's, of rhythmic and pitch organization.

The increasing rhythmic complexity in Carter's mature works arose from his dissatisfaction with the limited range of rhythm and modes of continuity in even the most "advanced" scores of Western music, and from his perception of the broader rhythmic repertory in such other musics as Indian *talas,* Arabic *durub,* Balinese "tempi," and Watusi drum-pieces of Africa. While composing the Cello Sonata he worked out a manner of *evolving* rhythms and tempos, a constant change of pulse, based on a technique called by Richard Franko Goldman metric modulation—"a means of going smoothly, but with complete accuracy, from one absolute metronomic speed to another, by lengthening or shortening the value of the basic note unit."[7] This technique ensures the most precise temporal controls over a music in rhythmic flux while permitting the greatest degree of independence among the separate voices in Carter's favored contrapuntal textures. Example 10-3, from the sixth variation of the Variations for Orchestra, shows one use of the technique. Each six-measure period accelerates gradually from ♩ =80 to ♩ =240: as the cello breaks into triplet eights at measure 301, the viola begins the theme again in quarters, at the initial ♩ =80 tempo. The undulating, fluid effect of wavelike overlappings of voices at different tempos is unique; it suggests Carter's extraordinary rhythmic imagination, apparent in every work. Example 10-3 can also suggest the thoroughgoing chromaticism, not quite twelve-tone in organization, of Carter's mature

EXAMPLE 10-3. E. Carter, Variations for Orchestra, measures 295–307. Copyright 1957 Associated Music Publishers, Inc. Used by permission.

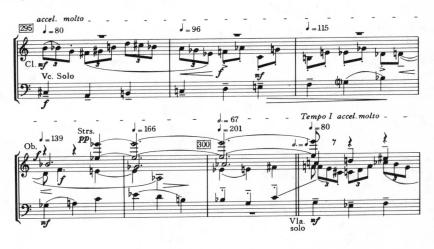

[7] Richard Franko Goldman, "The Music of Elliott Carter," *MQ,* XLIII (1957), 161.

style, and its energetic, strongly directional melodic motion, which contributes to the sense of dynamism and "expressivity" in his work.

SYSTEMATIC SERIAL COMPOSITION: MILTON BABBITT

Schoenberg's "method of composing with twelve tones which are related only with one another," as he called it, was initially a substitute for the comprehensive principles of pitch organization of Classic-Romantic tonality, in which the twelve tones were related to *one*, the tonic. The twelve-tone method sought to come to terms with the chromatic vocabulary of music and to ensure a continuing and total chromaticism in the realm of pitch organization. However, just as tonality had affected aspects of music other than pitch, so too did the new "atonal" method. More consciously than Schoenberg, Webern explored these implications of serial technique. In a work like Webern's Symphony, Op. 21 (1928), the structure of the pitch row affects aspects of rhythm, dynamics, phrase-structure, counterpoint, orchestration, and over-all form; in the second movement, even the choice of row-transpositions used in each variation derives from the shape of the pitch row itself. It was this logical extension of the serial principle that made Webern, not Schoenberg, the hero of a whole generation of composers after World War II, the "post-Webernites" of the 1950's headed by the French composers Olivier Messiaen and Pierre Boulez and the German Karlheinz Stockhausen. However, even before these Europeans began working out the implications of Webern's later works the American Milton Babbitt (b. 1916) was moving in a similar direction, suggested to him, however, perhaps more by Schoenberg than by Webern.

A trained mathematician, Babbitt saw not just a "method" in twelve-tone music but a real *system* (a concept denied by Schoenberg) and in the pitch row not just a "series" but an ordered *set*, in the definitive mathematical sense. As early as the mid-1940's Babbitt was using the serial principle to structure durational and other nonpitch components of his music. He was also addressing himself to control of the two dimensions of pitch, horizontal-linear and vertical-harmonic, in such a way that every note—or, to use a newer and more precise terminology, every pitch-class (C, E♭, etc., the register not specified)—was not only a member of an unfolding linear set but of another, related set, governing and in fact creating the vertical dimension. This kind of thinking led him to a study of the structure of twelve-tone sets themselves, and to an extension of a principle advanced first by Schoenberg: that of "combinatoriality" (as Babbitt termed it), the combining of various forms of a set without note-duplication between simultaneous hexachords (half-rows), or, in short, the production of twelve-tone *aggregates*.

Babbitt developed further Schoenberg's discovery, formulating methods for constructing pitch sets that would be "semi-combinatorial" or "all-combinatorial." A semi-combinatorial set is so constructed that one of its transformations (besides its retrograde) can be transposed so that the first hexachord includes the same notes as the last hexachord of the original set; it can then be combined with that transposed version without destroying the ideal of total chromaticism. The all-combinatorial set is so constructed that *all* of its transformations and one or more of its transpositions achieve the same end. These sorts of sets open up vast possibilities for contrapuntal techniques that still maintain total chromaticism.

The earliest works to be based on these ideas were *Three Compositions for Piano* (1947–48), *Composition for Four Instruments* (1947–48), and *Composition for Twelve Instruments* (1948). In the first of the *Three Compositions*, the pitch set is an all-combinatorial set. Four forms only (and their retrogrades) are used; as Example 10-4 shows, various pairs of these may be combined without duplicating the pitch-content of corresponding hexachords (compare "A" and "B" in the example). Constant rotation of the chromatic total in the music is ensured not only by

EXAMPLE 10-4. Pitch-set forms used in M. Babbitt, *Three Compositions for Piano*, No. 1.

consistent aggregate-formations but also, in single voices, by following one set linearly with another whose first hexachord is the "opposite" of the one just completed: in the lower voice of measures 1–8, for example, the prime form of the set at the "zero" level (P-O; A-B hexachord order), then the retrograde inversion at the first transposition, up a semitone (RI-1; A-B order), the inversion at the seventh transposition (I-7; A-B order), and the retrograde at the sixth transposition (R-6; A-B order) appear successively (see Example 10-5); the order of successive set-forms is constantly varied as the composition proceeds. In addition to pitch, Babbitt serializes other components in this movement: aspects of duration, of dynamics, and of the formation of the three-note simultaneities characteristic of this piece.

EXAMPLE 10-5. M. Babbitt, *Three Compositions for Piano* (Hillsdale, N.Y.: Boelke-Bomart, Inc., 1957), No. 1, measures 1–8. Quoted by permission.

The numerical series 5 1 4 2 (= 12, or the number of sixteenth-notes in a measure of $\frac{3}{4}$, which is the meter of the piece) is chosen as the prime form of a "durational set"; 2 4 1 5 is its retrograde, 1 5 2 4 its inversion, and 4 2 5 1 its retrograde inversion. The form of the movement, in six sections, is determined by the various uses of this set: in measures 1–8, it controls the grouping of even attacks (Example 10-6a); in mea-

sures 9–18, the articulations between groups of even sixteenths (Example
10-6b); in measures 20–28, accents and repeated notes (Example 10-6c);
in measures 29–48, temporal durations between attack points (Example
10-6d). In measures 49–56 an effect of recapitulation is achieved by a return to the manner of measures 1–8. It will be noticed that the "durational set" forms parallel those of the pitch set: when for example an RI
form of the pitch set appears, it is associated with the 4 2 5 1 (RI) form
of the "durational set" (see Example 10-6c).

EXAMPLE 10-6. Uses of the "durational set" in M. Babbitt, *Three Compositions for Piano*, No. 1.

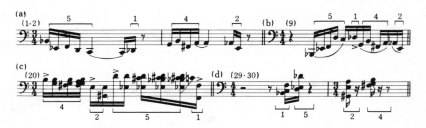

Dynamics are also determined to reflect and confirm the serial
ordering of pitch materials in the piece. The *mezzo piano* of measure
1 is associated with the prime form of the pitch set; *mezzo forte* with the
retrograde; *forte* with the inversion; and *piano* with the retrograde inversion. This holds true up to the "recapitulation" of measures 49–56,
when the "dynamics set" is "transposed."

Finally, the three-note chords—or better, simultaneities—that appear frequently in the composition reveal a serial approach: the register
chosen for the notes of each is determined by the following scheme:

$$
P = \begin{array}{cccc} \uparrow 2 & 3 & \uparrow 8 & 9 \\ 1 & 4 & 7 & 10 \\ 0 & \downarrow 5 & 6 & \downarrow 11 \end{array} \qquad R = \begin{array}{cccc} \uparrow 9 & \uparrow 6 & 5 & 2 \\ 10 & 7 & 4 & 1 \\ 11 & 8 & \downarrow 3 & \downarrow 0 \end{array}
$$

$$
I = \begin{array}{cccc} \uparrow 0 & \uparrow 5 & 6 & \uparrow 11 \\ 1 & 4 & 7 & 10 \\ 2 & 3 & \downarrow 8 & 9 \end{array} \qquad RI = \begin{array}{cccc} 11 & 8 & \downarrow 3 & \uparrow 0 \\ 10 & 7 & 4 & 1 \\ \downarrow 9 & \downarrow 6 & 5 & 2 \end{array}
$$

Thus, in measure 11 (Example 10-7) the upper part is an expression of
the pitch set I-1 and the particular registration of the notes of each three-
note group follows the I version of the "registral set" scheme given

above; the lower part, built from the pitch set RI-1, forms its simultaneities according to the RI version of that scheme.

EXAMPLE 10-7. Serial approach to three-note simultaneities in M. Babbitt, *Three Compositions for Piano*, No. 1, measure 11.

In his *Composition for Twelve Instruments* (1948; revised 1954) Babbitt went further to integrate the pitch and durational components of his music by deriving a durational set from the pitch set and composing not only in terms of a twelve-*tone* system but of a twelve-*duration* system as well. Example 10-8 shows (a) the prime pitch set, with each note defined by its *order* number and its *pitch* number (the latter measured in semitones from the first note); (b) the pitch set transposed up two semitones, thus altering the pitch numbers of the tones; and (c) the durational set, based on a sixteenth-note unit, that corresponds to pitch-set P-2.

EXAMPLE 10-8. Pitch and duration sets in M. Babbitt, *Composition for Twelve Instruments* (1948).

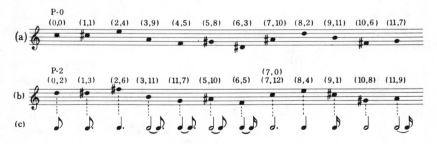

The musical expression in *Composition for Twelve Instruments* is one emphasizing single-impluse events; the pointillistic texture has been likened to a bank of different colored lights, of varied wattage, flashing on and off at different rates. Later works by Babbitt have demonstrated that other textures, other expressive qualities are perfectly possible. *All Set,* for instance, written in 1957 for a Brandeis University arts festival, is scored for a seven-piece jazz ensemble and is based metrically, rhythmically, melodically, and even at some points harmonically on the style of the "progressive jazz" of the 1940's. Several works have included voice, with a frankly *espressivo* line. Such are the song cycle *DU* (1951), the *Composition for Tenor and Six Instruments* (1960), and *Two Sonnets* for baritone, clarinet, viola, and cello (1955). In these, duration is not serially organized, Babbitt believing that correct prosody should be the primary rhythmic determinant. Nevertheless, various linked chains of pitch relationships exist in them, as can be heard in the opening measures of *DU* (Example 10-10), which also can exemplify Babbitt's expressive, sensitively rhythmed and contoured vocal line, reminiscent of the lyric art of Webern.

The voice exposes the prime set in four phrases of three notes each. This set is all-combinatorial and is furthermore an "all-interval" set; that is, it can be presented in such a way that every possible interval within an octave occurs once, and only once (Example 10-9). Such a set

EXAMPLE 10-9. The all-interval set of M. Babbitt's *DU* .

ensures a variety of interval-structures in the music and allows a linear deployment free from built-in symmetries and other form-dictating repetitions. Each vocal phrase of three notes is accompanied by piano music with the nine other chromatic notes; vertical dotted lines in Example 10-10 show the four twelve-tone aggregates thus created. Within each aggregate, three-note interval-structures are formed by voice and piano (circled in Example 10-10); they are the *same* structures within each aggregate; in the first aggregate, for example, the four interval-structures ("molecules" might be an apposite word for them) are all based on the intervals of a major third (or its inversion, a minor sixth), a minor second (or major seventh), and a perfect fifth (or perfect fourth). Finally, the nature of the accompaniment is such that we hear it as having three "voices": a high treble voice beginning B-F♯-A, a middle-register voice (E-G-D), and a bass voice (A♭-C♯-B♭). Tracing each of these voices through the excerpt, we discover that each is itself a twelve-tone set, related directly to the prime set of the singer. Moreover, within each of the four chromatic aggregates, each of the accompanying voices is a different form of the singer's three-note phrase: the piano's treble "voice" is an intervallic retrograde, the middle-register line an inversion, and the

bass a retrograde inversion. These linear relationships have been bracketed in Example 10-10.

EXAMPLE 10-10. M. Babbitt, *DU* (Hillsdale, N.Y.: Boelke-Bomart, Inc., 1957),
measures 1–5. Quoted by permission.

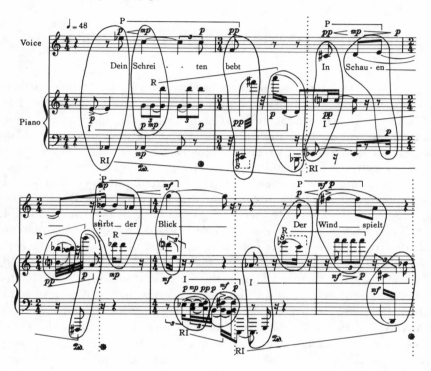

Through such extensions of the serial principle, not only to both
the horizontal and vertical dimensions of pitch but to other realms as
well, Babbitt has created music with a staggeringly complex network of
inter-relationships. Not only are these relationships complex: they *are*
the music; the interlocked components are inseparable; it is no longer
meaningful to speak of one, or to hear one, separate from the others; the
music, approaching "total organization," demands total hearing.[8]

Babbitt has been second only to Schoenberg himself as formulator
and codifier of serial concepts. He has also been an influential teacher of

[8] Some critics would add ". . . or none at all," claiming that *analyzing*
totally organized music is a more meaningful exercise than experiencing it aurally.
Babbitt has countered this view in the article "Who Cares if You Listen?" *High
Fidelity Magazine,* VIII, 2 (February 1958); reprinted in *ACS,* pp. 235–44. The question of "the perception and cognition of complex music" is thoroughly and provoc-
atively discussed in chapter 11 of Leonard B. Meyer's *Music, the Arts, and Ideas*
(Chicago: The University of Chicago Press, 1967).

younger composers, from a base at Princeton. Among those who, taught by both Sessions and Babbitt, constitute what has been called a "Princeton school," are Peter Westergaard (b. 1931), Henry Weinberg (b. 1931), Donald Martino (b. 1931), Benjamin Boretz (b. 1934), and James K. Randall (b. 1929).

ELECTRONIC, CONCRÈTE, *AND COMPUTER MUSIC*

Babbitt's interest in "total control" over musical materials led him perhaps inevitably to the medium of electronic music, and in the late 1950's he became one of the directors of the first major American electronic studio, co-sponsored by Princeton and Columbia and an outgrowth of the studio established at Columbia somewhat earlier.

Electronic music and tape-recorder music had begun in Europe. Pioneers in *musique concrète* (composition from pre-taped and stored sound materials, electronically manipulated and reassembled) were some French composers, notably Pierre Henry, working at the Paris studio of La Radiodiffusion Française in the late 1940's. Pioneers in *elektronische Musik* (composition directly onto magnetic tape of electronically generated sound materials) were some Germans, notably Herbert Eimert and Karlheinz Stockhausen, working at the Cologne studio of the Westdeutscher Rundfunk in the early 1950's. John Cage was the first American actually to prepare a "score for making a recording on tape" (*Imaginary Landscape No. 5*, 1951–52), but two other composers began about the same time to work systematically in tape-music composition: Otto Luening (b. 1900) and Vladimir Ussachevsky (b. 1911), both professors at Columbia. Working singly and together, Luening and Ussachevsky had produced enough compositions by the fall of 1952 to present the first American tape-music concert (at The Museum of Modern Art in New York, November 22). Luening's first tape pieces were *musique concrète* based on solo flute sounds: *Fantasy in Space, Low Speed,* and *Invention* (all 1952). Ussachevsky's early work culminated in *A Piece for Tape Recorder* (1956), which combined electronically generated sounds with prerecorded sounds on file in a library of sound-on-tape maintained at the Columbia studio; some of the latter had been used for his earlier pieces *Sonic Contours* and *Underwater Waltz.* The two composers collaborated in 1954 in two "concertos" for tape-recorded sounds and orchestra, *Rhapsodic Variations* and *A Poem in Cycles and Bells.*

The basic equipment for these composers of early electronic/tape music consisted of two or more tape recorders; an electronic generator of periodic sound signals, whether sine-wave (a fundamental pitch with no overtones), square-wave (fundamental with odd-numbered upper partial tones), or sawtooth-wave (fundamental with all upper partials); a generator of noise, whether the hissing steam-like sound of "white noise" (an infinite number of signals over the entire range of the audible sound spectrum) or the cloud-like band-of-sound of "colored noise" (an infinite number of signals within a *limited* range of frequencies); various sound-filtering and reverberating devices; scissors, razor blade, splicing block, and a supply of magnetic tape. With such equipment the composer was for the first time in the same position as the painter or sculptor: able to create directly and concretely in his medium, not subject to re-interpretation by a performer.

Understandably, Edgard Varèse, who more than 30 years earlier had dreamed of "instruments obedient to my thought" and of music invigorated by science, turned enthusiastically to tape music, creating three major works in the new medium before his death. One was *Déserts* (1950–54), for a group of wind and percussion instruments alternating with "organized sound" material on tape, in a big A B A C A B A form, "A" standing for the sections played by instruments, "B" for tape music based on raw sounds collected by Varèse in a foundry, a sawmill, and several factories, and "C" for tape music based on percussion-instrument sounds. The work seems wholly integrated; the electronic interpolations simply broaden the expressive range of Varèse's "sound-mass" techniques of the 1920's, and the music has a power of almost terrifying dimension. In 1958, working together with the architect Le Corbusier for the Brussels World's Fair pavilion of the Philips Corporation, a Dutch radio and electronic firm, Varèse composed *Poème électronique*. Here finally all his ideas of music as spatial, of sound as "living matter," could be realized. The music was planned for tape-recorded performance through some 425 loudspeakers arranged in 15 "tracks" and embedded in the looping curves of the ceiling and walls of Le Corbusier's building; the sound could actually sweep in great circles around and overhead, at different speeds and along various tracks simultaneously. Varèse composed the piece in a great variety of sounds, including a mysterious frictional sound originating in a tape-recording of his rubbing his palms together and also including the human voice, which lends an awesome presence to the work. In *Poème électronique* even more than in *Déserts*, Varèse approached the realization of his vision for a work never finished (*Espace*) of an apocalyptic sound montage in space: "voices in the sky, filling all space, crisscrossing, overlapping, penetrating each other, splitting up, superimposing, repulsing each other, colliding, crashing together."[9]

At the Columbia studio, as elsewhere in the 1950's, electronic

---

[9] Quoted in Chou Wen-chung, "Varèse: A Sketch of the Man and His Music," *MQ*, LII (1966), 166. Varèse's third electronic work, little-known, was composed for a brief portion of Thomas Bouchard's film, *Around and About Joan Miró* (1956).

music composition was a tedious task involving recording and re-recording on magnetic tape, then manually splicing together bits of tape to really "compose" a work. A great step in reducing such laborious techniques was taken with the development by the Radio Corporation of America of an electronic sound synthesizer (originally designed for use in speech synthesis), an advanced model of which, the Mark II, was installed in the Columbia studio in July 1959, under the direction of Luening, Ussachevsky, and Babbitt. The R.C.A. Synthesizer allowed Babbitt to pursue his ideal of a totally organized music, for it made possible the most precise control not only of the pitch components but those of rhythm, dynamics, and·timbre as well. "Control," however, was of no importance to Babbitt without perception, and his work in the 1960's was strongly conditioned by a typically thoroughgoing investigation of the fundamental human capabilities of perception and relation, within the extraordinarily wide boundaries of the Synthesizer's productive capacity. The result, in works like *Composition for Synthesizer* (1961) and *Ensembles for Synthesizer* (1962–64), was a music of great lucidity sonorously and architectonically, in striking contrast to the music of both Luening and Ussachevsky, which seldom loses sight of its non-electronic musical sources, and the music of Varèse, with its cosmic stridency and gestural dynamism. Other works by Babbitt combined synthesized sound with live performance: *Vision and Prayer* (1961), *Philomel* (1964), and *Correspondences* (1966–68). In these a new vitality appeard. In *Vision and Prayer*, Dylan Thomas's poem is set against a wholly synthesized accompaniment; the voice moves from recitation through speech-song and back again. *Philomel*, a wondrously musical poem by John Hollander on the transformation into a nightingale of the ravished and speechless Philomela, is set by Babbitt for live voice, taped and electronically altered voice, and synthesized sound. Composed for the remarkable soprano Bethany Beardslee, Babbitt's music for *Philomel* is as precisely ordered and as full of structural subtleties as any of his music; at another level it is a profoundly moving, "expressive" work. One critic has remarked that Philomela's "final triumphant phrase [Example 10-11], her ultimate recognition of her vocal powers, celebrates Mr. Babbitt's new-found voice as well."[10]

A five-year grant from the Rockefeller Foundation in 1959 enabled the Columbia-Princeton Electronic Music Center to invite many composers to use its facilities; ten years later, a survey listed as the result some 225 compositions by more than 60 composers from 11 countries.[11] A few composers closely identified with the Center (besides its directors) have come to special prominence as makers of electronic com-

[10] Richard F. French, in "Current Chronicle," *MQ*, L (1964), 382–88.

[11] See the list of "Compositions Created at the Center," in the informative brochure issued with *Columbia-Princeton Electronic Music Center Tenth Anniversary Celebration* (Composers Recordings Inc. album SD 268).

EXAMPLE 10-11. M. Babbitt, *Philomel*, conclusion (live voice part only).
Copyright Associated Music Publishers, Inc. Used by permission.

positions. Walter Carlos (b. 1939) has produced probably the best-known
of all electronic music thus far: the synthetically re-composed Baroque
works on the best-selling recordings *Switched-On Bach* and *The Well-
Tempered Synthesizer*. Mario Davidovsky (b. 1934), originally from Ar-
gentina, began with some purely electronic works (Electronic Studies
Nos. 1 and 2; 1960 and 1962) but has since concentrated on an integration
of electronic sounds with music for live performers, in a series of *Syn-
chronisms*. Jacob Druckman (b. 1928) too has emphasized live/electronic
confrontations in some brilliantly conceived, powerful, close-to-theatri-
cal works like *Animus I* (trombone and tape; 1966), *Animus III* (clarinet
and tape; 1969), and *Valentine* (double-bass and tape; 1970). Charles
Wuorinen (b. 1938), better-known as a performer, conductor (as co-
director of the Group for Contemporary Music at Columbia from 1962 to
1971, at the Manhattan School of Music thereafter), and composer of
non-electronic music, was able easily—like Babbitt—to turn his serially
oriented style to the electronic medium (*Symphonia Sacra* of 1960–61;
Orchestral and Electronic Exchanges of 1965); his *Time's Encomium*
(1968–69), commissioned by Nonesuch Records, won the 1970 Pulitzer
Prize in music—the first time a wholly electronic work, existing only in
recorded form, gained that prize.

Even if, as mentioned above, the R.C.A. Synthesizer marked a
great step forward in reducing the laborious, time-taking job of electronic
composition in a "classic" studio, it was a super-costly, bulky, and
literally unique machine. However, during the 1960's, technologists aided
by the invention of tiny transistors and solid-state circuitry developed
smaller, less expensive, and easier-to-operate synthesizers. These were
based on a principle of voltage control and consisted of a group of
modules—sound generators, sound modifiers (filters, amplifiers, mixers,
reverberators, and the like), control voltage generators, and control voltage processors. The first of these modular, voltage-controlled synthesizers were those of Robert Moog, working in upstate New York, and
Donald Buchla, of the San Francisco area; other makes—the ARP, the
Putney, the ElectroComp, and others—were soon on the market.

It is hard to say whether these small synthesizers came into exis-

tence out of composers' needs or whether their invention spurred composers into making electronic music—probably a bit of both. But by the
early 1970's electronic studios built around Moog or Buchla or other
equipment were to be found all across the country; hardly any college
music department was without one. Electronic-music composition had
entered a new phase of widespread practice.

Some composers associated with this development should be mentioned. Morton Subotnick (b. 1933) was one of the founders of the
San Francisco Tape Center. He and other composers in the area—notably Pauline Oliveros (b. 1932) and Larry Austin (b. 1930)—actually collaborated with Buchla in the development of his synthesizer equipment.
Subotnick's *Silver Apples of the Moon* (1966) symbolized the new status
of electronic music and was in fact a "first": in a happy and (with hind-
sight) seemingly inevitable marriage of technology, commerce, and art,
it was specifically commissioned by the enterprising firm of Nonesuch
Records and was planned to fill the two sides of an LP record. A second
Nonesuch commission, *The Wild Bull* (1967), and *Touch* (for Columbia
Records; 1968) share with *Silver Apples* Subotnick's fondness for lengthy
sequential patterns and multiple ostinatos (arising partly, at least, out of
characteristics of the Buchla equipment). Kenneth Gaburo (b. 1926) has
been interested in electronic/live works: *Antiphony III* (1962–63), composed at the Yale and University of Illinois studios, grew out of an idea
to produce a concerto for voices and electronic sounds; *Antiphony IV
(Poised)* (1968) assigns a singer to the left speaker system, has her project
the phonemes of a short poem at widely separated time- and pitch-inter-
vals, and alternates or opposes her with sounds of piccolo, bass, trombone, double-bass, and electronics from the right speaker system (with
occasional crossovers to the left). Roger Reynolds (b. 1934), one of a
lively group of composers in the San Diego area, moves beyond live/
electronic antiphony into multi-media in *Ping* (1968), which calls for
slide projections, film, and combined instrumental, *concrète*, and electronic sound; Reynolds's complementary *Traces* (1969) is for piano, flute,
cello, and six separate channels of taped sounds (both *concrète* and
electronic), so planned that a rich tapestry of combination-tones, differ-
ence-tones, and other "residues" (traces) of musical events is woven.

Related to tape-recorder and electronic music is computer music,
which may be defined as the programming of an electronic computer to
generate music or, in the early stages (from which we have hardly
emerged), to generate material that can be transcribed into musical
notation. The first serious experiments in computer composition were
carried out in 1955–56 by the composer-mathematician team of Lejaren Hiller (b. 1924) and Leonard Isaacson, working with the Illiac automatic high-speed digital computer at the University of Illinois. Their
first product was a four-movement *Illiac Suite* (1956) for string quartet,

each movement titled "Experiment," intended to show the compositional possibilities of one or another aspect of computer programming. Anything but radical in sound and structure, the *Illiac Suite* was more a technological breakthrough than anything else. Hiller later produced a *Computer Cantata* (1963), much more sophisticated musically, in conjunction with Robert Baker and a more advanced (IBM 7090) computer. More recently, various composers, mathematicians, and engineers are progressing rapidly toward a combination of sound-synthesizer and computer to provide a studio for the composer "controlled from a central console that will be the only instrument with which the composer will come into contact. . . . All that will be necessary, after composing the piece, is to push the button."[12]

EXPERIMENTAL MUSIC; MUSIC AS PROCESS AND ACTION

At precisely the same time that composers like Babbitt, Ussachevsky, and Hiller were working to increase the composer's personal control over musical materials and their realization in sound, an apparently opposite impulse was leading other composers in a different direction. In their music the will and determination of the composer were *reduced:* either he found ways of producing his music by chance or random methods (thus minimizing his role in the choice of the notes to be played or sung) or he produced not the actual note-symbols in ordered relationships but just musical raw material, to be ordered by the performer; for some works, not even the raw material was provided, only suggestions about the physical activity to initiate it, or about the environment in which it was to take place.

Several adjectives have been used to define this music: "aleatory," "indeterminate," "chance," "random," "improvisatory" are some of them. The different connotations of each of these are subsumed, however, under the more general term *experimental,* in the precise meaning defined by John Cage when he writes: "An experimental action is one the outcome of which is unforeseen."[13] The "action" here is that of musical composition; the "outcome" is the musical performance. It is in this sense that the music to be discussed in this section is "experimental."

Undisputed leader of such experimental music from the early

[12] Joel Chadabe, "New Approaches to Analog-Studio Design," *PNM*, VI, 1 (Fall–Winter 1967), 107–13.

[13] "Composition as Process," three lectures given at Darmstadt in September 1958; reprinted in Cage, *Silence* (Middletown: Wesleyan University Press, 1961), pp. 18–55.

1950's was Cage himself. In the summary of his compositional methods partially quoted above (p. 214), Cage lists the post-war "paths my musical thought has taken" as these:

> . . . composition using charts and moves thereon (1951); composition using templates made or found (1952–   ); composition using observation of imperfections in the paper upon which it is written (1952–   ); composition without a fixed relation of parts to score (1954–   ); composition indeterminate of its performance (1958–   ).

Underlying all these means for reducing his dominance over the musical experience and letting the music "happen"[14] was Cage's discovery in 1951 that there is no silence. Previously, he had organized his music on the assumptions that the opposite of sound was silence; that duration was the only characteristic of sound measurable in terms of silence; that therefore any valid musical structure (a work of sounds and silences) must be based not on frequency, as traditionally it had been, but on duration. Then in 1951 Cage entered a soundproof and anechoic chamber, as silent as technologically possible. He heard two sounds, one high, one low; the engineer in charge explained that the high sound was his nervous system in operation, the low sound his blood circulating. Cage's reactions:

> The situation one is clearly in is not objective (sound-silence), but rather subjective (sounds only), those intended and those others (so-called silence) not intended. If, at this point, one says, "Yes! I do not discriminate between intention and non-intention," the splits, subject-object, art-life, etc., disappear, an identification has been made with the material, and actions are then those relevant to its nature, i.e.:
> *A sound does not view itself as thought, as ought, as needing another sound for its elucidation, as etc. . . .*
> *A sound accomplishes nothing; without it life would not last out the instant.*
> *Relevant action is theatrical (music [imaginary separation of hearing from the other senses] does not exist), inclusive and intentionally purposeless. . . .*[15]

The most dramatic, certainly the most famous, application by Cage of these ideas is the work *4′33″* (1952), a three-part piece for any instrument or combination of instruments. In its most familiar version,

[14] Cage's influence on the mixed-media, unmatrixed, often improvisational form of theater called Happenings has been very strong, since his organization at Black Mountain College in 1952 of an event involving painting, dance, piano-playing, poetry, films, slides, phonorecordings, radios, and a lecture by himself. See Michael Kirby, *Happenings* (New York: E. P. Dutton & Co., 1965).

[15] From an article of 1955, reprinted as "Experimental Music: Doctrine" in *Silence,* pp. 13–17. The bracketed phrase is Cage's.

by pianist David Tudor (who was a constant associate of Cage for many years), the performer seats himself, stopwatch nearby; indicates the beginning of each part by closing, the end by opening, the keyboard cover; and plays . . . nothing. But if he makes no intentional sounds, there are other sounds to be heard, and the audience, in the traditional listening situation of a piano recital, is invited to listen to them. As Tudor puts it: "It is one of the most intense listening experiences one can have. You really listen. You're hearing everything there is. Audience noises play a part in it. It is cathartic—four minutes and thirty-three seconds of meditation, in effect."[16]

Cage could hardly repeat himself as a composer of "silent" music. From the theoretical and philosophical position so vividly dramatized by *4'33"*, and aided by certain ideas of Zen Buddhism and other Oriental and speculative sources, he sought to find other ways to remove himself —his memory, taste, will—from the act of "composition" in a traditional sense. The "charts and moves thereon [and the] templates made or found" that he mentions were themselves prepared by chance operations, typically by tossing coins and translating the results into visual diagrams according to an intricate system based on the Chinese *I Ching* (Book of Changes); the diagrams were then translated into conventional notation. Such was the composing method for *Music of Changes* (1951) for piano. Coin-tossing together with notational "decisions" derived from the specks appearing on imperfectly printed music paper is the method for *Music for Piano 21–52* (1955), two groups of sixteen pieces which may be played alone or together in an indeterminate time-span; the duration and dynamics of individual notes are free.

A next step was to suggest the notes of a score by dropping an *I Ching*-derived stencilled diagram onto graph paper and plotting the result in "graph notation," from which then the performer might make any version he wished. *Music for Carillon* (1952) is an example: Cage published it in graph notation and also in two different versions conventionally notated, one with a two-octave range for the bells, another with three. For the *Concert for Piano and Orchestra* (1957–58) there is no master score; indeed, the work may be realized as a piano solo (the pianist being "free to play [from a 'book' of eighty-four different kinds of composition] any elements of his choice, wholly or in part, and in any sequence") or as a chamber work, a piece for symphony orchestra, one for piano with orchestra, etc. This is a work, in other words, not only "without a fixed relation of parts to score" but one also "indeterminate of its performance." Together with the *Concert* may be performed an *Aria*

[16] Quoted in Harold Schonberg, "The Far-out Pianist," *Harper's*, CXXX (June 1960), 49. The original version of *4'33"*, which shows its relation to earlier (nonexperimental) music by Cage and is different from the published "score," is reproduced in *Source*, I, 2 (July 1967), 46–55.

(1958) in which Cage leaves many aspects of performance undetermined. The *Aria* may also be sung with the tape-recorder piece *Fontana Mix* (1958), itself experimental in that the "sound sources, their mechanical alteration, changes of amplitude, frequency, overtone structure, the use of loops [for continuous repetition of taped material], special types of splicing, etc. may be determined" by the producer from graph-notated drawings and point-speckled transparent sheets. The voice-tape montage "is intended seriously to be fun, to provoke the audience to audible response, to break down the standard notion of performance in one dimension and an audience confined silently in another dimension."[17]

With such a conception, Cage had reached that point of indeterminacy where composer, performer, and listener meet and mingle in producing the musical experience. The means for obtaining such an experience were refined in such later works as *Theatre Piece* (1960), and Cage attained his ideal of non-self-expression as a composer: "I have no desire to improve on creation."[18] The paradox of this sentence is that in it lies perhaps the *most* creative aspect of Cage's "many paths": a profound humanism aimed at freeing man by removing the artificial barriers of his own making that surround him and permitting him to experience life with re-awakened sensitivity. His existential goal is essentially "to introduce us to the very life we are living."

Three composers closely associated with Cage and his experimental music ideas in the 1950's were Christian Wolff (b. 1934), Morton Feldman (b. 1926), and Earle Brown (b. 1926). Both Wolff and Feldman seemed most interested in extending Cage's ideas about setting sounds free, free from *intended* inter-relationships. Wolff spoke of "a concern for a kind of objectivity, almost anonymity—sound come into its own. The 'music' is a resultant existing simply in the sounds we hear, given no impulse by expression of self or personality."[19] In a number of chamber pieces, some indeterminate not only as to duration of tones but as to instrumentation, Wolff developed a notation whereby the players, responding to each other spontaneously like basketball or hockey players, could seem to *pass* notes to each other, loosing them as an arrow is loosed rather than propelled. Typically, Wolff's music in performance included more "silence" than sound, the notes hovering separately in the air almost as autonomous intelligences.

Feldman too developed new notations in the early 1950's for "allowing the sounds to be free," often suggesting through graphic means generalized areas (of register, for instance: high, medium, or low) within which the performer has a free choice of specifics (*Projections*, for cham-

---

[17] Peter Yates, "Music," *Arts and Architecture*, LXXVII, 7 (July 1960), 4, 32.

[18] Quoted in *Time*, LXXV, 12 (March 21, 1960), 46.

[19] Quoted by Cage in "History of Exeprimental Music in the United States," *Silence*, p. 68.

ber ensembles; *Intersection I* and *Marginal Intersection,* for orchestra; all 1951). By the 1960's he had achieved "a more complex style in which each instrument is living out its own individual life in its own individual sound world," often by virtue of Feldman's "choosing intervals that seemed to erase or cancel out each sound as soon as we hear the next"[20] (*Durations,* a series of five chamber pieces; 1960–61). In *The Swallows of Salangan* (1961), for wordless chorus and instruments, all the performers are given a music of successive notes; no rests are specified; there are precise pitch indications but no rhythmic ones. The conductor initiates the performance with a slow downbeat; he gives no others. Within the general tempo thus cued, the performers move through their parts, determining for themselves the actual durations of the slow, successive tones. The result, different in detail with every performance, is comparable to a cloud-mass whose precise outlines are constantly, almost imperceptibly shifting from moment to moment but which retains its identity as it moves through space. Feldman has spoken of the effect as being "very much like a series of reverberations from a common sound source." Although various details of Feldman's music are experimental (their exact results unforeseen), he has a clear generalized image of a work. His musical personality is a distinctive one as well, tending to favor slow rhythms, very soft dynamics, and what Cage has called "tender" sonorities. In some later pieces (e.g., *Structures for Orchestra,* 1960–62) Feldman came full circle, notating rhythms and pitches precisely again but in such a way as to create the same kind of ethereal but intense atmosphere, the weightless but clustered density, the non-periodic but fluid rhythmic flow of his experimental music.

Earle Brown was influenced in his musical ideas by artists, especially the sculptor Alexander Calder and the painter Jackson Pollock. In the mobiles of Calder he saw the possibilities of a work's never being the same twice yet always being the same work. In Pollock's "action" paintings he saw possibilities for a work's being spontaneously realized, either by composer or by performer, on the basis of graphic cues given by the composer. In a remarkable group of compositions published as a *Folio* (1952–53) Brown presented his first "open-form" music on the mobile principle: *1953* for piano, a study for the larger *Twenty-five Pages.* The score may be read either side up; in the complete work, the twenty-five pages may be played in any sequence; the two-stave systems may be read in either treble or bass clef; each system may be determined to last a certain time by the performer. Thus four aspects of the music—inversion, page sequence, clef disposition, and time—are "mobile." The notation, original with Brown, is "time notation": the horizontal length of a

[20] Feldman, jacket notes for a recording of *Durations,* Time Records No. 58007.

note suggests its duration relative to other notes and to the time-span determined for each system. *Folio* also includes Brown's first Pollock-like pieces, *MM 87 and MM 135* for piano, "composed very rapidly and spontaneously and . . . in that sense performances rather than compositions," and the celebrated work *December 1952*, the score of which is reproduced as Example 10-12. "Score" is not quite the word: *December 1952* is a single page of unruled paper constituting either/both score and/or parts for (any) performer(s), on which are drawn lines and rectangles, both horizontal and vertical, of various lengths and thicknesses. The lines and rectangles may be read as implying direction, loudness, duration, and pitch. The performer is to "track" his way around the page (which may be held in any position), realizing spontaneously (or under the control of a conductor reacting to the sheet as to a score) the sonorous implications of the markings and the "tracks" he chooses to follow. Vaguely reminiscent of a composition by Mondrian, *December 1952* has been exhibited as a work of graphic art and has historical significance as the first wholly graphic music (at least since the staffless neumes of the earlier Middle Ages).

EXAMPLE 10-12. Earle Brown, *December 1952*. Reproduced by permission of Associated Music Publishers, Inc.

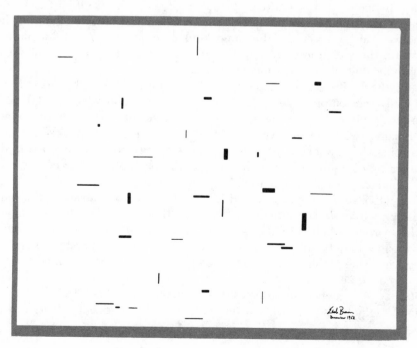

Utilizing various idioms of experimental and non-experimental music and various methods of notation, Brown developed further his mobile, open-form ideas in such works as *Available Forms I* for chamber ensemble (1961) and *Available Forms II* (1962) "for large orchestra four hands," i.e. with two conductors. In each of these works, Brown composed a number of brief musical events, sharply differentiated in character. These may be sounded in any order, repeated, combined, cut off in the middle, taken at different tempos, all at the discretion of the conductor, who thereby realizes one version of the work from the "available forms." Maximum possibilities of transformation and mobility (cf. Calder) exist in these works, which are formed spontaneously in performance (cf. Pollock).

Other groups of composers in the late 1950's and '60's developed Cage's idea that "relevant action is theatrical (music [imaginary separation of hearing from the other senses] does not exist), inclusive and intentionally purposeless." Viewing the way of the future as leading to a sort of *Gesamtkunstwerk*-like Happening, radically anti-Establishment, reminiscent in their mockery and humor of the Dada artists earlier in the century, these composers joined other artists in sound-and-environment events so diverse as to preclude any sort of categorization here. Although New York City was a major center, with an American wing of an international group called Fluxus particularly active, similar groups existed in Ann Arbor, Michigan (the ONCE group), Seattle ("Dimensions of New Music"), and elsewhere in the country. The subtitle of *An Anthology* (1963) edited by composer La Monte Young (b. 1935) suggests the "theatrical . . . inclusive and intentionally purposeless" diversity of this music-as-process-and-action movement:

Chance operations / Concept art / Meaningless work / Natural disasters / Indeterminacy / Anti-art / Plans of action / Improvisation / Stories / Diagrams / Poetry / Essays / Dance constructions / Compositions / Mathematics / Music

Among the contributors, who included Cage, Brown, and Wolff, were Joseph Byrd, Toshi Ichiyanagi, Richard Maxfield, Nam June Paik, and James Waring. Young himself included a number of his compositions of 1960. *Composition 1960 #10* is reproduced below, in its entirety:

Draw a straight line and follow it.

October 1960

Composition 1960 #7—" to be held for a long time"—was performed in New York in 1961 by a string trio; its duration was 45 minutes; it evoked a large number of ancillary sounds, mostly audience noises, but also revealed to those who continued to listen a whole inner world of fluctuating overtones in the open fifth as sustained by the players.

Among the ONCE group composers, Robert Ashley (b. 1930) and Gordon Mumma (b. 1935) were the leaders. A typical piece of Ashley's is *Public Opinion Descends Upon the Demonstrators* (1961), for a single operator of complex electronic playback equipment with a large variety of pre-recorded sounds, and an audience. The audience is seated unconventionally so that its members can observe each other and so that the operator can observe their reactions. The operator determines the sounds of the piece according to audience activity: there are specific sound-complexes for him to produce when each of the following actions is "performed" by a member of the audience: (1) leave the auditorium; (2) walk around in the auditorium; (3) speak aloud or laugh; (4) whisper (audibly or noticeably); (5) make any kind of exaggerated gesture; (6) make any kind of secretive gesture; (7) glance "meaningfully" at another member of the audience; (8) seek a remote visual diversion (through the windows, about the ceiling, etc.); (9) look toward a loudspeaker; (10) make an involuntary physical gesture (yawn, scratch, adjust clothing, etc.); (11) show an enforced physical rigidity (waiting it out.) Things get lively as soon as the audience begins to understand that in some mysterious way *it* is creating the piece: exhibitionists, angry resenters, and shrinking violets all contribute to a lively interaction between "audience" and "performer" in which traditional roles are thoroughly confused and in which no one is really certain who the "composer" is. Like Ashley, Mumma has been concerned with activating the musical experience: *Meanwhile, A Twopiece* (1961) for grand piano, percussion, pre-recorded electronic sounds, and "another instrument on which one of the performers is proficient" is written in a notation that indicates only the physical gestures to be made by the two players, with cues for them to move from instrument to instrument at certain points. In speaking of the ideology of such a piece, Mumma has said that its physicality, free choice of sounds, and interaction between performers respond partly to the fact that "with the widespread use of 'canned' music (radio, phonograph, and tape playback in serious music, commercial popular music, jazz, and electronic music) the visual or theatrical aspect of the performance of music has lost much of its significance."[21] In *Meanwhile* and in a work like *Gestures II* for two pianos (1962), Mumma strikes back, as do Ashley and other composers of "action and gesture" music.

[21] Private communication, February 23, 1962.

BIBLIOGRAPHICAL NOTES

The music discussed in this (and the following) chapter is also treated extensively, in the broader context of Western music in general, in Eric Salzman's companion volume, *Twentieth-Century Music: An Introduction* (2nd ed.; Englewood Cliffs: Prentice-Hall, Inc., 1974). The book by Leonard Meyer cited in footnote 8 is an important critical-aesthetic contribution.

In addition to the three essays by Carter mentioned in footnote 6, *Flawed Words and Stubborn Sounds: A Conversation with Elliott Carter,* ed. Allen Edwards (New York: W. W. Norton & Company, Inc., 1971), is illuminating.

Milton Babbitt's theoretical writings, for many readers almost impenetrably detailed and complex, have appeared in various journals: *Journal of the American Musicological Society,* III (1950); *The Score and I.M.A. Magazine,* June 1955; *MQ,* XLVI (1960); *Journal of Music Theory,* V (1961); *PNM,* I (1962); *Journal of the International Folk Music Council,* XVI (1964). (Of these, the *PNM* article has been perhaps the most influential among other composers.) A good discussion of Babbitt's 36-measure, serial *Semi-Simple Variations* for piano (1957) is offered by Elaine Barkin in her too-modestly-titled "A simple approach to Milton Babbitt's semi-simple Variations," *Music Review,* 28, No. 4 (November 1967), 316–22.

Elliott Schwartz's *Electronic Music: A Listener's Guide* (New York: Praeger Publishers, 1973) is informed and comprehensive; its Part IV includes "observations" on the subject by 23 composers. *Electronic Music* (Washington: Music Educators National Conference, 1968) is a reprint of the November 1968 issue of the *Music Educators Journal;* it is one of the most accessible introductions available. Babbitt has written a lucid account of the R.C.A. Synthesizer's contribution in "The Revolution in Sound: Electronic Music," *University, A Princeton Magazine,* IV (April 22, 1960), 8–16. Otto Luening pinpoints the chronology of electronic-music development in "Some Random Remarks about Electronic Music," *Journal of Music Theory,* VIII, 1 (Spring 1964), 89–98.

Hiller and Isaacson's *Experimental Music* (New York: McGraw-Hill Book Company, 1959) relates in detail the problems and progress of early computer composition. Chapter 5 of the book by Elliott Schwartz cited above is on "Computer-generated Sound"; it is the best introductory account in print.

Cage's own essays and lectures are unparalleled sources for his ideas on the experimental music of chance and indeterminacy; they have been collected in two books, *Silence* (Middletown: Wesleyan University Press, 1961) and *A Year from Monday* (same publisher, 1968). See also his *Notations* (West Glover: Something Else Press, Inc., 1969), a book with facsimiles of 263 contemporary composers' manuscript pages plus commentary, typographically fascinating, by them and the editors (Cage and Alison Knowles).

ELEVEN

INTERSECTIONS, INTERACTIONS, PROJECTIONS

Each of the words in the title of this last chapter might be found as heading for a musical work of the 1960's or early '70's. The decade after World War II had seen extraordinary activity in American music, along apparently widely divergent lines; another ten to fifteen years later, however, it was possible to perceive some new syntheses—or, if that term suggests too strongly ultimate mergers wholly completed, at least "intersections" and "interactions" among different trends and kinds of music; and perhaps these "projected" some syntheses lying ahead. As one composer-critic of the period put it: "For the younger composers, and many of the older ones, the barriers are down, the categories destroyed. . . . Any kind of statement is possible."[1] In all the areas of American music—jazz, popular music and musical theater, concert music —one of the most striking trends of the later 1950's and 1960's was the intermingling of musical techniques, languages, and even worlds that had seemed separate before.

[1] Salzman, *Twentieth-Century Music* (2nd ed.), p. 200.

JAZZ AND THE THIRD STREAM

In the jazz field, three principal post-war types—cool jazz, hard bop or funky jazz, and "the new thing"—arose from interactions of attitude and intersections of style. Cool jazz may be dated from a famous series of recordings made early in 1949 by a nine-man group led by trumpeter Miles Davis (b. 1926), later gathered together in an album titled *Birth of the Cool* (Capitol Records album T-762). Based on sophisticated arrangements by Gil Evans (b. 1912) for an unusual ensemble of solo instruments including French horn and tuba, this was a chamber jazz of great musical elegance, if also of great restraint expressively compared to the contemporaneous bop style. The ruminative, often gutturally soliloquizing trumpet of Davis and the thin, pale tone of alto saxophonist Lee Konitz (b. 1927) were characteristic. Pianist in the performances of *Venus de Milo* by Gerry Mulligan (b. 1927) and in his own *Rouge* was John Lewis (b. 1920). In 1952, Lewis founded the Modern Jazz Quartet; its light sound (piano, vibraphone, bass, and drums) and a style often including contrapuntal devices like canon and fugue and based on such non-traditional source materials as Elizabethan virginal music (*The Queen's Fancy*), Bach (*Vendôme*), and an old Christmas carol (*God Rest Ye Merry, Gentlemen*) made it the epitome of cool jazz. Related in its breadth of style-sources was the music of a quartet organized by pianist Dave Brubeck (b. 1920), who had studied with both Milhaud and Schoenberg. Typical was a verson of *Perdido*, recorded at a 1953 Oberlin College concert, in which the Brubeck group included witty improvisatory quotations from a 1928 Broadway show tune (*Crazy Rhythm*), a popular song of 1935 (*The Music Goes 'Round and 'Round*) and Stravinsky's *Petrushka,* plus a fugal exposition in the manner of Baroque-era music. Brubeck later broke out of the traditional $\frac{4}{4}$ meter of jazz with a number of works in $\frac{5}{4}$ and $\frac{7}{4}$, issued in a record album titled *Time Out.* Even more eclectic, sophisticated, and intellectualized was the piano jazz of Lennie Tristano (b. 1919), noted as a teacher of vanguard jazz style in the 1950's.

Perhaps in reaction to such a cultivated chamber jazz, there emerged in the mid-1950's a hard, harsh, leather-lunged style sometimes called "hard bop" or "funky" jazz. The latter term, an old colloquialism for "smelly" with sexual implications like the original ones of "jazz" itself, suggested the back-to-the-roots aim of the style. As expressed first by Horace Silver (b. 1928), pianist and musical director of the Jazz Messengers of drummer Art Blakey (b. 1919); by another pianist, Thelonious Monk (b. 1918); and by bassist Charlie Mingus (b. 1922), hard bop combined the chromaticism, the asymmetrical phrases, and the sharp punctuation of the bop style with the old earthiness of New Orleans jazz. The result was a tough, angular, honking music as complex harmonically as bop and cool jazz but also as expressionistically fervent and powerfully communicative as the early jazz of the 1920s.

With the appearance in the late 1950's of saxophonists John Coltrane (1926–1967) and Ornette Coleman (b. 1930), some jazz approached the ultra-chromatic, even atonal style of certain non-jazz. This "new thing" ("free-form jazz," "atonal jazz," "the new wave" were other attempts to name it) gave up the traditional basis of jazz in a pre-existent "tune" and a steady, even beat and turned to an almost wholly spontaneous, rhapsodic, and passionately expressive style in which the players relied on virtually extra-sensory perception to follow each other's ideas. Men like saxophonists Albert Ayler (1934–1970) and Archie Shepp (b. 1937) identified the searing expressionism of the "new thing" with the struggles of the American Negro and with the militant Black Nationalism of the 1960's. Ayler commented, "It's not about notes anymore. It's about feelings!" The black poet and playwright Le Roi Jones said: "You hear . . . poets of the Black Nation."[2] One of Shepp's early pieces had the title *Rufus;* this was an abbreviation for *Rufus Swung His Face at Last to the Wind, Then His Neck Snapped,* and the idea behind the piece was a lynching.

At about this time the identity of jazz and its very existence as a separate music were threatened by extraordinary developments in the world of popular music. The following section of this chapter describes these; here it should be pointed out that no longer were black singers of jazz-related music identified—as had been blues and swing singers like Bessie Smith (1895–1937), Billie Holiday (1915–1959), Jimmy Rushing (1903–1972), and Ella Fitzgerald (b. 1918)—with jazz itself. Rather, such spectacular black vocalists as Mahalia Jackson (1911–1972) and Ray Charles (b. 1932), James Brown (b. 1934) and Aretha Franklin (b. 1942) were heard (depending on their emphasis of religious or secular songs) as "gospel" or "soul" singers, part of the broader picture of American popular music.

Several composers of the period moved freely from jazz to non-jazz or the reverse. Gunther Schuller (b. 1925) saw in the intersection of these two mainstreams of American music possibilities for a "Third Stream," as he termed it in 1957. His *Transformation* (1957) for an eleven-piece jazz-like ensemble was conceived as "a kind of musical reflection (in general terms) of the issue . . . namely, the continuing process of amalgamation of jazz and contemporary 'classical' music."[3]

---

[2] Both quotations from the jacket notes of *The New Wave in Jazz,* Impulse Records album A-90.

[3] Schuller, jacket notes for *Modern Jazz Concert: Six Compositions Commissioned by the 1957 Brandeis University Festival of the Arts,* Columbia recording WL-127.

Conversations and *Concertino* (both 1959) set a jazz quartet (with the make-up of the Modern Jazz Quartet) against, respectively, string quartet and symphony orchestra. In these works "amalgamation" is a misnomer: the two styles are kept discrete; they intersect but are not synthesized. In later works like *Seven Studies on Themes of Paul Klee* (1959) and his First Symphony (1965), Schuller moved closer to a real synthesis. A substantial number of other composers also utilized jazz elements. Their incentive seemed to spring not at all from an "Americanist" ideal, nor perhaps even the Third Stream envisioned by Schuller. Some of them, practiced jazz musicians themselves, simply found the repertory of jazz idioms and inflections to be promising, natural, and viable foundations for more formal composition: among these were Hall Overton (1920–1972) and Francis Thorne (b. 1922); the latter's witty chamber work, punningly titled *Six Set Pieces* (1967), combined serial techniques with jazz-derived ideas easily and naturally, even in two movements called "Jam Sessions." Others seemed more interested in the vitalizing possibilities of improvisation in general, without, however, Cage's aesthetic of an "experimental" indeterminacy. Among these composers are Larry Austin (b. 1930), Meyer Kupferman (b. 1926), Michael Colgrass (b. 1932), Peter Phillips (b. 1930), and David Reck (b. 1935).

Another composer well-versed in ragtime and jazz (as a pianist), an arranger of skill and taste, and a connoisseur of American popular music in general is William Bolcom (b. 1938). This orientation has influenced much of his music. Bolcom had his first critical success with *Dynamite Tonite* (1963), subtitled "opera for actors"; its relationship to musical comedy is implicit in the subtitle (but so is the aspiration to an artistic integrity surpassing that of the usual musical). Bolcom provided much of the impetus for the ragtime revival of the early 1970's, both as a performer and as a composer of new rags like *Seabiscuits* (1967) and the delicate *Graceful Ghost* (1970). Together with William Albright (b. 1944) he also wrote *Brass Knuckles* (1969), a rollicking rag which is, however, studded with cluster-chord crashes; they evoke the spirit of the deadpan surprises (in the form of sudden *sforzando* eruptions) in the piano-playing of a Eubie Blake.

Although not ordinarily a composer of jazz-related music, Salvatore Martirano (b. 1927) exploited, in *Ballad* for amplified singer and chamber ensemble (1966), the extraordinary vocal agility, range, and varied tonal nuance of young rock-and-roll singers in a work combining lacerating intensity and good humor. Similar elements of virtuosity and expressivity are demanded in Martirano's *O, O, O, O, that Shakespeherian Rag* (1958), the title from T. S. Eliot, the texts from Shakespeare, and the music, for chorus and instrumental ensemble, a "so elegant, so intelligent" commentary on the verses.

THE REVOLUTION IN POPULAR MUSIC: FROM POP TO ROCK

If jazz underwent rapid changes in the two decades after World War II, an even more violent upheaval occurred in American popular music. With the exception of a continuing undercurrent of sweet, romantic, conservative, virtually "traditional" song—heard from such older performers as Lawrence Welk (b. 1903), Perry Como (b. 1912), and Frank Sinatra (b. 1917)—American popular music was transformed entirely, from "pop" to "rock."

As had happened before in popular-music development (and may well happen again), the main source of the transformation was the music of blacks, this time the "rhythm-and-blues" of black dance music on recordings.[4] The term covered several kinds of music American blacks were making and enjoying in the postwar years: the strong-rhythmed dance music of big bands, which was rooted in the Kansas City swing style (Andy Kirk, Jay McShann, Erskine Hawkins, and others); the urban blues of band-backed showmen in big-city dance halls and auditoriums (T-Bone Walker, Louis Jordan, B. B. King, Bobby Bland, and others), which were rooted in the personal laments or exultations of the self-accompanied singers of country blues (Lightnin' Hopkins, Mississippi John Hurt, Muddy Waters, Blind Lemon Jefferson, Big Bill Broonzy, and others); and the close harmony of singing groups (The Ink Spots, The Dominos, The Ravens, The Drifters, The Orioles, and others), which was rooted in the gospel singing of rural evangelistic and urban storefront churches (recorded by such soloists and groups as Sister Rosetta Tharpe, Mahalia Jackson, Dorothy Love Coates, and James Cleveland; The Soul Stirrers, The Dixie Hummingbirds, the Clara Ward Singers, the Sallie Martin Singers, the Roberta Martin Singers; and others).

Another source of the new popular music was the hillbilly style of southern upland whites—or, as it would be called when the folkish music became known more widely, "country-and-western" (or just "country")—and a variant of it, "bluegrass" music.

These two musics—rhythm-and-blues and country-and-western—had some stylistic characteristics in common which made their marriage a potentially happy one: they both emphasized a highly personal, grass-

---

[4] "Rhythm-and-blues" was a name coined by the record industry (along with others that did not catch on, like "sepia" and "ebony") as a substitute for "race music," which with the growing social consciousness of the late 1940's came to be viewed as offensive.

roots earthiness of vocal style; they both were based rhythmically on a powerful and danceable instrumental background; and they both tended to favor the guitar, whether the electrically amplified guitar of the urban blues singers, the natural "acoustic" guitar (long prominent as a rural, folkish instrument) of country blues, or the steel guitar, sometimes amplified, of country-and-western music.

The transformation of American popular music through the marriage of black rhythm-and-blues and white country-and-western music was owed primarily to a new phenomenon in American society: a self-conscious, self-aware, and economically strong "youth culture" of rebellious teenagers—that generation of Americans born just before World War II or during the baby boom immediately after it, raised in the postwar economic boom, and come to adolescence in the 1950's. Early in that decade, rhythm-and-blues records began to attract white teenagers, especially as a music for dancing. A few alert disc jockeys began to program the records for a general audience, not just for the black community; one of them, Alan Freed, broadcasting out of Cleveland in 1952, was instrumental in popularizing the name "rock 'n' roll" for this music.[5] Soon, record manufacturers were marketing rhythm-and-blues/rock-and-roll recordings generally, not just to blacks. And soon they were employing white musicians to "cover" black hits—to record copies or new (smoother-edged, somewhat diluted, and generally more commercially successful) versions of them—or were searching for white musicians whose styles were based on, or close to, black music. White rock-and-roll hits in turn awakened interest in the black music and musicians they had imitated. Before long, much American popular music was moving in the direction of rock-and-roll.

The first indication at the national level of the change in popular-music taste was the appearance in 1953 of a rock-and-roll song on the weekly list of best-selling records published in *Billboard* magazine: it was *Crazy Man Crazy*, by Bill Haley and His Comets (a white group). Haley was even more successful the following year with *Shake, Rattle and Roll* (a cover for black Joe Turner's recording of it earlier in 1954).

Haley's was primarily a northern style based on the heavy rolling beat of rhythm-and blues, with however a slight twang of guitars from country-and-western. The opposite balance typified the songs of his successor in popularity (and in fact the most spectacularly successful rock-and-roll star of the 1950's and early '60's), Elvis Presley. Born in 1935 in East Tupelo, Mississippi, Presley sang (and played guitar to) a music blending a dash of rhythm-and-blues with large amounts of country-and-

[5] Freed did not invent the term, although he claimed to have and has been credited with it. See Charlie Gillett, *The Sound of the City*, 2nd ed. (New York: Dell Publishing Company, 1972), p. 9.

western; some called the style "rockabilly," others "country rock." After cutting five songs for Sun Records, a Memphis firm, and building a reputation by 1955 as the nation's most promising country musician, Presley was signed by a major record company, RCA Victor. In early 1956 he recorded the song *Heartbreak Hotel* for them; they arranged television appearances for him and put together an LP album by him, partly from material recorded earlier.[6] Within a few weeks, both the single of *Heartbreak Hotel* and the LP album were leading the *Billboard* lists. Presley had reached the top; for eight years, into 1963, he was to remain there.

If Presley and other white rock-and-roll stars—notably Pat Boone (b. 1934) and Johnny Cash (b. 1932)—were the national favorites, some black musicians were more inventive. One whose originality, power, and wit can be measured by his enormous impact on later musicians was Chuck Berry (b. 1926). His first record, *Maybellene* (1955), was about sex and speed; others spoke directly to, and for, the youth culture, like *School Day* (1957) or *Almost Grown* (1959) (". . . Don't bother me, leave me alone/Anyway I'm almost grown"). In *Roll Over, Beethoven* (1956), Berry opted for popular as against high culture (". . . Roll over, Beethoven, and tell Tchaikowsky the news") in an unconscious echo of earlier American vernacular-culture champions (see p. 109). He sounded yet other notes of protest in his songs, and, with his powerful shouting-blues voice, the brassy sound of his amplified guitar, and his drummer's bombshell beats, he helped to confirm rock-and-roll as a music of rebellious youth. Bo Diddley (b. 1930 as Ellas McDaniel), Fats Domino (b. 1928), Sam Cooke (1935–1964), and Little Richard (b. 1934) were other blacks who, although heard mainly within the Negro community during the 1950's, would provide materials for nationally—even internationally—popular covers later. (Many in the black community complained bitterly about this cultural, and commercial, robbery.) More versatile than they, able to adapt to a variety of styles (popular ballads, gospel songs, and jazz as well as rock-and-roll) and thus able to win a national audience more easily, was Ray Charles, the blind singer-pianist-organist-saxophonist who along with Presley dominated the pop-music field in the early 1960's.

By the late 1950's a new trend in popular music—by no means unrelated to rock-and-roll—was visible. This was an interest in folk music, especially that of the American past, and in folkish songs newly written.

---

[6] The album's songs clearly reveal Presley's models: *Blue Suede Shoes* (based on the original by white country-and-western singer Carl Perkins), *I Got a Woman* (originally recorded in 1955 as a rhythm-and-blues number by Ray Charles), *Tutti Frutti* (originally recorded by the black urban-blues singer "Little Richard" Penniman), *Money Honey* (originally recorded in 1954 by the black gospel-influenced group The Drifters); in addition, there were rockabilly-tinged slow ballads and even a version of Rodgers and Hart's *Blue Moon*.

Pete Seeger (b. 1919) and The Weavers, strongly influenced by the leftist, Depression-era folk singing of Woody Guthrie (1912–1967), turned *Goodnight, Irene,* which had been recorded in the early 1930's by country-blues singer Huddie Ledbetter (1885–1949), known as Leadbelly, into a hit as early as 1950. But it was not until several years later that folk or folk-derived music began to rival rock-and-roll in national popularity; The Kingston Trio's *Tom Dooley* (1958), based on a late nineteenth-century ballad, was a landmark. By the middle 1960's, the folk-music revival had progressed so far that perhaps the most universally well-known song in the country was an earlier labor-movement song with a tune of uncertain origins, its words adjusted by Pete Seeger and others to relate it to the major socio-political drives of the time for civil rights and world peace: *We Shall Overcome* (Example 11-1).[7]

EXAMPLE 11-1. *We Shall Overcome.* New Words and Music Arrangement by Zilphia Horton, Frank Hamilton, Guy Carawan & Pete Seeger. TRO © Copyright 1960 and 1963, LUDLOW MUSIC, INC., New York, N.Y. USED BY PERMISSION. Royalties derived from this composition are being contributed to The Freedom Movement under the trusteeship of the writers.

Among the leading figures in the folk revival were Harry Belafonte (b. 1927), who popularized the calypso style of the West Indies in 1957; Joan Baez (b. 1941), who came to prominence in 1960 with her first LP album (including *Donna, Donna* and *House of the Rising Sun*); the trio of Peter, Paul, and Mary, whose first hit (a version of Pete Seeger's *If I Had a Hammer*) was recorded in 1962; and Bob Dylan (b. 1941 as Robert Zimmerman).

[7] Although often identified as deriving from *I'll Overcome Some Day* (1900–1) by the black gospel-song composer C. Albert Tindley, the melody of *We Shall Overcome* has no relationship to Tindley's; the text, however, is close to that of the chorus of his hymn ("I'll overcome some day,/I'll overcome some day;/If in my heart I do not yield/I'll overcome some day"). I am grateful to Wayne D. Shirley of the Library of Congress's Music Division for providing me with a copy of Tindley's hymn; it was he too who informed me that the Library's Folk Song Archive has recordings of *We Shall Overcome* being sung as a song of the labor movement in the 1940's.

Dylan began his career as a New York coffee-house balladeer in 1960. His model was Woody Guthrie; he sang in a high, harsh, somewhat tuneless voice that sounded very "old-timey," very "country," and he played an acoustic guitar, sometimes punctuating his songs with wails on a harmonica hung on a frame around his neck. He had a unique poetic sensibility, and a number of his songs stated unforgettably some major themes of the 1960's—at least those of the disillusioned, alienated youth, sick of the country's domination by the military-industrial complex, its undeclared wars, and its racial strife. Some of these were *Blowin' in the Wind* (1963), against racial prejudice; *Hard Rain's A-Gonna Fall* (1963), against the nuclear bombing threat; *It Ain't Me Babe* (1964), about superficial boy-girl relationships; *Mr. Tambourine Man* (1965), about alienation; *Subterranean Homesick Blues* (1965), about the absurdity of it all.

Among many others influenced by Dylan was the team of Paul Simon and Art Garfunkel (both born in 1942). They treated topics as timely as Dylan's, if in a less poetically unique and musically uncompromising and individualistic way, in such songs as *The Sound of Silence* (1964), *Scarborough Fair/Canticle* (1966), and *Mrs. Robinson* (from the film *The Graduate* of 1968).[8] In fact, one of the most striking things about the new popular songs of the later 1960's was the quality and significance of their lyrics: they spoke of serious matters both timely and timeless, and in a more poetically artful way than had the popular songs of a generation earlier.[9]

Ironically, the team of musicians which most clearly personified the intersections of black and white, urban and country, folk and pop, and pop and art in American "popular" music of the later 1960's—and a group which even surpassed Presley in popular success—was not American at all but British: The Beatles (John Lennon, Paul McCartney, George Harrison, and Ringo Starr). Early in 1964 their recording of *I Want to Hold Your Hand* reached Number 1 on the "charts" (the *Billboard, Cashbox,* and *Variety* best-seller lists); during one week in March the top five records were all by them; and for the whole period from

[8] Hollywood was slow to adopt the new pop music: apart from some films with Elvis Presley as male lead, beginning with *Love Me Tender* (1956), few Hollywood products used rock on their soundtracks until the late 1960's. The first film with an all-rock score was Richard Lester's *A Hard Day's Night* (1964), a British production starring The Beatles (and their music).

[9] This claim, a generalization only, is borne out by the large number of published discussions, criticism, and analysis of the song texts of the period. Framing these are two key articles, one on the absence of sincerity, variety, and realism in popular songs as of 1954, the other on their presence in songs as of 1970. See S. I. Hayakawa, "Popular Songs vs. The Facts of Life," *Etc.*, XII (1955), 83–95; reprinted in *Mass Culture*, ed. Bernard Rosenberg and David Manning White (New York: The Free Press, 1957), pp. 393–403; and Charles Hamm, "Rock and The Facts of Life," *Yearbook for Inter-American Musical Research*, VII (1971), 5–15.

February to July songs by them led all others.[10] This fantastic popularity, absolutely without historical precedent, was maintained by The Beatles for years, in fact virtually until the group dissolved in 1970; it was due to several factors, among them the inventiveness of song-writers Lennon and McCartney, canny management and promotion of the group, and their studied eclecticism, always seeming to be one step ahead of the expanding stylistic range of rock-and-roll.

Indeed, variants of rock-and-roll were multiplying so fast by the late 1960's, each seeming another step removed from the ultimate source (rhythm-and-blues/country-and-western), that the new pop music came to be called simply "rock," plus one of any number of qualifying adjectives. There was folk rock (The Byrds, The Band, Country Joe & The Fish). There were blues rock (Ike and Tina Turner, The Righteous Brothers) and hard rock (The Doors, The Jimi Hendrix Experience). There was acid rock from San Francisco groups like Jefferson Airplane; the term referred to the drug LSD, to songs which spoke positively of such drugs (like singer Grace Slick's *White Rabbit*) or hinted at their use, and to the delirious experience of rock concerts which combined ear-splitting, consciousness-numbing amplification, hypnotically repetitive rhythms and static or constantly revolving harmonies, and kaleidoscopic, psychedelic light-shows.[11] There were Bach rock (*A Whiter Shade of Pale*, by the British group, Procol Harum) and Renaissance rock (*Pavan for My Lady*, by the short-lived American one, Ars Nova). There was even rock that was not—or, as one critic described it, "unpopular pop"[12]— in the complex, Varèse- and Stravinsky- and Cage-influenced music of Frank Zappa (b. 1940) and his group, The Mothers of Invention; their early concerts were precursors of the cynical grotesqueries of what, in the early 1970's, was called variously "rock 'n' rouge," "deca-rock" (for

---

[10] Gillett, *The Sound of the City*, p. 286; *Lillian Roxon's Rock Encyclopedia* (New York: Grosset & Dunlap, 1969), *s.v.* "The Beatles." It was perhaps due to The Beatles' unparalleled popularity that the most common instrumental make-up of a rock group came to be a foursome of lead guitar, rhythm guitar, and bass guitar (all three heavily amplified and armed with various devices for timbral changes), plus a drummer.

[11] Such concerts were by no means unique to acid rock. After The Beatles' examples (especially the concert by them that filled New York's Shea Stadium, fall of 1966), rock concerts and festivals were a commonplace in giant interior halls like Fillmore Auditorium in San Francisco and Fillmore East in New York. The peak of rock-concert productions occurred in a field near Woodstock, New York in the summer of 1969, when more or less 450,000 young people gathered in a three-day "festival of love" and rock; the nadir at Altamont Speedway, California, later that year, when many members of an audience of 300,000 experienced bad drug "trips," violence, and rioting (with a few deaths).

[12] Lawrence Gushee, paper delivered at the annual meetings of the American Musicological Society, November 4, 1972. David Walley implies somewhat the same thing in the title of his biography of Zappa, *No Commercial Potential* (New York: Outerbridge & Lazar, Inc., 1972).

"decadent"), or "glitter rock": the homo-erotic, sado-masochistic, chaotic unisex spectacles of performers like David Bowie and Alice Cooper (both males).

By the mid-1970's, it seemed that this glut of rock offshoots might be presaging the decline of the genre and the dawn of a new cycle of American popular music. One critic forecast a renaissance of lyricism, seeing in the melodious songs of Joni Mitchell (*Clouds, The Circle Game, Chelsea Morning*), Carly Simon (*Anticipation, A Legend in Your Own Time*), Carole King (*You've Got a Friend, I Feel the Earth Move*), and Randy Newman (*I Think It's Going to Rain Today*) successors to those of Gershwin, Porter, and Rodgers.[13] And perhaps this lyric renaissance would come out of the musical, which had finally begun to reflect the transformation of American popular music.

The rock revolution had effected a decentralization of the geographical sources (in performance, recording, and publishing) of popular music: Nashville, Memphis, Detroit, and San Francisco were as important breeding-grounds and distribution centers as New York. The American musical comedy, however, with its center of gravity at Broadway and Times Square, remained dominated by New York's tendency to a narrow if sophisticated insularity and for a long time tended to maintain the aesthetic and the musical style of pre-World War II productions. Only in 1967, in *Hair* (music composed by Galt MacDermot), did the popular lyric theater begin to catch up with the new pop music. *Hair*, although not the revolutionary work it seemed at first to be (partly because of one semi-nude scene), was at least perceptibly tinged with rock, in such songs as *Aquarius* and *Electric Blues*, and with rock's themes of protest from the youth culture.

At least one brilliant new composer of musicals (as well as other kinds of works) appeared in the immediate post-war years: Leonard Bernstein (b. 1918). A pupil of Piston at Harvard with prodigious gifts as pianist, conductor, and composer, Bernstein moved easily from one to another of America's worlds of music, "classical" and popular. His Second Symphony, "The Age of Anxiety" (1949), includes a lengthy jazz-piano solo; his ballet score *Fancy Free* was amplified into a musical, *On the Town* (both 1944). With a style that might be described as out of Stravinsky by Copland, and with complete fluency in the pre-rock popular-music idiom, Bernstein created in *West Side Story* (1957) the freshest musical of the post-war period. A recasting of the Romeo and Juliet story in terms of the ethnic melting-pot of Manhattan's upper west side, *West Side Story* was an evocative portrait of post-war urban America;

---

[13] Don Heckman, "You Like to Recognize the Tune? You Will," *The New York Times*, September 24, 1972.

its finely-balanced interaction between ballet and drama owed much to choreographer Jerome Robbins, who had also conceived the dances of *Fancy Free*. And with *Mass* (composed for the opening in 1971 of the John F. Kennedy Center for the Performing Arts in Washington, D.C.) Bernstein wrote a work that had some relationship, at least, with avant-garde impulses toward a new, "third music theater" (see p. 273). The only other post-war musical to rival (and even out-do) the success of *West Side Story* was *My Fair Lady* (1956), composed by Frederick Loewe (b. 1904) to Alan Jay Lerner's book after Shaw's *Pygmalion*. Perhaps the American audience that responded by the millions to this near-operetta was identifying with the guttersnipe-turned-lady of the heroine; musically speaking it had little to identify with, for like all the other musicals of the late 1950's and most of the '60's *My Fair Lady* shared in no way in in the popular-music revolution.

By the early 1970's, however, a second new figure in musical comedy seemed especially promising as a composer with staying power. This was Stephen Sondheim (b. 1920). Sondheim had written the lyrics of the songs in *West Side Story*. Later he went on independently to compose the scores for a series of musicals of high inventiveness and artistry (*Gypsy, Company, Follies*) which culminated in a fresh and elaborate work, *A Little Night Music* (1972). Its clever patter songs, contrapuntal duets and trios, a quartet, and even a double quintet suggested once again (as with *Oklahoma!* almost 30 years earlier) that the musical might be aspiring to a new high-mindedness.

OTHER NEW MUSIC

Other new music of the 1960's and early '70's revealed a further development of trends already seen in the 1950's, with important intersections and interactions between them. Some new emphases were visible (and at least one de-emphasis in the case of serialism, which seemed to be declining in importance by the early 1970's). Besides the rapid expansion of electronic music composition, which I have discussed above, the most important developments seemed to be a "new virtuosity" in composing and performing live music; a new interest in the interplay of popular and "serious" music; and extensions in two directions of ideas that had been expressed, if not originated, by John Cage—toward a new "minimalism" on the one hand and, on the other, toward collage techniques, mixed-media productions, and a new music theater. And, although these developments seemed often superficially contrasting, antithetical, they all bespoke a new sort of expressionism, one which however had deep roots in the American musical past.

The New Virtuosity

Much of the new music put unprecedented demands on performers' abilities; it almost seemed to create a new virtuosity, displayed dazzlingly by such singers as Bethany Beardslee, Cathy Berberian, and Jan DeGaetani, such pianists as David Tudor, Paul Jacobs, and Robert Miller, and such others as violinist Matthew Raimondi, double-bassist Bertram Turetzky, flutist Harvey Sollberger, and percussionists Max Neuhaus and Raymond DesRoches. And these in turn extended the range of performance possibilities envisioned by composers. This is suggested in the works of the fluent composer Charles Wuorinen (who, as co-director with Sollberger of the Columbia Group for Contemporary Music, was intimately acquainted with many of these performers). Although temperamentally and intellectually inclined to "a very detailed structuring of events [in a composition] down to a very small scale, as well as on a very large scale" (and thus sympathetic to Babbitt's serial approach), Wuorinen also believed that "since even the most detailed score still represents an assemblage of generalities . . . it should always be possible to reinterpret compositions."[14] It was ironic, then, that he was awarded the Pulitzer Prize for an all-electronic composition (see above, p. 241), especially since the overwhelming majority of his works are for live performers, like the *Piano Variations* (1964), several chamber concertos with different solo instruments (cello, flute, oboe, and others), and the masque *The Politics of Harmony* (1966–67). In these, Wuorinen writes a music sometimes of ferocious intensity and furious activity, sometimes of complex lacy delicacy, that both responds to and demands more of the new virtuosity, approaching at times the outer limits of interpretative possibility and perception.

Equally demanding of performers' virtuosity but much more accessible to listeners than Wuorinen's music (and, for complicated reasons, to the performers themselves) has been a series of works by George Crumb (b. 1929) so well received that he was unquestionably the most highly acclaimed "young" American composer of the early 1970's. A former pupil of Ross Lee Finney, Crumb matured rapidly; by 1968, he had won a Pulitzer Prize for *Echoes of Time and the River: Four Processionals for Orchestra*. A large number of his works are settings of the Spanish poems of Federico García Lorca: four books of *Madrigals* (I and II, 1965; III and IV, 1969); *Songs, Drones and Refrains of Death* (1968); *Night of the Four Moons* (1969); and *Ancient Voices of Children* (1970). All of these reveal an extraordinarily subtle and adventuresome tonal imagination, a unique "ear," especially for tiny and delicate shades of

[14] Benjamin Boretz, "Conversation with Charles Wuorinen," *Contemporary Music Newsletter*, III, 7–8 (November–December 1969), 4–8.

timbre. To realize his sonorous visions, Crumb has called on an immense range of new performance techniques: humming into wind-instrument mouthpieces, vocalizing into undamped (and amplified) piano strings, whispering, shouting, microtonal "bending" of pitch (by, for example, turning the tuning-pegs of a double-bass), and so forth. And from the worlds of traditional and popular music he has borrowed many instruments: banjo, mandolin, toy piano, jew's harp, musical saw, cowbells, electric guitar, and other amplified instruments. *Black Angels* ("1969, *in tempore belli*" is the composer's dating, referring to the undeclared war in Vietnam) is for electric string quartet; *Vox Balaenae* (1972) is for flute, cello, and piano, each electrically amplified. In the latter work, the players are to wear black half-masks; the depersonalization of the human components eerily increases the "personalization" (à la Carter) of the music.

Another, older composer who came to prominence in the 1960's after building an earlier reputation as a neo-Classic *Wunderkind* was Lukas Foss (b. 1922). In 1957, inspired by the improvisatory vitality of jazz, Foss organized an Improvisation Chamber Ensemble in Los Angeles, hoping to develop principles of non-jazz improvisation. This had a marked effect on the music that he composed. *Time Cycle* (1959–60), four songs on texts having to do with time, clocks, or bells, appeared in two different versions—"the occasion, the size of the hall," said Foss, "will call for one or the other"—one of them for soprano and orchestra with improvisatory interludes between the songs (the other without them). *Echoi* (1961–63), for piano, percussion, clarinet, and cello, in four movements, includes not only conventionally "precise" notation but also "proportional" notation which, barless and beatless, requires the performers to view the entire score and to follow each others' playing; passages of "no coordination" and free re-ordering of given pitches; passages with random, aperiodic assortments of dynamics, articulations, pitches, or all three; and percussion passages written as stems without note-heads, inviting performance on any of the drums at hand, in any order. Toward the end of *Echoi IV*, two pre-recorded but uncoordinated tape tracks, one of clarinet music, the other of cello, are turned on; the live performers are to echo in a free manner the taped sounds of their own instruments. There are other aspects of choice and chance in *Echoi* (no two performances will ever be the same) but the composer's ideas dominate throughout. Example 11-2 can at least suggest some of the aspects of notation I have mentioned: the notation is proportional; large notes stand for longer time, small notes for shorter; dotted lines show the moments of coordination among performers; "c. 1s." represents a rest of "about one second"; noteless stems on the vibraphone staff indicate general melodic contour but no specific pitches.

EXAMPLE 11-2. L. Foss, *Echoi,* first movement excerpt. © Copyright 1964 by Carl Fischer, Inc., New York. Reproduced by permission.

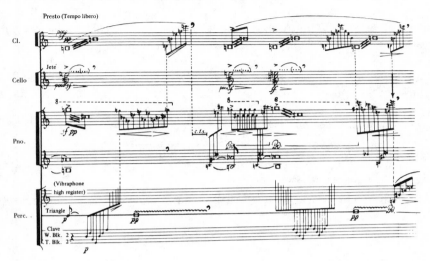

Traditionally, at least in Western music, composers have considered music to be a temporal art: time was the only continuum in which music was perceived to exist. There have been a few exceptions, notably the conscious planning in spatial terms of the polychoral music of Venice and Rome in the sixteenth and seventeenth centuries, or of similarly multi-group music by Berlioz, but these have proved the rule. However, in much recent music, composers have conceived of sound itself as spatialized as well as temporalized. That is, the musical discourse, no longer shaped according to principles of harmonic continuity or of underlying omnipresent "beat," is essentially one of discrete sounds or blocks of them, shaping time rather than being shaped by it. The result is an effect of sound in space more than in time, for the whole perception of time's passing is altered and attenuated by the discreteness of the sonorous events. Some composers no longer even speak of "sonorities" (let alone "chords" or "harmonies") but of "densities," "sound structures," or "sound objects." Formal principles often rest on the intersection and interaction of such sound structures, or on the equally spatial images of textures thick or thin, fluctuating or constant, combined or opposed. High-low contrasts are heard in spatial terms, as are timbral shifts. In some music, physical space itself has become crucial: symptomatically, an older composer like Henry Brant (b. 1913) who has been interested for a long time in varied placement of instrumentalists and singers in halls, auditoriums, and even the out-of-doors—e.g., *Millenium 1* (1950), *The Grand Universal*

Circus (1959), *Fire in Cities* (1961), and *Voyage Four* (1964)—has achieved new recognition. Ralph Shapey (b. 1921) similarly divides performers into sub-groups disposed in different, spatially separated positions. Thus his *Ontogeny* (1958) for orchestra calls for a division of the symphonic ensemble into seven sub-orchestras, re-positioned on stage. Another orchestral work, *Rituals* (1958), is similarly conceived. In speaking of his *Incantations* (1961) for soprano and ten instruments, Shapey articulated this new spatial concept of music:

> music as an object in Time and Space
>
> aggregate sounds structured into concrete sculptured forms
>
> images existing as a totality from their inception, each a self-involved unit of individual proportions
>
> related, inter-related, and unrelated images organized into an organic whole
>
> permutations occurring only within each self-contained unit . . .[15]

In several imaginative works by Roger Reynolds, including *The Emperor of Ice Cream* (1963) and *Blind Men* (1966), not only is the spatial distribution of the performers specified but the scores show their movement from one area of the stage to another.

Minimalism

Cage's idea that "music (imaginary separation of hearing from the other senses) does not exist" had led, as we have seen (p. 249) to many kinds of activity. Among them were the "static" drone-pieces of La Monte Young—which, however, to anyone who really listened were not in fact static: like "real" music, they pulsed and "moved," but with a strange inner life of minutely shifting timbres arising from the slight variations of overtone-structure in the tone(s) sounded—as, for example, when a violinist's bow moves across the string with ever-so-slight changes of pressure not willed by the performer but simply the result of his human "imperfection." Young went on to compose a whole series of non-melodic drone-music compositions on this phenomenon, rationalized and informed by his thorough study of classical Indian acoustical and intervallic theory (which is the basis of much of the music from India that sounds "static" to Western ears). One example is *The Second Dream of the High-Tension Line Stepdown Transformer*, from *The Four Dreams of China* (1962). It is based on four pitches in frequency ratios of 36/35/32/24. Example

---

[15] Quoted in "Music Programs and Notes," University of Illinois 1965 Festival of Contemporary Arts, p. 23.

11-3a gives a rough approximation of the pitches; 35 is less than a quarter-tone away from 36, hence the arrows in the example. Example 11-3b illustrates the just-intoned second, fourth, and fifth among several of the tones. In performing the composition, strict rules dictate which tones may be sounded together; otherwise, each tone may enter or exit at will. An apparently static "harmonic" music results—harmonic in the sense of the intervals formed not only between the basic tones but between their upper partials and the combination tones that are produced when these simple fundamental tones are dwelt on. But, as the per-

EXAMPLE 11-3. Basis of L. M. Young's *Second Dream of the High-Tension Line Stepdown Transformer* (1962). (a) Pitches to be sounded (approximate; just intonation is to be used); (b) interval-ratios produced.

formers develop their own sensitivity to such "harmonies," and to the degree that the listener does also, the music is not at all static; a strange, hypnotic, dream-like succession of delicate sound-images unfolds in shimmering, undulating procession.

A few others besides Young have pursued similar paths of minimal drone-music, notably Terry Riley (b. 1935) in works like *In C* for orchestra (1965), Dick Higgins (b. 1938), and Philip Glass (b. 1937).[16]

Steve Reich (b. 1936) has claimed (in an unpublished set of "optimistic predictions [1970] about the future of music") that "the pulse and the drone will re-emerge as basic sources of new music." His major interest has been in the pulse, especially of the sort heard all about us as machines beat against each other in shifting, out-of-phase relationships— two windshield wipers on a bus, two warning bells at a railroad crossing, and the like. *Come Out* (1966) is a piece based entirely on a tape-recording of one spoken phrase, ". . . come out to show them." The making of this phrase into a 13-minute work involved a tape-loop technique, whereby the phrase is repeated endlessly, and multi-track stereo playback. The tracks begin together—the phrase is "in unison" rhythmically with itself—then one is slightly speeded up and begins to move gradually,

[16] Higgins has written a provocative essay on "Boredom and Danger" in which he calls attention to this music's ultimately producing "a very strange, euphoric acceptance and enjoyment"; reprinted in *Source*, No. 5 (III, 1; January 1969), 14–17.

almost imperceptibly, out of phase with the other. Soon, in this remarkable "modern mensuration canon" technique, the resultant pulsation of
out-of-phase channels produces a kind of rhythmic combination-tone
effect. And eventually, as the two voices divide into four, then into eight,
a thick tapestry of multiple pulsations is perceived, as hypnotic and
euphoric rhythmically as Young's music is harmonically. Reich developed
techniques for live performance of similar minimal pulse-music in such
works as *Piano Phase* for two pianists (1967), *Four Organs* for electric
organs and maracas (1970), and *Phase Patterns* (also 1970) for four or
more identical keyboards, each performer repeating a few notes in a
basic drumstroke pattern (the paradiddle) but in slowly shifting tempo,
thus changing the phase in intricate oscillations.

Collage, Mixed-media, and Music Theater

Intersection and interaction are by definition the common ground
among various kinds of works, produced increasingly in recent years, that
may otherwise be vastly dissimilar: collage pieces (from the French word
for "paste-up"), mixed-media productions (an offshoot of the earlier Happenings but often more carefully structured), and a new kind of music
theater (closely related to mixed-media). Although many influences con-
joined to stimulate such works, their recent prominence is certainly
indebted to precepts and examples offered by John Cage.

In composing—or, rather, giving directions for—such a work as
his *Imaginary Landscape No. 4* (1951) for 12 radio receiving sets (24
performers), Cage effectively set the stage for a collage piece. The
"found objects" comparable to the bits of wood, newspaper, ribbon,
and what not in a collage by Picasso or Braque (or, more apposite to
Cage, his contemporary and friend Robert Rauschenberg) are the bits
of broadcast sound picked up by the various radios from different stations.
These sonorous "objects" both *represent* (are part of a total auditory
image) and *present* (are themselves). Like the musical quotations in works
of Ives (who may in fact be the American ancestor of the collage technique) or the pre-recorded materials of a *concrète* piece, such objects
make for a double level of perception: one experiences a new work but
at the same time is invited or made willy-nilly to perceive or remember
others.

In Crumb's *Ancient Voices of Children*, for example, evocative
fragments of other music are imbedded like flickerings of memory in the
matrix of the composition—flamenco music, *Bist du bei mir* from the
Notebook for Anna Magdalena Bach, a reminiscence of Mahler. Mahler
also figures in one startling movement of *Sinfonia* (1968), by Luciano Berio
(born in Italy in 1925 but since 1965 a musically influential American resi-

dent): against a playing of the entire third movement of Mahler's Second Symphony, countless references to other music proliferate, some spoken or sung, some played: Bach, Schoenberg, Debussy, Ravel, Strauss, Berlioz, Brahms, Berg, Hindemith, Beethoven, Stravinsky, Boulez, Stockhausen, Ives, Berio himself, and others. Berio remarked that the movement could be considered "a documentary on an *objet trouvé* recorded in the mind of the listener."[17] Foss's *Phorion* (1967), based on one movement of a violin partita by Bach (the title can be translated as "stolen goods"), and his *Geod* (1969) based (depending on the location of any given performance) on different patriotic/national materials, can be considered in the same way.

The collage technique is a naturally inviting one for live/electronic music, especially because it lends itself so well to a kind of abstract musical drama: juxtaposition can easily lead to opposition and conflict. Man-against-machine is embodied in the last movement of Foss's *Echoi*, when the live performers struggle against pre-recorded tapes of their own performance. Man-against-machine is also the theme of Druckman's *Animus I* (see above, p. 241); the composer describes the dramatic result:

> . . . After the first splitting off of the tape and the ensuing dialogue the [trombone] player sits while the electronic sounds move too quickly for him to compete. The man begins again with angrier, more animal-like material; the tape again enters . . . this time driving him off the stage. The tape exhausts itself, the man re-enters, the two finish in a tenuous balance.[18]

Like collage in their purposeful juxtaposition of disparate materials, but extended out beyond sound-materials to those in other media, have been various mixed-media productions. These had their origin in the Happenings of the 1950's and early '60's and in the action-music and environmental art of the ONCE, Fluxus, and other such groups. They also reflected, or at least paralleled, the multiple bombardment of the senses of a typical rock concert. And of course they flowed from Cage's dictum that "relevant action is theatrical (music [imaginary separation of hearing from the other senses] does not exist)."

Cage himself was co-producer with Lejaren Hiller of one of the most spectacular examples of mixed-media events, HPSCHD ("harpsichord" in the six-letter form that is the maximum necessary for computer coding), which was premiered at the University of Illinois in May 1969. The production lasted about five hours; it involved seven harpsichordists,

---

[17] From jacket notes by the composer for the Columbia recording (MS 7268).
[18] Jacket notes for *Electronic Music III* (Turnabout album TV 34177).

computer-generated sounds on fifty-one tapes, fifty-two slide projectors, a battery of colored spotlights, and an audience of several thousand who variously sat, stood, danced, and wandered through the environment. The sound-materials of the work themselves, and their organization, were an extraordinary mix. Three of the (amplified) harpsichordists played material based on the *Introduction to the Composition of Waltzes by Means of Dice* attributed to Mozart; another played any Mozart music of his choice; two others began with material by Mozart and moved on through music by Beethoven, Chopin, Schumann, Gottschalk, Ives, Schoenberg, Cage, and Hiller; the seventh played a computer-generated repertory of materials in equal-tempered twelve-tone tuning. Meanwhile, each of the fifty-one tapes produced sound-material based on a different equal-tempered division of the octave, from five to fifty-six tones (excluding the usual one of twelve). When HPSCHD was recorded—or at least a twenty-minute segment of it—a further nicety was added: along with the recording (Nonesuch H-71224) came a computer-output sheet which, if followed by the listener, enable him to "perform" the work by manipulating the knobs and buttons of his stereo set. (This acknowledgment and utilization of the new "medium" of the piece in its recorded form was a brilliant and genial idea of Cage and Hiller.)

An increasing number of other composers have been producing mixed-media works. Pauline Oliveros is one. Her *Valentine for SAG* (1968)—the acronym refers to the Sonic Arts Group, which developed out of ONCE—is based on an actual game of hearts played onstage, with the four players' heartbeats amplified. At the same time a narrator discusses the history of card games; two carpenters build a picket fence downstage; a croquet player hits a few balls; projections of giant playing-cards are visible.

In *Spider Song*, by Stanley Lunetta (b. 1937), two composer/performers are to compose, perform, and record a rock song onstage, in the presence of an audience; meanwhile, other participants are altering the stage environment visually and sonically. In the first two presentations of *Spider Song* (New York and Buffalo, December 1968), the songs *Carnegie Hall* and *Why Can't You Sit Still?* were created and preserved.

Morton Subotnick, whom we have met above (see p. 242) as a composer of electronic music, has also worked in mixed-media. In his *Mandolin* (1963), subtitled "a theater piece for viola, projections, and tape," the viola plays the role of a kind of musical narrator to a larger musical drama. The work is a kind of nineteenth-century theater piece with a piano composition of Liszt emerging in the middle. In *An Electric Christmas* (1967), Subotnick organized one of the most unusual demonstrations of interactions and intersections of the late 1960's. Clearly indebted to the format and setting of a rock concert, *An Electric Christmas* mingled in one evening-long event the medieval music of the New York Pro Musica ensemble, rock from a group called Circus Maximus, Subotnick's own electronic music (mostly composed and played on the spot), film projections, and a light-show; it culminated in a joyous, intermixed, semi-improvisatory version by the whole crowd of the fourteenth-century love-song, *Douce dame jolie*, by Guillaume de Machaut.

Sydney Hodkinson (Canadian-born in 1934) has produced many mixed-media works, including *Organasm* (1968) for solo organist and many "assistants." The latter bedevil the long-suffering soloist in a crescendo of torments to a peak of pandemonium, when suddenly the organ power is cut off, the assistants dash away, and all that is left is a tranquil recorded organ voluntary.

Obviously, there is an element of theatricality in such works as these. One composer, Eric Salzman (b. 1933), has claimed that they represent a "third music theater—neither opera nor musical—that [is] in the process of finding itself[:] a primarily non-verbal art integrating sound, movement, image, music, language, idea, thinking, feeling."[19] Salzman has pursued his vision by organizing a special music-theater group called Quog and by composing a number of music-theater pieces. Among them are *Verses and Cantos* (1967) for voices, rock and non-rock instrumental groups, and electronic sounds; and *The Nude Paper Sermon* (1968–69), "tropes" for actor, Renaissance consort, chorus, and electronic sounds. Just as media are mixed in these works, so are musical styles, in a dramatic (and theatrical) response to the experiential situation, when everyone has access through modern technology to a virtually limitless range of musics. As Salzman puts it:

> Multi-track, multi-layer experience becomes the norm: Ravi Shankar, John Cage, the Beatles, Gregorian chant, electronic music, Renaissance madrigals and motets, Bob Dylan, German *Lieder*, soul, J. S. Bach, jazz, Ives, Balinese gamelan, Boulez, African drumming, Mahler, *gagaku*, Frank Zappa, Tchaikowsky, Varèse . . . all become part of the common shared experience.[20]

The New Expressionism

One of the most powerful, if paradoxical, effects of the new ideas of time and space in music, of "concrete sculptured forms," of the new

---

[19] *The New York Times*, December 12, 1972.

[20] From the composer's jacket notes for *The Nude Paper Sermon* (Nonesuch recording H-71231). The same point, put in almost the same way, is made by composer Ben Johnston in a thoughtful essay "On Context," *Source*, No. 4 (II, 2; July 1968), 44–45: "Machaut, the Beatles, Wagner, Ravi Shankar, Pete Seeger, Bach, and Xenakis meet . . . only as far from me as my record player."

virtuosity, and also of the music involving chance and performer-choice in a context of composer-controlled image of sound, is of a new expressionism. Unlike the post-Romantic expressionism of a Strauss or a Schoenberg, it is not the composer's feelings but those of the performers or, even more potently, of the sounds themselves that seem to be loosed. Not only do the performers seem more alive, flexible, responsive to each other, but in a peculiarly palpable way the music itself takes on an unprecedented sentience, personalization, willfulness. Hear Lukas Foss, speaking of the second movement of *Echoi:*

> . . . vibraphone shadowing clarinet (close canon at the unison) sticks to him like glue. clarinet should make futile attempts to escape its own shadow, like an insect trying to extricate itself from a spider web. cello joins in the pursuit. . . . pitchless percussion also shadowing, imitating. everyone wanting to get in on the act.[21]

Or hear Chou Wen-chung (b. 1923), a former pupil of Varèse whose Chinese origins allow him to relate what seems new in American music to some very old Oriental ideas, speaking of his orchestral works *All in the Spring Wind* (1953) and *And the Fallen Petals* (1954):

> . . . a tonal brushwork in space—with ever-changing motion, tension, texture, and sonority. . . . The ancient Chinese musician believed that each single tone or aggregate of tones is a musical entity in itself and a living spark of expression as long as it lasts. Therefore, it was also believed that the meaning in music lies intrinsically in the tones themselves, that maximum expressiveness can be derived from a succession of tones without resorting to extraneous procedures.[22]

Or think of the abstract musical drama in Druckman's *Animus I*, when the tape "drives" the trombonist offstage and then "exhausts itself," or of the musical self-commentary inherent in quotation and collage techniques.

Many present-day American composers are building a whole new musical aesthetic on an assumption of the potential *vitality*—in a literal sense—of sounds themselves. This is especially true of those working in electronic or *concrète* music who no longer have to think, and who choose not to think, in terms of twelve-tone equal temperament, Classic-Romantic or "neo-" tonalities, metrical rhythm, traditional instruments, standardized instrumentation, or even "performance." Suggestive in this

---

[21] "Work-Notes for *Echoi*," *PNM*, III, 1 (Fall–Winter 1964), 54–61.

[22] "Towards a Re-Merger in Music," *Contemporary Composers on Contemporary Music*, ed. Elliott Schwartz and Barney Childs (New York: Holt, Rinehart and Winston, 1967), pp. 309–15.

connection is a set of hints to beginning electronic-music composition students for shaping their works, a guide written by a young composer who is also a teacher. She suggests working toward any of four "forms"—static, evolutionary, climactic, and dialog. "Dialog form" she defines as "two or more distinctly separate sounds or textures brought into inter-action." This interaction can be realized in different ways; some that she suggests (and note the personalization):

   a. they [the sounds] begin as separate but eventually merge into one, or find some relationship to each other;

   b. one of several equals [sounds again] eventually dominates over others;

   c. one texture breaks up into several components which exhibit increasing individuality;

   d. a sound originally by itself begins to be accompanied (or possibly attacked) by another. . . .[23]

All these kinds of ideas have a familiar ring to us who have surveyed American music of the past century. They remind us of Carter's "auditory scenarios, for performers to act out with their instruments." They relate to Cage's ideas of "giving up control so that sounds can be sounds" and to Wolff's concern for "a kind of objectivity, almost anonymity—sound come into its own." They go back to Varèse, who liked to quote a nineteenth-century Polish scientist's definition of music as "the corporealization of the intelligence that is in sounds" (University of Southern California lecture, 1939). They go further back ultimately to Ives and his faith in "the large unity of a series of particular aspects of a subject rather than [in] the continuity of its expression," his "discussions and arguments" among musical protagonists, and the spatially separated, semi-coordinated components of *The Unanswered Question*.

Furthermore, in the action-music, the "music as process," the mixed-media events, the new music theater, even the rock concert—all of which invite the listener to be not just a passive recipient but an active participant in the musical experience (even, in *4'33"*, to be the "composer")—and in the world of electronic and tape music, adapted best not to a formal concert situation but to home listening through recordings, we have come almost full circle, to the situation of the singing schools of the eighteenth century or the household music of the nineteenth. In sum, far from being outlandishly new, the anticlassic, asymmetrical, expressionistic, self-defining architecture of sound in both time and space that is the new American music relates to an older world view of musical ex-

---

[23] Laurie Spiegel, ". . . Some Possible Shapes for Sound Composition (or music). . . ." Ms. Spiegel has kindly allowed me to quote from her unpublished guide.

pression and to a tradition of American music; it projects—experimentally, in Cage's sense of the word—ahead into the future as well.

BIBLIOGRAPHICAL NOTES

Jazz of the post-World War II era is discussed from the biographical-critical standpoint (not the analytic) in Joe Goldberg's *Jazz Masters of the Fifties* (1965) and Martin Williams's *Jazz Masters in Transition, 1957–69* (1970); both books are published by The Macmillan Company.

The works that seem to me to be the best on the background-musics of rhythm-and-blues are the following: on country blues, Samuel B. Charters, *The Country Blues* (New York: Rinehart, 1959); on urban blues, Charles Keil, *Urban Blues* (Chicago: The University of Chicago Press, 1966); on gospel song, Tony Heilbut, *The Gospel Sound* (New York: Simon and Schuster, 1971); on big-band dance music, Ross Russell, *Jazz in Kansas City and the Southwest* (Berkeley: University of California Press, 1971).

Country-and-western's development since about 1920 is definitively chronicled in Bill C. Malone's *Country Music U.S.A.* (Austin and London: University of Texas Press, 1968).

Of the many books on the development from rhythm-and-blues through rock-and-roll to rock, the best in my opinion (because most thorough and objective) is Charlie Gillett's *The Sound of the City* (2nd ed.; New York: Dell Publishing Company, 1972); in his second edition, Gillett candidly revises some of his opinions in the first (1970). *Popular Music and Society* (1971–   ) is a scholarly quarterly on the subject; it has included a number of articles on recent pop music and rock. Richard Goldstein's *The Poetry of Rock* (New York: Bantam Books, Inc., 1969) is an anthology of rock lyrics; the author's comments may profitably be read against a background of the views of H. F. Mooney on earlier popular-song texts, published in two articles in *American Quarterly:* "Songs, Singers and Society, 1890–1954," VI/3 (Fall 1954), 221–32; and "Popular Music Since the 1920s: The Significance of Shifting Taste," XX/1 (Spring 1968), 67–85.

Elliott Schwartz's *Electronic Music* (New York: Praeger Publishers, 1973) is valuable for material discussed in this chapter as well as the preceding; it has a useful bibliography and a discography.

Avant-garde developments, especially mixed-media and new music theater, are dealt with extensively and enthusiastically by Eric Salzman in the second edition (1974) of his companion volume in the Prentice-Hall History of Music Series, *Twentieth-Century Music*. Another basic resource is *Source* (1967–   ), the issues of which are apt themselves to be multi-media productions, with recordings, templates, scores, and other bits of material as well as essays and articles. More in-depth analytic discussions of recent music are contained in every issue of *Perspectives of New Music* and of the unpretentious and slight (but valuable) *Contemporary Music Newsletter* (1967–   ), available from the Department of Music, Washington Square College, New York University.

INDEX